A SERIOUS OCCUPATION

A SERIOUS OCCUPATION

Literary Criticism by Victorian Women Writers

edited by

SOLVEIG C. ROBINSON

broadview press

National Library of Canada Cataloguing in Publication

A serious occupation : literary criticism by Victorian women writers / edited by Solveig C. Robinson.

Includes bibliographical references.
ISBN 1-55111-350-3

1. English literature—19th century—History and criticism.
2. Criticism—Great Britain—History—19th century—Sources. 3. Women critics—Great Britain—History—19th century. I. Robinson, Solveig C., 1962–

PR463.S47 2003   820.9'008   C2002-905560-1

Broadview Press Ltd. is an independent, international publishing house, incorporated in 1985. Broadview believes in shared ownership, both with its employees and with the general public; since the year 2000 Broadview shares have traded publicly on the Toronto Venture Exchange under the symbol BDP.

We welcome comments and suggestions regarding any aspect of our publications–please feel free to contact us at the addresses below or at broadview@broadviewpress.com.

North America
PO Box 1243, Peterborough, Ontario, Canada K9J 7H5
3576 California Road, Orchard Park, NY, USA 14127
Tel: (705) 743–8990; Fax: (705) 743–8353
email: customerservice@broadviewpress.com

UK, Ireland, and continental Europe
Thomas Lyster Ltd., Units 3 & 4a, Old Boundary Way
Burscough Road, Ormskirk
Lancashire, L39 2YW
Tel: (01695) 575112; Fax: (01695) 570120
email: books@tlyster.co.uk

Australia and New Zealand
UNIREPS, University of New South Wales
Sydney, NSW, 2052
Tel: 61 2 9664 0999; Fax: 61 2 9664 5420
email: info.press@unsw.edu.au

www.broadviewpress.com

Broadview Press Ltd. gratefully acknowledges the financial support of the Government of Canada through the Book Publishing Industry Development Program for our publishing activities.

This book is printed on acid-free paper containing 30% post-consumer fibre.

Eco-Logo Certified
30 % Post.

PRINTED IN CANADA

For Peter

CONTENTS

ACKNOWLEDGMENTS

THANKS ARE DUE to many organizations and individuals for research assistance and encouragement. I am especially grateful to the American Council of Learned Societies (ACLS) for fellowship support in 1998–99. I would also like to thank my colleagues at Pacific Lutheran University and at Mary Washington College for their support and assistance, and the library staffs at Pacific Lutheran University, the University of Puget Sound, and Mary Washington College for their fine work in locating source materials. Further thanks are due the members of the Research Society for Victorian Periodicals (RSVP) and of VICTORIA for their interest, support, and material assistance with this project. For extra assistance, special thanks go to Ellen Jordan, University of Newcastle, Australia, for sharing work in progress on Anne Mozley; Thomas J. Tobin, William Morris Society, for tracking an Alice Meynell quotation; and Mark Jensen and Eric Nelson, Pacific Lutheran University, for help with translations.

INTRODUCTION

ALTHOUGH LITERARY CRITICISM by Victorian men of letters has always been widely available, the literary criticism written by Victorian women has remained relatively obscure. In large part, this has been the result of cultural biases about who was entitled to write criticism. Criticism has always been a high-prestige genre, because the critic by definition assumes a position of authority relative to the text, the author, and the reader. In her study of *The Woman Reader, 1837–1914*, Kate Flint notes that *any* kind of reading is bound up in questions of authority: "authority to speak, to write, to define, to manage, and to change not just the institutions of literature, but those of society itself" (43). During the Victorian period, when authors as diverse as Sarah Stickney Ellis, Alfred Tennyson, and John Ruskin reiterated the theme that woman's proper place was in a domestic, supporting role to masculine authority, women's ability to judge for others was assumed to be strictly limited, and such assumptions about the rigidity of the Victorian separate spheres persisted into the late twentieth century. The persistence of these assumptions helps to account for the fact that, until recently, very few scholars have even looked for criticism by Victorian women. Indeed, in a 1989 study of the Victorian novel-publishing industry, *Edging Women Out*, sociologist Gaye Tuchman simply voiced what was considered to be a truism when she stated flatly that "Unlike men, women never possessed the power to define the nature of good literature" (204).

But these assumptions about Victorian women's power to influence both society and literature as critics have been proven wrong.

Feminist scholarship from the 1970s onward has recalled to view a considerable number of Victorian women who worked openly in numerous areas in the public sphere, from art to politics to science, as well as many more whose work was performed more discreetly but who were, nonetheless, very influential in their particular fields. Ongoing research in literary studies, particularly in the field of Victorian periodicals, has brought to light a considerable number of powerful and respected women who met the challenges of the serious occupation of literary criticism.

Scholarship in Victorian periodicals has been crucial to the rediscovery of women critics. Literary historian Margaret Beetham points out the role played by periodicals in nineteenth-century cultural definition, arguing that the periodical was the locus at which "writers, editors, publishers and readers engaged in trying to understand themselves and their society ... to make their world meaningful." Those who controlled the *location* of the defining process also controlled the definition itself: "Those who owned, edited and wrote for the nineteenth-century periodical press had more power to define their world and 'make their meanings stick'" (20). Because the great power wielded by periodical editors and contributors in defining Victorian literary norms and tastes has long been recognized, extraordinary efforts have been undertaken since the mid-twentieth century to identify both who those individuals were and precisely what their influence was. Beginning with the Wellesley Project and continuing in the work of the Research Society of Victorian Periodicals (RSVP), the Society for the History of Authorship, Reading, and Publishing (SHARP), and others, scholars have continued to identify the anonymous contributors to nineteenth-century reviews and magazines and to publicize their work. As the identification process has continued, dozens of influential women critics have emerged from obscurity.

Of course, the cloak of anonymity was one of the major reasons so many Victorian women were able to establish themselves firmly within the critical field: until the last decades of the century, the identities of most periodical contributors—men and women—were concealed. Anonymous publication helped to preserve a sense of corporate identity for the different periodicals: the *Saturday Review* or *Blackwood's*

Edinburgh Magazine, for example, presented an outward consistency reinforced by the magazine's suppression of its individual contributors' identities. This practice of anonymity meant that a woman contributor who could write well in a particular periodical's style or tone was not automatically barred from assuming the critical pen; indeed, in some cases, individual women writers were explicitly sought out. Geraldine Jewsbury reviewed fiction for the *Athenaeum* for decades, due to her presumed insight into what women novel-readers would prefer, and Eliza Lynn Linton was invited to join the staff of the *Saturday Review* because the editor knew she could adopt the magazine's acerbic style. The identities of Jewsbury, Lynn Linton, and other contributors were frequently known to publishing insiders, but by not calling attention to the names—and thus the genders—the illusion that women were not in fact influential critics could be sustained.

Ironically, yet another factor in some women's success as critics was the very cultural bias against women as authorities that sought to bar them from criticism. Historian Judith Newton suggests that women's position as consummate outsiders gave them the necessary critical distance to comment objectively on both social and literary matters: "Their more marginal position in relation to the market and the professional public world made them even better placed than professional men to enact the role of social 'crank,' to offer social analyses and critiques of the very market or social relations on which their class position to some degree hinged" (2). The benefits of being an outsider were attested to by Harriet Martineau, who in her *Autobiography* credited her invalidism and subsequent withdrawal from London to the countryside with providing her the necessary distance from events to see and comment on them more clearly. It may also explain the case of Anne Mozley, who continued to shield her identity even when republishing her critical essays in book form.

The 18 Victorian women critics brought together in the pages of this anthology assumed their positions of authority for a variety of reasons and adapted to or challenged Victorian gender ideology to very different degrees. The two earliest critics, Anna Jameson and Harriet Martineau, turned to writing out of financial need and were relatively undaunted by Victorian assumptions about women's authority: both published (or republished) their work under their own names without apology. A significant number of the women capitalized on the fact that they had already established their literary reputations in other genres, most notably fiction. Charlotte Brontë, Dinah Mulock Craik, M.E. Braddon, Margaret Oliphant, and Eliza Lynn Linton all assumed their critical authority to one degree or another on the basis of their insider's knowledge of how novels worked; Eliza Cook and Janet Hamilton made their reputations first as poets, adding criticism to their oeuvres later in their careers. George Eliot reversed the trend by serving her literary apprenticeship first as translator, editor, and critic, and then turning to fiction, where her expertise quickly catapulted her to the top of her profession. Family connections played a major role in creating professional opportunities for several of the women: Anne Thackeray Ritchie and Mary Augusta Ward had illustrious literary relatives (Ritchie's father was novelist William Makepeace Thackeray, and Ward was the niece of poet and critic Matthew Arnold); Anne Mozley came from a family of publishers and booksellers and followed her brothers into journalism; and Alice Meynell collaborated with her journalist husband. Elizabeth Rigby Eastlake and Elizabeth Julia Hassell both showed extraordinary promise as scholars and turned to critical writing as a natural outlet for their intellectual abilities. Helen Blackburn moved into journalism as an extension of her activism within the Langham Place women's movement.

Not only are the backgrounds and motivations of these critics quite different, but their styles and perspectives are as well. The essays included here range from topical reviews of particular texts to appreciations of individual authors to character studies to assessments of the state of contemporary literature and criticism. Martineau highlights Scott's contributions to the development of the realist novel, while Eastlake, Jewsbury, and Oliphant predict the demise of the form in the wake of the new sensation fiction. Charlotte Brontë, Craik, Ritchie, and Ward offer examples of biographical criticism, locating the works of Emily Brontë, George Eliot, and Jane Austen in the contexts of their lives and times. Hasell and Meynell both offer critical reappraisals of major poets of the day; in Hasell's case, she offers one of the earliest reassessments of Robert Browning's work. Writing in a very different key, Eliot, Cook, and Braddon employ wit to brilliant effect in satirical critiques of women's fiction, utilitarian philosophy, and the state of contemporary criticism. Jameson, Eliot, and Blackburn all expressly concern themselves with the status of women in society, Jameson through the lens of Shakespeare's characterization of Portia, and Eliot and Blackburn through analyses of women's achievements in literature. Hamilton, herself a self-educated working-class poet, lauds the benefits of literature for other working-class individuals, and Mozley stresses the benefits of fiction in fostering the next generation of poetic genius.

Between them, these women represent the full spectrum of Victorian society—from the self-taught working-class poet Hamilton to the manor-born Hasell, from the stubbornly antifeminist Lynn Linton to the radical Blackburn, from the self-effacing Mozley and Oliphant to the self-promoting Braddon. Arranged in chronological order by date of publication, the essays gathered together here reveal just how rich and diverse Victorian women's critical prose truly is. To borrow from Helen Blackburn's conclusion in her essay imagining a library of books by women authors, such essays as these "should tend to heighten the increasing respect for women's capacities, increase respect for their latent powers in the hearts of women themselves, and respect for the value of women's work in the hearts of men."

REFERENCES

Beetham, Margaret. "Towards a Theory of the Periodical as a Publishing Genre." *Investigating Victorian Journalism.* Ed. Laurel Brake, Aled Jones, and Lionel Madden. New York: St. Martin's Press, 1990. 19–32.

Flint, Kate. *The Woman Reader, 1837–1914.* Oxford: Oxford University Press, 1993.

Newton, Judith. "Engendering History for the Middle Class: Sex and Political Economy in the *Edinburgh Review.*" *Rewriting the Victorians: Theory, History, and the Politics of Gender.* Ed. Linda M. Shires. New York: Routledge, 1992. 1–17.

Tuchman, Gaye, with Nina E. Fortin. *Edging Women Out: Victorian Novelists, Publishers, and Social Change.* New Haven: Yale University Press, 1989.

CHARACTERS OF INTELLECT: PORTIA
(1832)

Anna Jameson

ANNA BROWNELL MURPHY (1794–1860) was born in
Dublin, the daughter of an Irish portrait painter and his
English wife. After working some years as a governess, she
married barrister Robert Jameson in 1825. The marriage was
unsuccessful, and the couple lived apart for many years before
formally separating in 1837. Driven by a need to support
herself, she early turned to writing. While her first published
work was fiction—*The Diary of an Ennuyée* (1826) was based on
a travel journal she kept while working as a governess—she
made her mark as an author of nonfiction prose.

Although she made significant contributions to the fields
of biography and travel writing during the 1820s and 1830s,
Jameson is probably best remembered for her aesthetic and
social criticism, which she began writing in the 1840s. Based
on research conducted during her extensive travels in Britain
and on the Continent, she published several popular gallery
guides, numerous articles, and an important four-volume
work on *Sacred and Legendary Art* (1848–64). (The final
volume, *The History of Our Lord as Exemplified in Works of Art*,
was completed after her death by her friend and fellow critic,
Lady Elizabeth Rigby Eastlake.) Jameson was acknowledged
as an important art critic during her lifetime and was widely
read and admired both in Europe and in the United States.

Jameson was also an important figure in the nineteenth-
century women's movement. Her own experiences convinced

her of the importance of expanding educational and employment opportunities for women, and several of her early publications focused on the condition of women both in the past and during her own time. The biographical sketches *The Loves of the Poets* (1829) and *Memoirs of the Celebrated Female Sovereigns* (1831) presented historical women and paved the way for *Characteristics of Women* (1832), an examination of how Shakespeare's heroines exemplified aspects of women's lives and opportunities. In the 1840s and 1850s she was an active mentor of the Langham Place feminists, presenting and publishing two influential lectures, *Sisters of Charity* (1855) and *The Communion of Labour* (1856), on the importance of women leading useful lives.

Jameson died in 1860 from pneumonia, after having caught cold while working in the British Library on the last volume of *Sacred and Legendary Art*. Her obituary in the London *Daily News*, written by Harriet Martineau, declares that "long after [her works] have ceased to be sought and regularly read, some touch of nature in them, some trait of insight, or ingenuity of solution will come up in fireside conversation, or in literary intercourse, and remind a future generation that in ours there was a restless, expatiating, fervent, unreasoning, generous, accomplished Mrs. Jameson among the lights of the time."

The following excerpt is taken from *Characteristics of Women*, which was issued in later editions as *Shakespeare's Heroines*. As the title suggests, Jameson uses fictional figures to analyze how real women's characters and behaviours are shaped by circumstance and experience. In the process, as critic Anne E. Russell notes, she simultaneously holds up models of ideal feminine behaviour and challenges the assumptions upon which traditional models of womanliness are based. In the first chapter of *Shakespeare's Heroines*, Jameson examines Portia (from *The Merchant of Venice*), Isabella (*Measure for Measure*), Beatrice (*Much Ado About Nothing*), and Rosalind (*As You Like It*) as exemplary "Characters of Intellect." Portia embodies what Jameson considers to be an especially womanly form of intellect: while she exhibits intellectual powers comparable to any man's, these powers are less "self-directed" and instead "in a much greater degree modified by the sympathies and moral qualities." Yet while Jameson admires Portia for her sweetness and skill in employing her intellect on others' behalf, she warns that a Portia in the Victorian age would be not victor but victim, doomed by "Opinion" either to suppress her own nature or, in affirming and exercising it, to become rebellious, proud, and rigid.

WE HEAR IT ASSERTED, not seldom by way of compliment to us women, that intellect is of no sex. If this mean that the same faculties of mind are common to men and women, it is true; in any other signification it appears to me false, and the reverse of a compliment. The intellect of woman bears the same relation to that of man as her physical organization;—it is inferior in power, and different in kind. That certain women have surpassed certain men in bodily strength or intellectual energy does not contradict the general principle founded in nature. The essential and invariable distinction appears to me this: in men, the intellectual faculties exist more self-poised and self-directed—more independent of the rest of the character, than we ever find them in women, with whom talent, however predominant, is in a much greater degree modified by the sympathies and moral qualities.

In thinking over all the distinguished women I can at this moment call to mind, I recollect but one who, in the exercise of a rare talent, belied her sex; but the moral qualities had been first perverted.[1] It is from not knowing, or not allowing this general principle, that men of genius have committed some signal mistakes. They have given us exquisite and just delineations of the more peculiar characteristics of

---

[1] Artemisia Gentileschi, an Italian artist of the seventeenth century, painted one or two pictures, considered admirable as works of art, of which the subjects are the most vicious and barbarous conceivable. I remember one of these in the gallery of Florence, which I looked at once, but once, and wished then, as I do now, for the privilege of burning it to ashes. [Author's note.]

women, as modesty, grace, tenderness; and when they have attempted
to portray them with the powers common to both sexes, as wit, energy,
intellect, they have blundered in some respect; they could form no
conception of intellect which was not masculine, and therefore have
either suppressed the feminine attributes altogether and drawn
coarse caricatures, or they have made them completely artificial.[1]
Women distinguished for wit may sometimes appear masculine and
flippant, but the cause must be sought elsewhere than in nature, who
disclaims all such. Hence the witty and intellectual ladies of our come-
dies and novels are all in the fashion of some particular time; they are
like some old portraits which can still amuse and please by the beauty
of the workmanship, in spite of the graceless costume or grotesque
accompaniments, but from which we turn to worship with ever new
delight the Floras and goddesses of Titian, the saints and the virgins
of Raffaelle and Domenichino. So the Millamants and Belindas, the
Lady Townleys and Lady Teazles, are out of date, while Portia and
Rosalind, in whom nature and the feminine character are paramount,
remain bright and fresh to the fancy as when first created.

Portia, Isabella, Beatrice, and Rosalind, may be classed together as
characters of intellect, because, when compared with others, they are
at once distinguished by their mental superiority. In Portia, is intellect kindled into romance by a poetical imagination; in Isabel, it is
intellect elevated by religious principle; in Beatrice, intellect animated
by spirit; in Rosalind, intellect softened by sensibility. The wit which
is lavished on each is profound, or pointed, or sparkling, or playful—
but always feminine: like spirits distilled from flowers, it always
reminds us of its origin; it is a volatile essence, sweet as powerful; and
to pursue the comparison a step further, the wit of Portia is like attar
of roses, rich and concentrated; that of Rosalind, like cotton dipped
in aromatic vinegar; the wit of Beatrice is like sal-volatile, and that of

---

[1] Lucy Ashton, in the *Bride of Lammermoor,* may be placed next to Desdemona; Diana
Vernon is (comparatively) a failure, as every woman will allow; while the masculine Lady
Geraldine, in Miss Edgeworth's tale of *Ennui,* and the intellectual Corinne, are consis-
tent, essential women: the distinction is more easily felt than analyzed. [Author's note.]
Diana Vernon and Corinne are characters in Walter Scott's *Rob Roy* (1817) and in the
French-Swiss writer Germaine de Staël's (1766–1816) 1807 novel by that name.

Isabel like the incense wafted to heaven. Of these four exquisite characters, considered as dramatic and poetical conceptions, it is difficult to pronounce which is most perfect in its way, most admirably drawn, most highly finished. But if considered in another point of view, as women and individuals, as breathing realities, clothed in flesh and blood, I believe we must assign the first rank to Portia, as uniting in herself, in a more eminent degree than the others, all the noblest and most lovable qualities that ever met together in woman, and presenting a complete personification of Petrarch's exquisite epitome of female perfection:

> Il vago spirito ardento,
> E'n alto intelletto, un puro core.[1]

It is singular that hitherto no critical justice has been done to the character of Portia; yet more wonderful that one of the finest writers on the eternal subject of Shakespeare and his perfections should accuse Portia of pedantry and affectation, and confess she is not a great favorite of his—a confession quite worthy of him who avers his predilection for servant-maids, and his preference of the Fannys and the Pamelas over the Clementinas and Clarissas. Schlegel,[2] who has given several pages to a rapturous eulogy on the *Merchant of Venice*, simply designates Portia as a "rich, beautiful, clever heiress." Whether the fault lie in the writer or translator, I do protest against the word clever.[3] Portia *clever*! What an epithet to apply to this heavenly compound of talent, feeling, wisdom, beauty, and gentleness! Now would it not be well if this common and comprehensive word were more accurately defined, or at least more accurately used? It signifies properly, not so much the possession of high powers as dexterity in the adaptation of certain faculties (not necessarily of a high order) to a certain end or aim—not always the worthiest. It implies something commonplace,

---

[1] "The wandering ardent spirit, with a pure heart within a high intellect." Jameson combines lines from two of Petrarch's (1304–74) poems idealizing Laura.

[2] August Wilhelm von Schlegel (1767–1845), German scholar and critic.

[3] I am informed that the original German word is *geistreiche*, literally "rich in soul or spirit," a just and beautiful epithet. [Author's note.]

inasmuch as it speaks the presence of the *active* and *perceptive*, with a deficiency of the *feeling* and *reflective* powers; and, applied to a woman, does it not almost invariably suggest the idea of something we should distrust or shrink from, if not allied to a higher nature? The profligate French women who ruled the councils of Europe in the middle of the last century, were clever women; and that *philosopheress*, Madame du Châtelet,[1] who managed at one and the same moment the thread of an intrigue, her cards at piquet, and a calculation in algebra, was a very clever woman! If Portia had been created as a mere instrument to bring about a dramatic catastrophe—if she had merely detected the flaw in Antonio's bond and used it as a means to baffle the Jew, she might have been pronounced a clever woman. But what Portia does is forgotten in what she *is*. The rare and harmonious blending of energy, reflection, and feeling, in her fine character, makes the epithet *clever* sound like a discord as applied to *her*, and places her infinitely beyond the slight praise of Richardson[2] and Schlegel, neither of whom appears to have fully comprehended her.

These and other critics have been apparently so dazzled and engrossed by the amazing character of Shylock, that Portia has received less than justice at their hands; while the fact is, that Shylock is not a finer or more finished character in his way than Portia is in hers. These two splendid figures are worthy of each other—worthy of being placed together within the same rich framework of enchanting poetry and glorious and graceful forms. She hangs beside the terrible inexorable Jew, the brilliant lights of her character set off by the shadowy power of his, like a magnificent beauty-breathing Titian by the side of a gorgeous Rembrandt.

Portia is endued with her own share of those delightful qualities which Shakespeare has lavished on many of his female characters; but besides the dignity, the sweetness, and tenderness which should distinguish her sex generally, she is individualized by qualities peculiar to herself; by her high mental powers, her enthusiasm of temperament,

---

[1] Emilie du Châtelet (1706–49), mathematician and physicist, companion of Voltaire, and translator of Newton.

[2] Samuel Richardson (1689–1761), English novelist.

her decision of purpose, and her buoyancy of spirit. These are innate; she has other distinguishing qualities more external, and which are the result of the circumstances in which she is placed. Thus she is the heiress of a princely name and countless wealth; a train of obedient pleasures have ever waited round her; and from infancy she has breathed an atmosphere redolent of perfume and blandishment. Accordingly there is a commanding grace, a high-bred, airy elegance, a spirit of magnificence, in all that she does and says, as one to whom splendor had been familiar from her very birth. She treads as though her footsteps had been among marble palaces, beneath roofs of fretted gold, o'er cedar floors and pavements of jasper and porphyry; amid gardens full of statues, and flowers, and fountains, and haunting music. She is full of penetrative wisdom, and genuine tenderness, and lively wit; but as she has never known want, or grief, or fear, or disappointment, her wisdom is without a touch of the sombre or the sad; her affections are all mixed up with faith, hope, and joy; and her wit has not a particle of malevolence or causticity.

It is well known that the *Merchant of Venice* is founded on two different tales; and in weaving together his double plot in so masterly a manner, Shakespeare has rejected altogether the character of the astutious lady of Belmont with her magic potions, who figures in the Italian novel. With yet more refinement, he has thrown out all the licentious part of the story, which some of his contemporary dramatists would have seized on with avidity, and made the best or the worst of it possible; and lie has substituted the trial of the caskets from another source.[1] We are not told expressly where Belmont is situated; but as Bassanio takes ship to go thither from Venice, and as we find them afterwards ordering horses from Belmont to Padua, we will imagine Portia's hereditary palace as standing on some lovely promontory overlooking the blue Adriatic, with the Friuli mountains or the Euganean hills for its background, such as we often see in one of Claude's or Poussin's elysian landscapes. In a scene, in a home like

---

[1]   In the *Mercatante di Venezia*, of Ser. Giovanni, we have the whole story of Antonio and Bassanio, and part of the story but not the character of Portia. The incident of the caskets is from the *Gesta Romanorum*. [Author's note.]

this, Shakespeare, having first exorcised the original possessor, has placed his Portia: and so endowed her, that all the wild, strange, and moving circumstances of the story become natural, probable, and necessary in connection with her. That such a woman should be chosen by the solving of an enigma is not surprising: herself and all around her, the scene, the country, the age in which she is placed, breathe of poetry, romance, and enchantment.[1]

· · ·

The sudden plan which she forms for the release of her husband's friend, her disguise, and her deportment as the young and learned doctor, would appear forced and improbable in any other woman, but in Portia are the simple and natural result of her character.[2] The quickness with which she perceives the legal advantage which may be taken of the circumstances; the spirit of adventure with which she engages in the masquerading, and the decision, firmness, and intelligence with which she executes her generous purpose, are all in perfect keeping, and nothing appears forced—nothing is introduced merely for theatrical effect.

But all the finest parts of Portia's character are brought to bear in the trial scene. There she shines forth all her divine self. Her intellectual powers, her elevated sense of religion, her high, honorable principles, her best feelings as a woman, are all displayed. She maintains at first a calm self-command, as one sure of carrying her point in the end! yet the painful heart-thrilling uncertainty in which she keeps the whole court, until suspense verges upon agony, is not contrived for effect merely; it is necessary and inevitable. She has two objects in view—to deliver her husband's friend, and to maintain her husband's honor by the discharge of his just debt, though paid out of her own wealth ten times over. It is evident that she would rather owe

---

[1] See *Merchant of Venice* 2.7.39–47.

[2] In that age, delicate points of law were not determined by the ordinary judges of the province, but by doctors of law, who were called from Bologna, Padua, and other places celebrated for their legal colleges. [Author's note.]

the safety of Antonio to anything rather than the legal quibble with which her cousin Bellario has armed her, and which she reserves as a last resource. Thus all the speeches addressed to Shylock in the first instance are either direct or indirect experiments on his temper and feelings. She must be understood, from the beginning to the end, as examining with intense anxiety the effect of her own words on his mind and countenance; as watching for that relenting spirit which she hopes to awaken either by reason or persuasion. She begins by an appeal to his mercy, in that matchless piece of eloquence which, with an irresistible and solemn pathos, falls upon the heart like "gentle dew from heaven":—but in vain; for that blessed dew drops not more fruitless and unfelt on the parched sand of the desert, than do these heavenly words upon the ear of Shylock. She next attacks his avarice:

Shylock, there's *thrice* thy money offer'd thee.

Then she appeals, in the same breath, both to his avarice and his pity:

Be merciful!
Take thrice thy money. Bid me tear the bond.

All that she says afterwards—her strong expressions, which are calculated to strike a shuddering horror through the nerves; the reflections she interposes, her delays and circumlocution to give time for any latent feeling of commiseration to display itself; all, all are premeditated, and tend in the same manner to the object she has in view. Thus—

You must prepare your bosom for his knife.
Therefore lay bare your bosom!

These two speeches, though addressed apparently to Antonio, are spoken *at* Shylock, and are evidently intended to penetrate *his* bosom. In the same spirit she asks for the balance to weigh the pound of flesh; and entreats of Shylock to have a surgeon ready—

> PORTIA: Have by some surgeon, Shylock, on your charge,
> To stop his wounds lest he do bleed to death!
> SHYLOCK: Is it not so nominated in the bond?
> PORTIA: It is not so express'd—but what of that?
> 'Twere good you do so much, for *charity*.

So unwilling is her sanguine and generous spirit to resign all hope, or to believe that humanity is absolutely extinct in the bosom of the Jew, that she calls on Antonio, as a last resource, to speak for himself. His gentle yet manly resignation—the deep pathos of his farewell, and the affectionate allusion to herself in his last address to Bassanio—

> Commend me to your honourable wife;
> Say how I loved you, speak me fair in death, &c.

are well calculated to swell that emotion which through the whole scene must have been laboring suppressed within her heart.

At length the crisis arrives, for patience and womanhood can endure no longer; and when Shylock, carrying his savage bent "to the last hour of act," springs on his victim—"A sentence! come, prepare!" then the smothered scorn, indignation, and disgust burst forth with an impetuosity which interferes with the judicial solemnity she had at first affected; particularly in the speech—

> Therefore, prepare thee to cut off the flesh.
> Shed thou no blood; nor cut thou less, nor more,
> But just the pound of flesh: if thou tak'st more
> Or less than a just pound—be it but so much
> As makes it light, or heavy, in the substance,
> Or the division of the twentieth part
> Of one poor scruple; nay, if the scale do turn
> But in the estimation of a hair,—
> Thou diest, and all thy goods are confiscate.

But she afterwards recovers her propriety, and triumphs with a cooler scorn and a more selfpossessed exultation.

It is clear that, to feel the full force and dramatic beauty of this marvellous scene, we must go along with Portia as well as with Shylock; we must understand her concealed purpose, keep in mind her noble motives, and pursue in our fancy the undercurrent of feeling, working in her mind throughout. The terror and the power of Shylock's character,—his deadly and inexorable malice—would be too oppressive; the pain and pity too intolerable, and the horror of the possible issue too overwhelming, but for the intellectual relief afforded by this double source of interest and contemplation.

I come now to that capacity for warm and generous affection, that tenderness of heart, which render Portia not less lovable as a woman than admirable for her mental endowments. The affections are to the intellect what the forge is to the metal; it is they which temper and shape it to all good purposes, and soften, strengthen, and purify it. What an exquisite stroke of judgment in the poet, to make the mutual passion of Portia and Bassanio, though unacknowledged to each other, anterior to the opening of the play! Bassanio's confession very properly comes first:—

BASSANIO: In Belmont is a lady richly left,
And she is fair, and fairer than that word,
Of wondrous virtues; sometimes from her eyes
I did receive fair speechless messages;

and prepares us for Portia's half-betrayed, unconscious election of this most graceful and chivalrous admirer—

NERISSA: Do you not remember, lady, in your father's time, a Venetian, a scholar, and a soldier, that came hither in company of the Marquis of Montferrat?
PORTIA: Yes, yes, it was Bassanio; as I think, so he was called.
NERISSA: True, madam; he of all the men that ever my foolish eyes looked upon was the best deserving a fair lady.
PORTIA: I remember him well; and I remember him worthy of thy praise.

Our interest is thus awakened for the lovers from the very first; and what shall be said of the casket scene with Bassanio, where every line which Portia speaks is so worthy of herself, so full of sentiment and beauty, and poetry, and passion? Too naturally frank for disguise, too modest to confess her depth of love while the issue of the trial remains in suspense, the conflict between love and fear, and maidenly dignity, cause the most delicious confusion that ever tinged a woman's cheek or dropped in broken utterance from her lips.[1]

· · ·

The short dialogue between the lovers is exquisite.

BASSANIO: Let me choose;
For, as I am, I live upon the rack.
PORTIA: Upon the rack, Bassanio? Then confess
What treason there is mingled with your love.
BASSANIO: None, but that ugly treason of mistrust,
Which makes me fear the enjoying of my love.
There may as well be amity and life
'Tween snow and fire, as treason and my love.
PORTIA: Ay! but I fear you speak upon the rack,
Where men enforced do speak anything,
BASSANIO: Promise me life, and I'll confess the truth.
PORTIA: Well then, confess, and live.
BASSANIO: Confess and love
Had been the very sum of my confession!
O happy torment, when my torturer
Doth teach me answers for deliverance!

A prominent feature in Portia's character is that confiding, buoyant spirit which mingles with all her thoughts and affections. And here let me observe, that I never yet met in real life, nor ever read in tale

---

[1] See *Merchant of Venice* 3.2.1–18.

or history, of any woman, distinguished for intellect of the highest order, who was not also remarkable for this trusting spirit, this hopefulness and cheerfulness of temper, which is compatible with the most serious habits of thought and the most profound sensibility. Lady Wortley Montagu[1] was one instance; and Madame de Staël furnishes another much more memorable. In her Corinne, whom she drew from herself, this natural brightness of temper is a prominent part of the character. A disposition to doubt, to suspect, and to despond, in the young, argues, in general, some inherent weakness, moral or physical, or some miserable and radical error of education; in the old, it is one of the first symptoms of age: it speaks of the influence of sorrow and experience, and foreshows the decay of the stronger and more generous powers of the soul. Portia's strength of intellect takes a natural tinge from the flush and bloom of her young and prosperous existence, and from her fervid imagination. In the casket scene, she fears indeed the issue of the trial, on which more than her life is hazarded; but, while she trembles, her hope is stronger than her fear. While Bassanio is contemplating the caskets, she suffers herself to dwell for one moment on the possibility of disappointment and misery.

> Let music sound while he doth make his choice;
> Then if he lose, he makes a swan-like end,
> Fading in music: that the comparison
> May stand more proper, my eye shall be the stream
> And wat'ry death-bed for him.

Then immediately follows that revulsion of feeling, so beautifully characteristic of the hopeful, trusting, mounting spirit of this noble creature.

> But he may win!
> And what is music then?—then music is
> Even as the flourish, when true subjects bow

---

[1] Lady Mary Wortley Montagu (1689–1762), poet, letter-writer, and essayist.

> To a new-crowned monarch: such it is
> As are those dulcet sounds at break of day
> That creep into the dreaming bridegroom's ear
> And summon him to marriage. Now he goes
> With no less presence, but with much more love,
> Than young Alcides, when he did redeem
> The virgin tribute paid by howling Troy
> To the sea monster. I stand here for sacrifice.

Here, not only the feeling itself, born of the elastic and sanguine spirit which had never been touched by grief; but the images in which it comes arrayed to her fancy,—the bridegroom waked by music on his wedding-morn,—the new-crowned monarch,—the comparison of Bassanio to the young Alcides, and of herself to the daughter of Laomedon, are all precisely what would have suggested themselves to the fine poetical imagination of Portia in such a moment.

Her passionate exclamations of delight when Bassanio has fixed on the right casket, are as strong as though she had despaired before. Fear and doubt she could repel;—the native elasticity of her mind bore up against them; yet she makes us feel that, as the sudden joy overpowers her almost to fainting, the disappointment would as certainly have killed her.

> How all the other passions fleet to air,
> As doubtful thoughts, and rash-embrac'd despair,
> And shuddering fear, and green-ey'd jealousy!
> O love! be moderate, allay thy ecstasy;
> In measure rain thy joy, scant this excess:
> I feel too much thy blessing; make it less,
> For fear I surfeit!

Her subsequent surrender of herself in heart and soul, of her maiden freedom, and her vast possessions, can never be read without deep emotion; for not only all the tenderness and delicacy of a devoted woman are here blended with all the dignity which becomes the princely heiress of Belmont, but the serious, measured self-possession

of her address to her lover, when all suspense is over, and all conceal-
ment superfluous, is most beautifully consistent with the character. It
is, in truth, an awful moment, that in which a gifted woman first discovers, that, besides talents and powers, she has also passions and affections; when she first begins to suspect their vast importance in the sum
of her existence; when she first confesses that her happiness is no
longer in her own keeping, but is surrendered for ever and for ever
into the dominion of another! The possession of uncommon powers
of mind are so far from affording relief or resource in the first intox-
icating surprise—I had almost said terror—of such a revolution, that
they render it more intense. The sources of thought multiply beyond
calculation the sources of feeling; and mingled, they rush together, a
torrent as deep as strong. Because Portia is endued with that enlarged
comprehension which looks before and after, she does not feel the
less, but the more: because from the height of her commanding intellect she can contemplate the force, the tendency, the consequences of
her own sentiments—because she is fully sensible of her own situation
and the value of all she concedes—the concession is not made with
less entireness and devotion of heart, less confidence in the truth and
worth of her lover, than when Juliet, in a similar moment, but without
any such intrusive reflections—any check but the instinctive delicacy
of her sex, flings herself and her fortunes at the feet of her lover:

> And all my fortunes at thy feet I'll lay,
> And follow thee, my lord, through all the world.[1]

In Portia's confession, which is not breathed from a moon-lit balcony,
but spoken openly in the presence of her attendants and vassals, there
is nothing of the passionate self-abandonment of Juliet, nor of the
artless simplicity of Miranda, but a consciousness and a tender seriousness, approaching to solemnity, which are not less touching.[2]

---

[1] *Romeo and Juliet*, act ii. scene 2. [Author's note.]
[2] See *Merchant of Venice* 3.2.149–71.

• • •

We must also remark that the sweetness, the solicitude, the subdued fondness which she afterwards displays relative to the letter, are as true to the softness of her sex as the generous selfdenial with which she urges the departure of Bassanio (having first given him a husband's right over herself and all her countless wealth) is consistent with a reflecting mind, and a spirit at once tender, reasonable, and magnanimous.

It is not only in the trial scene that Portia's acuteness, eloquence, and lively intelligence are revealed to us; they are displayed in the first instance, and kept up consistently to the end. Her reflections, arising from the most usual aspects of nature and from the commonest incidents of life, are in such a poetical spirit, and are at the same time so pointed, so profound, that they have passed into familiar and daily application with all the force of proverbs.

> If to do were as easy as to know what were good to do, chapels
> had been churches, and poor men's cottages princes' palaces.

> I can easier teach twenty what were good to be done, than be
> one of the twenty to follow mine own teaching.

> The crow doth sing as sweetly as the lark,
> When neither is attended; and I think
> The nightingale, if she should sing by day,
> When every goose is cackling, would be thought
> No better a musician than the wren.
> How many things by season seasoned are
> To their right praise and true perfection!

> How far that little candle throws his beams!
> So shines a good deed in a naughty world.
> A substitute shines as brightly as a king,
> Until a king be by; and then his state
> Empties itself, as doth an inland brook
> Into the main of waters.

Her reflections on the friendship between her husband and Antonio are as full of deep meaning as of tenderness; and her portrait of a young coxcomb, in the same scene, is touched with a truth and spirit which show with what a keen observing eye she has looked upon men and things.

——I'll hold thee any wager,
When we are both accoutred like young men,
I'll prove the prettier fellow of the two,
And wear my dagger with a braver grace;
And speak between the change of man and boy
With a reed voice; and turn two mincing steps
Into a manly stride; and speak of frays
Like a fine bragging youth; and tell quaint lies—
How honourable ladies sought my love,
Which I denying, they fell sick and died;
I could not do with all: then I'll repent,
And wish, for all that, that I had not killed them:
And twenty of these puny lies I'll tell,
That men shall swear I have discontinued school
Above a twelvemonth.

And in the description of her various suitors, in the first scene with Nerissa, what infinite power, wit, and vivacity! She half checks herself as she is about to give the reins to her sportive humor: "In truth, I know it is a sin to be a mocker." But if it carries her away, it is so perfectly good-natured, so temperately bright, so lady-like, it is ever without offence; and so far most unlike the satirical, poignant, unsparing wit of Beatrice, "misprising what she looks on." In fact, I can scarce conceive a greater contrast than between the vivacity of Portia and the vivacity of Beatrice. Portia, with all her airy brilliance, is supremely soft and dignified; everything she says or does displays her capability for profound thought and feeling as well as her lively and romantic disposition; and as I have seen in an Italian garden a fountain flinging round its wreaths of showery light, while the many-colored Iris hung brooding above it, in its calm and soul-felt glory; so in Portia the wit is ever kept subordinate to the poetry, and we still feel the tender, the intellectual, and the imaginative part of the character, as superior to, and presiding over, its spirit and vivacity.

In the last act, Shylock and his machinations being dismissed from our thoughts, and the rest of the *dramatis personae* assembled together at Belmont, all our interest and all our attention are rivetted on Portia, and the conclusion leaves the most delightful impression on the fancy. The playful equivoque of the rings, the sportive trick she puts on her husband, and her thorough enjoyment of the jest, which she checks just as it is proceeding beyond the bounds of propriety, show how little she was displeased by the sacrifice of her gift, and are all consistent with her bright and buoyant spirit. In conclusion, when Portia invites her company to enter her palace to refresh themselves after their travels, and talk over "these events at full," the imagination, unwilling to lose sight of the brilliant group, follows them in gay procession from the lovely moonlight garden to marble halls and princely revels, to splendor and festive mirth, to love and happiness!

Many women have possessed many of those qualities which render Portia so delightful. She is in herself a piece of reality, in whose possible existence we have no doubt; and yet a human being, in whom the moral, intellectual, and sentient faculties should be so exquisitely blended and proportioned to each other—and these again, in harmony with all outward aspects and influences—probably never existed; certainly could not now exist. A woman constituted like Portia, and placed in this age and in the actual state of society, would find society armed against her; and instead of being like Portia, a gracious, happy, beloved, and loving creature, would be a victim, immolated in fire to that multitudinous Moloch termed Opinion. With her, the world without would be at war with the world within: in the perpetual strife, either her nature would "be subdued to the element it worked in," and, bending to a necessity it could neither escape nor approve, lose at last something of its original brightness, or otherwise—a perpetual spirit of resistance cherished as a safe-guard, might perhaps in the end destroy the equipage; firmness would become pride and self-assurance, and the soft, sweet, feminine texture of the mind settle into rigidity. Is there then no sanctuary for such a mind?—Where shall it find a refuge from the world?—Where seek for strength against itself? Where, but in heaven?

Camiola, in Massinger's *Maid of Honour*,[1] is said to emulate Portia; and the real story of Camiola (for she is an historical personage) is very beautiful. She was a lady of Messina, who lived in the beginning of the fourteenth century; and was the contemporary of Queen Joanna, of Petrarch, and Boccaccio. It fell out in those days that Prince Orlando of Arragon, the younger brother of the King of Sicily, having taken the command of a naval armament against the Neapolitans, was defeated, wounded, taken prisoner, and confined by Robert of Naples (the father of Queen Joanna) in one of his strongest castles. As the prince had distinguished himself by his enmity to the Neapolitans and by many exploits against them, his ransom was fixed at an exorbitant sum, and his captivity was unusually severe; while the King of Sicily, who had some cause of displeasure against his brother, and imputed to him the defeat of his armament, refused either to negotiate for his release or to pay the ransom demanded.

Orlando, who was celebrated for his fine person and reckless valor, was apparently doomed to languish away the rest of his life in a dungeon, when Camiola Turinga, a rich Sicilian heiress, devoted the half of her fortune to release him. But as such an action might expose her to evil comments, she made it a condition that Orlando should marry her. The prince gladly accepted the terms, and sent her the contract of marriage, signed by his hand; but no sooner was he at liberty than he refused to fulfil it, and even denied all knowledge of his benefactress.

Camiola appealed to the tribunal of state, produced the written contract, and described the obligations she had heaped on this ungrateful and ungenerous man: sentence was given against him, and he was adjudged to Camiola, not only as her rightful husband, but as a property which, according to the laws of war in that age, she had purchased with her gold. The day of marriage was fixed; Orlando

---

[1] Philip Massinger (1583–1640), English playwright. *The Maid of Honour* (ca. 1621–22) is based on a story by Boccaccio, and the heroine, Camiola, is considered one of Massinger's best characters.

presented himself with a splendid retinue; Camiola also appeared, decorated as for her bridal; but instead of bestowing her hand on the recreant, she reproached him in the presence of all with his breach of faith, declared her utter contempt for his baseness, and then freely bestowing on him the sum paid for his ransom, as a gift worthy of his mean soul, she turned away, and dedicated herself and her heart to heaven. In this resolution she remained inflexible, though the king and all the court united in entreaties to soften her. She took the veil; and Orlando, henceforth regarded as one who had stained his knighthood and violated his faith, passed the rest of his life as a dishonored man, and died in obscurity.

Camiola, in *The Maid of Honour*, is, like Portia, a wealthy heiress, surrounded by suitors, and "queen o'er herself": the character is constructed upon the same principles, as great intellectual power, magnanimity of temper, and feminine tenderness; but not only do pain and disquiet, and the change induced by unkind and inauspicious influences, enter into this sweet picture to mar and cloud its happy beauty, but the portrait itself may be pronounced out of drawing;—for Massinger apparently had not sufficient delicacy of sentiment to work out his own conception of the character with perfect consistency. In his adaptation of the story he represents the mutual love of Orlando and Camiola as existing previous to the captivity of the former, and on his part declared with many vows of eternal faith; yet she requires a written contract of marriage before she liberates him. It will perhaps be said that she has penetrated his weakness, and anticipates his falsehood. Miserable excuse!—how could a magnanimous woman love a man whose falsehood she believes but *possible?*— or loving him, how could she deign to secure herself by such means against the consequences? Shakespeare and Nature never committed such a solecism. Camiola doubts before she has been wronged; the firmness and assurance in herself border on harshness. What in Portia is the gentle wisdom of a noble nature appears in Camiola too much a spirit of calculation; it savors a little of the counting-house. As Portia is the heiress of Belmont, and Camiola a merchant's daughter, the distinction may be proper and characteristic, but it is not in favor of Camiola. The contrast may be thus illustrated:

CAMIOLA: You have heard of Bertoldo's captivity, and the king's neglect, the greatness of his ransom; *fifty thousand crowns*. Adorni! *Two parts of my estate*! Yet I so love the gentleman, for to you I will confess my weakness, that I purpose now, when he is forsaken by the king and his own hopes, to ransom him.—*Maid of Honour*, act iii.

PORTIA: What sum owes he the Jew?
BASSANIO: For me—three thousand ducats.
PORTIA: What? *no more*!
Pay him six thousand and deface the bond,
Double six thousand, and then treble that,
Before a friend of this description
Shall lose a hair thro' my Bassanio's fault.
　　　—You shall have gold
To pay the *petty debt* twenty times o'er.—*Merchant of Venice*.

Camiola, who is a Sicilian, might as well have been born at Amsterdam: Portia could only have existed in Italy. Portia is profound as she is brilliant; Camiola is sensible and sententious: she asserts her dignity very successfully; but we cannot for a moment imagine Portia as reduced to the necessity of *asserting* hers. The idiot Sylli, in *The Maid of Honour*, who follows Camiola like one of the deformed dwarfs of old time, is an intolerable violation of taste and propriety, and it sensibly lowers our impression of the principal character. Shakespeare would never have placed Sir Andrew Aguecheek[1] in constant and immediate approximation with such a woman as Portia.

Lastly, the charm of the poetical coloring is wholly wanting in Camiola, so that when she is placed in contrast with the glowing eloquence, the luxuriant grace, the buoyant spirit of Portia, the effect is somewhat that of coldness and formality. Notwithstanding the dignity and the beauty of Massinger's delineation, and the noble self-devotion of Camiola, which I acknowledge and admire, the two characters will admit of no comparison as sources of contemplation and pleasure.

---

[1]　Foolish suitor for Olivia in Shakespeare's *Twelfth Night*.

SOURCE

Shakespeare's Heroines: Characteristics of Women, Moral, Poetical and Historical (1832).

SELECTED SECONDARY READING

Johnstone, Judith. *Anna Jameson: Victorian, Feminist, Woman of Letters.* Aldershot: Scolar Press, 1997.

Russell, Anne E. "'History and Real Life': Anna Jameson, *Shakespeare's Heroines* and Victorian Women." *Victorian Review* 17.2 (Winter 1991): 35–49.

ACHIEVEMENTS OF THE GENIUS OF SCOTT
(DECEMBER 1832)

Harriet Martineau

HARRIET MARTINEAU (1802–76) was born in Norwich into a family of Unitarian textile manufacturers. Martineau's childhood was an unhappy one—in part because of her increasing deafness—but she early turned to education and study as a compensation for her feelings of isolation. She began her journalistic career in the 1820s, publishing articles about educational opportunities for women. Shortly after she began to write, her father's death and the failure of the family business freed her forever from the constraints of traditional middle-class feminine pursuits. As she described the situation in her *Autobiography*: "I, who had been obliged to write before breakfast, or in some private way, had henceforth liberty to do my own work in my own way; for we had lost our gentility"; this loss of caste ultimately enabled her to "have truly lived instead of vegetated" (1:108).

By the early 1830s, Martineau had become the only paid contributor to the newly reorganized *Monthly Repository*, and she became convinced that "authorship was my legitimate career" (*Autobiography* 1:156). With the encouragement of editor and mentor William Johnson Fox, in 1832 she launched her *Illustrations of Political Economy*, a series of fictionalized illustrations of the theories of Adam Smith that secured both her literary and financial success.

Martineau published influential works in a variety of nonfiction genres. (Her only noteworthy novel, *Deerbrook*, was published in 1839.) Her American travel books, *Society in America* (1837) and *A Retrospect of Western Travel* (1838), provided a foundation for modern sociological studies, and her *Life in the Sickroom* (1844) and *Letters on Mesmerism* (1845) did much to build sympathy and support for the sick and disabled, although the latter book caused a breach in her family. Martineau also wrote social and political history, most notably *The History of England During the Thirty Years' Peace, 1816–1846* (1849–50), and translated French philosopher Auguste Comte's *Positive Philosophy* in 1853.

What she regarded as her most important work was begun in 1852, when she joined the staff of the London *Daily News*. Over the next 14 years, Martineau wrote over 1,600 articles for the newspaper. The *Daily News* provided her a forum for discussing the many sociopolitical issues with which she was deeply engaged, including abolition, improved opportunities for women and the working classes, and industrial reform.

By her own assessment, Martineau was a popularizer of great ideas rather than an original thinker, although such an assessment downplays the cogency and force of her analyses. Her social and aesthetic criticism display a strong moral emphasis and surprisingly un-Victorian clarity of expression. In the following excerpt, taken from a series of articles originally published in *Tait's Magazine* in 1832, and republished as *Miscellanies* in 1836, Martineau discusses what she considers to be Sir Walter Scott's primary achievement: his use of fiction to address serious moral and societal questions. Her essay is not only an analysis of Scott's work, but a defence of fiction at a time when the novel was still a suspect genre. Martineau's appeal to other writers to apply Scott's techniques to "the present condition of society" is also an early recognition of the potential power of realist fiction to effect social change, and it prepares the way for such novelists as Dickens, Gaskell, and Eliot. Finally, her essay on Scott also serves to justify the strategy she was to employ in her *Illustrations of Political Economy*: in Martineau's analysis, fiction was the best way to reach the hearts and minds of lettered and unlettered alike, and thus anyone who wanted to educate— "the whole living phalanx of clergy, orthodox and dissenting, of moral philosophers, of all moral teachers"—"must yield the sceptre of moral sway" to Scott and his imitators.

THERE IS LITTLE REASON to question that Scott has done more for the morals of society, taking the expression in its largest sense, than all the divines, and other express moral teachers, of a century past. When we consider that all moral sciences are best taught by exemplification, and that these exemplifications produce tenfold effect when exhibited unprofessionally, it appears that dramatists and novelists of a high order have usually the advantage, as moralists, over those whose office it is to present morals in an abstract form. The latter are needed to systematize the science, and to prevent its being lost sight of as the highest of the sciences; but the advantage of practical influence rests with the former. When we, moreover, consider the extent of Scott's practical influence, and multiply this extent by its force, there will be little need of argument to prove that the whole living phalanx of clergy, orthodox and dissenting, of moral philosophers, of all moral teachers, except statesmen and authors of a high order, must yield the sceptre of moral sway to Scott. If they are wise, they will immediately acknowledge this, estimate his achievements, adopt, to a certain extent, his methods, and step forward to the vantage ground he has gained for them. If they be disposed to question the fact of the superiority of his influence, let them measure it for an instant against their own. Let them look to our universities, and declare whether they have, within a century, done much for the advancement of morals at home, or to bring morals into respect abroad. Let them look to the weight of the established clergy, and say how much they actually modify the thoughts and guide the conduct of the nation; taking into the account, as a balance against the good they do, the suspicion there exists against them in their character of a craft, and the disrepute which attaches itself to what they teach, through an admixture of abuses. Let them look to the dissenting clergy,—far more influential as they are than the established,—and say, whether they operate as extensively and benignantly upon the human heart, as he who makes life itself the language in which he sets forth the aims and ends of life; who not only uses a picture-alphabet, that the untutored and the truant may be allured to learn, but imparts thereto a hieroglyphic character, from which the most versed in human life may evolve continually a deeper and yet deeper lore. Let our moral philosophers (usefully employed though they be in arranging and digesting the science, and enlightened in modifying, from time to time, the manifestations of its eternal principles)—let our moral philosophers declare whether they expect their digests and expositions to be eagerly listened to by the hundred thousand families, collected, after their daily avocations, under the spell of the northern enchanter; whether they would look for thumbed copies of their writings in workshops and counting-houses, in the saloons of palaces, and under many a pillow in boarding-schools. Our universities may purify morals, and extend their influence as far as they can; their importance in this case runs a chance of being overlooked: for Scott is the president of a college where nations may be numbered for individuals. Our clergy may be and do all that an established clergy can be and do; yet they will not effect so much as the mighty lay preacher who has gone out on the highways of the world, with cheerfulness in his mien and benignity on his brow; unconscious, perhaps, of the dignity of his office, but as much more powerful in comparison with a stalled priesthood, as the troubadour of old,—firing hearts wherever he went with the love of glory,—than the vowed monk. Our dissenting preachers may obtain a hold on the hearts of their people, and employ it to good purpose; but they cannot send their voices east and west to wake up the echoes of the world. Let all these unite in a missionary scheme, and encompass the globe, and still Scott will teach morals more effectually than them all. They will not find audiences at every turn who will take to heart all they say, and bear it in mind for ever; and if they attempt it now, they will find that Scott has been before them every where. He has preached truth, simplicity, benevolence, and retribution, in the spicy bowers of Ceylon, and in the verandahs of Indian bungalowes, and in the perfumed dwellings of Persia, and among groups of settlers at the Cape, and amidst the pine woods and savannahs of the western world, and in the vineyards of the Peninsula, and among the ruins of Rome, and the recesses of the Alps, and the hamlets of France, and the cities of Germany, and the palaces of Russian despots, and the homes of Polish patriots. And all this in addition to what has been done in his native kingdom, where he has exalted the tastes, ameliorated the tempers, enriched the associations, and exercised the intellects of millions. This is already done in the short space of eighteen years; a mere span in comparison with the time that it is to be hoped our language and literature will last. We may assume the influence of Scott, as we have described it, to be just beginning its course of a thousand years; and now, what class of moral teachers (except politicians, who are not too ready to regard themselves in this light), will venture to bring their influence into comparison with that of the great lay preacher?[1]

· · ·

To do his next work of beneficence, this great moralist stepped beyond the Border, and over continents and seas. He implanted or nourished pure tastes, not only in a thousand homes, but among the homeless in every land. How many indolent have been roused to thought and feeling, how many licentious have been charmed into the temporary love of purity, how many vacant minds have become occupied with objects of interest and affection, it would be impossible to estimate, unless we could converse with every Briton, from the Factory Terrace at Canton round the world to the shores of the Pacific, and with every foreigner on the Continent of Europe whose countenance lights up at the name of Scott. If one representative only of every class which has been thus benefited were to repair to his grave, the mourning train would be of a length that kings might envy. There would be the lisping child, weeping that there should be no more tales of the

---

[1]   In the following omitted section, Martineau discusses Scott's "lesser" achievements of improving Scotland's image abroad and also positively influencing Scottish morals and manners.

Sherwood Foresters and the Disinherited Knight; there would be the school-boy, with his heart full of the heroic deeds of Coeur de Lion in Palestine; and the girl, glowing with the loyalty of Flora, and saddening over the griefs of Rebecca;[1] and the artisan who foregoes his pipe and pot for the adventures of Jeanie Deans;[2] and the clerk and apprentice, who refresh their better part from the toils of the counting-house amidst the wild scenery of Scotland; and soldier and sailor relieved of the tedium of barracks and cabin by the interest of more stirring scenes presented to the mind's eye; and rambling youth chained to the fireside by the links of a pleasant fiction; and sober manhood made to grow young again; and sickness beguiled, and age cheered, and domestic jars forgotten, and domestic sympathies enhanced;—all who have thus had pure tastes gratified by the creations of his genius, should join the pilgrim train, which will be passing in spirit by his grave for centuries to come. Of these, how many have turned from the voice of the preacher, have cast aside "good books," have no ear for music, no taste for drawing, no knowledge of any domestic accomplishment which might keep them out of harm's way, but have found that they have a heart and mind which Scott could touch and awaken! How many have thus to thank him, not only for the solace of their leisure, but for the ennobling of their toils!

Another great service rendered is one which could be administered only by means of fiction—a service respecting which it matters not to decide whether it was afforded designedly or unconsciously. We mean the introduction of the conception of nature, as existing and following out its own growth in an atmosphere of convention; a conception of very great importance to the many who, excluded from the regions of convention, are apt to lose their manhood in its contemplation. There is little use in assuring people of the middling ranks, that kings eat beef and mutton, and queens ride on horseback; they believe, but they do not realize. And this is the case, not only with the child who pictures a monarch with the crown on his head, on a

---

[1] Characters in *Waverley* and *Ivanhoe*.
[2] Heroine of *The Heart of Midlothian*.

throne, or with the maid-servant who gazes in awe on the Lord Mayor's couch; but to a much greater degree than is commonly supposed, with the father of the child, the master of the maid,—with him whose interests have to do with kings and courts, and who ought, therefore, to know what is passing there. It would be impossible to calculate how much patriotism has lain dormant, through the ignorance of the plain citizen, of what is felt and thought in the higher regions of society, to which his voice of complaint or suggestion ought to reach, if he had but the courage to lift it up. The ignorance may be called voluntary: it may be truly said that every one ought to know that human hearts answer to one another as a reflection in water, whether this reflection be of a glow-worm on the brink, or of the loftiest resplendent star. This is true; but it is not a truth easy in the use; and its use is all-important. The divine preaches it, as his duty, to humble courtly pride, and to remind the lowly of their manhood: but the divine himself realizes the doctrine better while reading *Kenilworth*, or *The Abbot*, than while writing his sermon; and his hearers use this same sermon as a text, of which Nigel and Peveril[1] are the exposition. Is this a slight service to have rendered?—to have, perhaps unconsciously, taught human equality, while professing to exhibit human inequality?—to have displayed, in its full proportion, the distance which separates man from man, and to have shown that the very same interests are being transacted at one and the other end of the line? Walter Scott was exactly the man to render this great service; and how well he rendered it, he was little aware. A man, born of the people, and therefore knowing man, and at the same time a Tory antiquarian, and therefore knowing courts, he was the fit person to show the one to the other. At once a benevolent interpreter of the heart, and a worshipper of royalty, he might be trusted for doing honor to both parties; though not, we must allow, equal honor. We cannot award him the praise of perfect impartiality in his interpretations. We cannot but see a leaning towards regal weaknesses, and a toleration of courtly vices. We cannot but observe, that the same licen-

---

[1] Heroes of *The Fortunes of Nigel* and *Peveril of the Peak*.

tiousness which would have been rendered disgusting under equal temptation in humble life, is made large allowance for when diverting itself within palace walls. Retribution is allowed to befall; but the vices which this whip is permitted to scourge are still pleasant vices, instead of vulgar ones. This is not to be wondered at; and perhaps the purity of the writer's own imagination may save us from lamenting it; for he viewed these things, though partially, yet too philosophically, to allow of any shadow of an imputation of countenancing, or alluring to vice, with whatever wit he may have depicted the intrigues of Buckingham, or whatever veil of tenderness he may have cast over the crimes of the unfortunate Mary. His desire was to view these things in the spirit of charity; and he was less aware than his readers of a humble rank, that he threw the gloss of romance over his courtly scenes of every character, and that, if he had drawn the vices of the lower classes, it would have been without any such advantage. Meanwhile, we owe him much for having laid open to us the affections of sovereigns,—the passions of courtiers,—the emotions of the hearts,—the guidance of the conduct,—the cares and amusements,— the business and the jests of courts. He has taught many of us how royalty may be reached and wrought upon; and has therein done more for the state than perhaps any novelist ever contemplated. That he did not complete his work by giving to courts accurate representations of the people, seems a pity; but it could not be helped, since there is much in the people of which Walter Scott knew nothing. If this fact is not yet recognised in courts, it soon will be; and to Walter Scott again it may be owing (as we shall hereafter show) that the true condition and character of the people will become better known in aristocratic regions than they are at present.[1]

· · ·

Another important moral service, which belongs almost exclusively to fiction, is that of satirizing eccentricities and follies, commonly

---

[1] In the following omitted section, Martineau discusses how Scott's fiction has exposed religious hypocrisy and superstition and thereby promoted greater religious tolerance.

thought too insignificant to be preached against, and gravely written about; but which exert an important influence on the happiness of human life. The oddities of women he has left almost untouched; but we have a brave assemblage of men who are safe from pulpit censure; (unless another Henry Warden should rise up to preach against the sixteen follies of a Roland Graeme under sixteen heads);[1] but who may be profited by seeing their own picture, or whose picture may prevent others becoming like them. Is it not wholesome to have a Malagrowther[2] before us on whom to exhaust our impatience, instead of venting it on the real Malagrowthers of society? Shall we not have fewer and less extravagant Saddletrees, and Shaftons, and Halcroes, and Yellowleys,[3] for these novels? and will not such bores be regarded with more good humor? Will not some excellent Jonathan Oldbuck now and then think of the Antiquary, and check his hobby?—and many a book-worm take a lesson from Dominie Sampson?[4] Whether such a direct effect be or be not produced, such exhibitions are as effectual as comedy ought to be on the stage, and mirthful raillery in real life, in enforcing some of the obligations, and improving the amenities of society. The rich variety of Scott's assemblage of oddities, and the exquisite mirth and good-humor with which they are shown off, are among the most remarkable particulars of his achievements. There is not only a strong cast of individuality (as there ought to be) about all his best characters; but his best characters are none of them representatives of a class. As soon as he attempted to make his personages such representatives, he failed. His ostensible heroes, his statesmen and leaders, his magistrates, his adventurers, his womankind, whether mistresses or maids, leave little impression of individuality; while his sovereigns, real heroes, and oddities are inimitable. The reasons of this failure may be found under our next head. The result is, that Walter Scott is not only one of the most amiable, but one of the most effective satirists that ever helped to sweep the path of life clear of the strewn follies under which many a thorn is hidden.

---

1   Characters in *The Monastery* and *The Abbott.*
2   Character in *The Fortunes of Nigel.*
3   Characters in *The Heart of Midlothian, The Monastery,* and *The Pirate.*
4   Characters in *The Antiquary* and *Guy Mannering.*

In ascending the scale of social services, for which gratitude is due to the illustrious departed, we next arrive at one which is so great that we cannot but mourn that it was not yet greater. There can be no need to enlarge upon the beauty and excellence of the spirit of kindliness which breathes through the whole of Scott's compositions; a spirit which not only shames the Malagrowthers of society, just spoken of, but charms the restless to repose, exhilarates the melancholy, rouses the apathetic, and establishes a good understanding among all who contemplate one another in these books. It is as impossible for any one to remain cynical, or moody, or desponding, over these books, as for an infant to look dismally in the face of a smiling nurse. As face answers to face, so does heart to heart; and as Walter Scott's overflowed with love and cheerfulness, the hearts of his readers catch its brimmings. If any are shut against him, they are not of his readers; and we envy them not. They may find elsewhere all imaginable proofs and illustrations of the goodliness of a kindly spirit; but why not add to these as perfect an exemplification as ever was offered? It may be very well to take one abroad in the grey dawn, and tell him that the hills have a capacity of appearing green, the waters golden, and the clouds rose-colored, and that larks sometimes sing soaring in the air, instead of crouching in a grassy nest; but why not let him remain to witness the effusion of light from behind the mountain, the burst of harmony from field and copse? Why not let him feel, as well as know, what a morning of sunshine is? Why not let him view its effects from every accessible point, and pour out his joy in snatches of song responsive to those which he hears around him, as well as his thankfulness in a matin hymn? If it be true, as no readers of Scott will deny, that it exhilarates the spirits, and animates the affections, to follow the readings of this great Enchanter, it is certain that he has achieved a great moral work of incitement and amelioration. The test of his merits here is, that his works are for the innocent and kindly-hearted to enjoy; and if any others enjoy them, it is by becoming innocent and kindly for the time, in like manner as it is for the waking flocks and choirs to welcome the sunrise: if the fox and the owl choose to remain abroad, the one must abstain from its prey, and the other hush its hootings.

The kindliness of spirit being of so bright a quality, makes us lament all the more, as we have said, that it had not the other excellence of being universally diffused. We know how unreasonable it is to expect every thing from one man, and are far from saying or believing that Walter Scott looked otherwise than benignantly on all classes and all individuals that came under his observation. What we lament is, that there were extensive classes of men, and they the most important to society, that were secluded from the light of his embellishing genius. His sunshine gilded whatever it fell upon, but it did not fall from a sufficient height to illuminate the nooks and valleys which he found and left curtained in mists. What is there of humble life in his narratives? What did he know of those who live and move in that region? Nothing. There is not a *character* from humble life in all his library of volumes; nor had he any conception that character is to be found there. By humble life we do not mean Edie Ochiltree's lot of privileged mendacity, nor Dirk Hatteraick's smuggling adventures, nor the Saxon slavery of Gurth, nor the feudal adherence of Dougal and Caleb Balderstone, and Adam Woodcock, nor the privileged dependance of Caxon and Fairservice.[1] None of these had any thing to do with humble life: each and all formed a part of the aristocratic system in which Walter Scott's affections were bound up. Jeanie Deans herself, besides being no original conception of Sir Walter's, derives none of her character or interest from her station in life, any farther than as it was the occasion of the peculiarity of her pilgrimage. We never think of Jeanie as poor, or low in station. Her simplicity is that which might pertain to a secluded young woman of any rank; and it is difficult to bear in mind—it is like an extraneous circumstance, that her sister was at service, the only attempt made throughout at realizing the social position of the parties. We do not mention this as any drawback upon the performance, but merely as saving the only apparent exception to our remarks, that Sir Walter rendered no service to humble life in the way of delineating its society. Faithful butlers and barbers, tricky lady's maids, eccentric falconers and gamekeepers, are not those among whom we should look for the strength of character, the sternness of passion, the practical heroism, the inexhaustible patience, the unassuming self-denial, the unconscious beneficence—in

---

[1] Characters in *The Antiquary, Guy Mannering, Ivanhoe, The Bride of Lammermoor, The Abbott,* and *Rob Roy.*

a word, the *true-heartedness* which is to be found in its perfection in humble life. Of all this Walter Scott knew nothing. While discriminating, with the nicest acumen, the shades of character, the modifications of passion, among those whom he did understand, he was wholly unaware that he bounded himself within a small circle, beyond which lay a larger, and a larger; that which he represented being found in each, in a more distinct outline, in more vivid coloring, and in striking and various combinations, with other characteristics of humanity which had never presented themselves to him. He knew not that the strength of soul, which he represents as growing up in his heroes amidst the struggles of the crusade, is of the same kind with that which is nourished in our neighbours of the next alley, by conflicts of a less romantic, but not less heroic cast. He knew not that the passion of ambition, which he has made to contend with love so fearfully in Leicester's bosom,[1] is the same passion, similarly softened and aggravated, with that which consumes the high-spirited working man, chosen by his associates to represent and guide their interests, while his heart is torn by opposite appeals to his domestic affections. He knew not that, however reckless the vice of some of his courtly personages, greater recklessness is to be found in the presence of poverty; that the same poverty exposes love to further trials than he has described, and exercises it into greater refinement; and puts loyalty more severely to the test, and inspires a nobler intrepidity, and nourishes a deeper hatred, and a wilder superstition, and a more inveterate avarice, and a more disinterested generosity, and a more imperturbable fortitude, than even he has set before us. In short, he knew not that all passions, and all natural movements of society, that he has found in the higher, exist in the humbler ranks; and all magnified and deepened in proportion as reality prevails over convention, as there is less mixture of the adventitious with the true. The effect of this partial knowledge is not only the obliteration to himself and to his readers, as far as connected with him, of more than half the facts and interests of humanity, but that his benevolence was stinted in its play. We find no philanthropists among his characters; because he had not the means of

---

[1]   Robert Dudley, Earl of Leicester (1533–88), courtier and favorite of Elizabeth I. He is a character in *Kenilworth*.

forming the conception of philanthropy in its largest sense. He loved men, all men whom he knew; but that love was not based on knowledge as extensive as his observation was penetrating; and it did not therefore deserve the high title of philanthropy. We have no sins of commission to charge him with, no breaches of charity, not a thought or expression which is tinged with bitterness against man, collectively or individually; but we charge him with omission of which he was unconscious, and which he would, perhaps, scarcely have wished to repair, as it must have been done at the expense of his Toryism, to which the omission and unconsciousness were owing. How should a man be a philanthropist who knows not what freedom is?—not the mere freedom from foreign domination, but the exemption from misrule at home, the liberty of watching over and renovating institutions, that the progression of man and of states may proceed together. Of this kind of freedom Sir Walter had no conception, and neither, therefore, are there any patriots in his *dramatis personae.* There are abundance of soldiers to light up beacons and fly to arms at the first notice of invasion; many to drink the healths and fight the battles of their chiefs, to testify their fidelity to their persons, and peril life and liberty in their cause; plenty to vindicate the honor of England abroad, and to exult in her glory at home. But this is not patriotism, any more than kindliness is philanthropy. We have no long-sighted views respecting the permanent improvement of society,— no extensive regards to the interests of an entire nation; and, therefore, no simple self-sacrifice, no steadfastness of devotion to country and people. The noble class of virtues, which go to make up patriotism, are not even touched upon by Scott. The sufferings of his heroes are represented to arise from wounded pride, and from the laceration of personal, or domestic, or feudal feelings and prepossessions; and in no single instance from sympathy with the race, or any large body of them. The courage of his heroes is, in like manner, compounded of instincts and of conventional stimuli; and in no one case derived from principles of philanthropy, or of patriotism, which is one direction of philanthropy. Their fortitude, howsoever steadfast, when arising from self-devotion at all, arises only from that unreasoning acquiescence in established forms, which is as inferior to the self-sacrifice of philanthropy, as the implicit obedience of a child is inferior to the concurrence of the reasoning man. None of Scott's personages act and suffer as members and servants of society. Each is for his own; whether it be his family, his chief, his king, or his country, in a warlike sense. The weal or woe of many, or of all, is the only consideration which does not occur to them—the only motive to enterprise and endurance which is not so much as alluded to. There is no talk of freedom, as respects any thing but brute force,—no suspicion that one class is in a state of privilege, and another in a state of subjugation, and that these things ought not to be. Gurth, indeed, is relieved from Saxon bondage, and Adam Woodcock is as imperious and meddling as he pleases, and the ladies' maids have abundant liberty to play pranks; but this sort of freedom has nothing to do with the right of manhood, and with what ought to be, and will be, the right of womanhood—it is the privilege of slavery, won by encroachment, and preserved by favor. Gurth got rid of his collar, but in our days he would be called a slave: and Adam Woodcock and Mistress Lilias lived by the breath of their lady's nostrils, in the same manner as the courtiers of Coeur de Lion gained an unusual length of tether from their lord's knightly courtesy, and those of the second Charles from his careless clemency. There is no freedom in all this. *Slave* is written on the knightly crest of the master, and on the liveried garb of the servitor, as plainly as even on the branded shoulder of the negro. But it must be so, it is urged, when times and scenes of slavery are chosen as the groundwork of the fiction.

We answer, Nay; the spirit of freedom may breathe through the delineation of slavery. However far back we may revert to the usages of the feudal system, there may be,—there must be, if they exist in the mind of the author,—aspirations after a state of society more worthy of humanity. In displaying all the pomp of chivalry, the heart ought to mourn the woes of inequality it inflicted, while the imagination revels in its splendors. But this could not be the case with Scott, who knew about as much of the real condition and character of the humble classes of each age as the Japanese; perhaps less, as he was a reader of Basil Hall.[1] Beyond that which seemed to him the outermost

---

[1] Captain Basil Hall (1788–1844), explorer and writer. Most of his books are about the Far East and North America.

circle, that of the domestics of the great, all was a blank; save a few vague outlines of beggar-women with seven small children, and other such groups that have by some chance found their way into works of fiction. His benignity, therefore, alloyed by no bitterness of disposition in himself, was so far restricted by the imperfection of his knowledge of life, as to prevent his conveying the conception of philanthropy in its largest sense. His services to freedom are of a negative, rather than a positive character; rendered by showing how things work in a state of slavery, rather than how they should work in a condition of rational freedom; and it follows, that his incitements to benevolence are also tendered unconsciously. Through an exhibition of the softening and brightening influence of benignity shed over the early movements of society, he indicates what must be the meridian splendor of philanthropy, penetrating every where, irradiating where it penetrates, and fertilizing, as well as embellishing whatever it shines upon.

Much has Walter Scott also done, and done it also unconsciously, for woman. Neither Mary Wollstonecraft, nor Thompson of Cork,[1] nor any other advocate of the rights of woman, pleaded so eloquently to the thoughtful,—and the thoughtful alone will entertain the subject,—as Walter Scott, by his exhibition of what women are, and by two or three indications of what they might be. He has been found fault with for the poverty of character of the women of his tales; a species of blame against which we have always protested. If he had made as long a list of oddities among his women as his men, he would have exposed himself to the reproach of quitting nature, and deserting classes for extravagant individualities; since there is much less scope for eccentricity among women, in the present state of society, than among men. But, it is alleged, he has made few of his female characters representatives of a class. True; for the plain reason, that there are scarcely any classes to represent. We thank him for the forcible exhibition of this truth: we thank him for the very term *womankind*; and can well bear its insulting use in the mouth of the scoffer, for the sake of the process it may set to

---

[1] William Thompson (1778–1883), radical Irish thinker.

work in the mind of the meditative and the just. There is no saying what the common use of the term *canaille* may in time be proved to have effected for the lower orders of men; or in what degree the process of female emancipation may be hastened by the slang use of the term *womankind*, by despots and by fools. It may lead some watchful intellects—some feeling hearts—to ponder the reasons of the fact, that the word *mankind* calls up associations of grandeur and variety,—that of *womankind*, ideas of littleness and sameness,—that the one brings after it conceptions of lofty destiny, heroic action, grave counsel, a busy office in society, a dignified repose from cares, a steadfast pursuit of wisdom, an intrepid achievement of good;—while the other originates the very opposite conceptions,—vegetation instead of life, folly instead of counsel, frivolity instead of action, restlessness in the palace of industry, apathy in that of repose, listless accomplishment of small aims, a passive reception of what others may please to impart; or, at the very best, a halting, intermitting pursuit of dimly-discerned objects. To some it may be suggested to inquire, Why this contrast should exist?—why one-half of the rational creation should be so very much less rational?—and, as a consequence, so much less good, and so much less happy than the other? If they are for a moment led by custom to doubt whether, because they are less rational, they are less happy and less good, the slightest recurrence to Scott's novels is enough to satisfy them, that the common notion of the sufficiency of present female objects to female progression and happiness is unfounded. They will perhaps look abroad from Scott into all other works of fiction—into all faithful pictures of life—and see what women are; and they will finally perceive, that the fewer women there are found to plead the cause of their sex, the larger mixture of folly there is in their pleadings; the more extensive their own unconsciousness of their wrongs, the stronger is their case. The best argument for Negro Emancipation lies in the vices and subservience of slaves: the best argument for female emancipation lies in the folly and contentedness of women under the present system,— an argument to which Walter Scott has done the fullest justice; for a set of more passionless, frivolous, uninteresting beings was never assembled at morning auction, or evening tea-table, than he has presented us with in his novels. The few exceptions are made so by the strong workings of instinct, or of superstition (the offspring of strong instinct and weak reason combined); save in the two or three instances where the female mind had been exposed to manly discipline. Scott's female characters are easily arranged under these divisions:—Three-fourths are *womankind* merely: pretty, insignificant ladies, with their pert waiting maids. A few are viragoes, in whom instinct is strong, whose souls are to migrate hereafter into the she-eagle or bear,—Helen M'Gregor, Ulrica, Magdalen Graeme, and the Highland Mother.[1] A few are superstitious,—Elspeth, Alice, Norna, Mother Nicneven. A few exhibit the same tendencies, modified by some one passion; as Lady Ashton, Lady Derby, and Lady Douglas.[2] Mary and Elizabeth are womankind modified by royalty. There only remain Flora M'Ivor, Die Vernon, Rebecca, and Jeanie Deans.[3] For these four, and their glorious significance, womankind are as much obliged to Walter Scott as for the insignificance of all the rest; not because they are what women might be, and therefore ought to be; but because they afford indications of this, and that these indications are owing to their having escaped from the management of man, and been trained by the discipline of circumstance. If common methods yield no such women as these; if such women occasionally come forth from the school of experience, what an argument is this against the common methods,—what a plea for a change of system! Woman cannot be too grateful to him who has furnished it. Henceforth, when men fire at the name of Flora M'Ivor, let women say, "There will be more Floras when women feel that they have political power and duties." When men worship the image of Die Vernon, let them be reminded, that there will be other Die Vernons when women are impelled to self-reliance. When Jeanie is spoken of with tender esteem, let it be suggested, that strength of motive makes heroism of action; and that as long as motive is confined and weakened, the very activity which should accomplish high aims must degenerate into puerile restlessness. When Rebecca is sighed for, as a lofty presence that has passed away, it should be asked, how she should possibly

---

[1] Characters in *Ivanhoe, The Abbott,* and *The Chronicles of the Canongate.*

[2] Characters in *The Bride of Lammermoor, Peveril of the Peak,* and *Castle Dangerous.*

[3] Characters in *Waverley, Rob Roy, Ivanhoe,* and *The Heart of Midlothian.*

remain or re-appear in a society which alike denies the discipline by which her high powers and sensibilities might be matured, and the objects on which they might be worthily employed? As a woman, no less than as a Jewess, she is the representative of the wrongs of a degraded and despised class: there is no abiding-place for her among foes to her caste; she wanders unemployed (as regards her peculiar capabilities) through the world; and when she dies, there has been, not only a deep injury inflicted, but a waste made of the resources of human greatness and happiness. Yes, women may choose Rebecca as the representative of their capabilities: first, despised, then wondered at, and involuntarily admired; tempted, made use of, then persecuted, and finally banished—not by a formal decree, but by being refused honorable occupation, and a safe abiding place. Let women not only take her for their model, but make her speak for them to society, till they have obtained the educational discipline which beseems them; the rights, political and social, which are their due; and that equal regard with the other sex in the eye of man, which it requires the faith of Rebecca to assure them they have in the eye of Heaven. Meantime, while still suffering under injustice, let them lay to heart, for strength and consolation, the beautiful commentary which Walter Scott has given on the lot of the representative of their wrongs. If duly treasured, it may prove by its effects, that our author has contributed, in more ways than one, to female emancipation; by supplying a principle of renovation to the enslaved, as well as by exposing their condition; by pointing out the ends for which freedom and power are desirable, as well as the disastrous effects of withholding them.[1]

• • •

These, then, are the moral services,—many and great,—which Scott has rendered,—positively and negatively,—consciously and unconsciously, to society. He has softened national prejudices; he has

---

[1] Martineau here quotes a long passage from Scott on *Ivanhoe*, in which he argues that allowing Rebecca to marry Ivanhoe would teach a false lesson, that virtue and self-denial are rewarded.

encouraged innocent tastes in every region of the world; he has imparted to certain influential classes the conviction that human nature works alike in all; he has exposed priestcraft and fanaticism; he has effectively satirized eccentricities, unamiableness, and follies; he has irresistibly recommended benignity in the survey of life, and indicated the glory of a higher kind of benevolence; and finally, he has advocated the rights of woman with a force all the greater for his being unaware of the import and tendency of what he was saying. The one other achievement which we attribute to him, is also not the less magnificent for being overlooked by himself.

By achieving so much within narrow bounds, he has taught how more may be achieved in a wider space. He has taught us the power of fiction as an agent of morals and philosophy; "and it shall go hard with us but we will better the instruction." Every agent of these master spirits is wanted in an age like this; and he who has placed a new one at their service, is a benefactor of society. Scott might have written, as he declared he wrote, for the passing of his time, the improvement of his fortunes, and the amusement of his readers: he might have believed, as he declared he believed, that little moral utility arises out of works of fiction: we are not bound to estimate his works as lightly as he did, or to agree in his opinions of their influences. We rather learn from him how much may be impressed by exemplification which would be rejected in the form of reasoning, and how there may be more extensive *embodiments* of truth in fiction than the world was before thoroughly aware of. It matters not that the truth he exemplified was taken up at random, like that of all his predecessors in the walks of fiction. Others may systematize, having learned from him how extensively they may embody. There is a boundless field open before them; no less than the whole region of moral science, politics, political economy, social rights and duties. All these, and more, are as fit for the process of exemplification as the varieties of life and character illustrated by Scott. And not only has he left the great mass of material unwrought, but, with all his richness of variety, has made but scanty use of the best instruments of illustration. The grandest manifestations of passion remain to be displayed; the finest elements of the poetry of human emotion are yet uncombined; the most various dramatic exhibition of events and characters is yet unwrought, for there has yet been no recorder of the poor; at least, none but those who write as mere observers; who describe, but do not dramatize humble life. The widest interests being thus still untouched, the richest materials unemployed, what may not prove the ultimate obligations of society to him who did so much, and pointed the way towards doing infinitely more; and whose vast achievements are, above all, valuable as indications of what remains to be achieved? That this, his strongest claim to gratitude, has not yet been fully recognised, is evident from the fact, that though he has had many imitators, there have been yet none to take suggestion from him; to employ his method of procedure upon new doctrine and other materials. There have been many found to construct fiction within his range of morals, character, incident, and scenery; but none to carry the process out of his range. We have yet to look for this legitimate offspring of the productions of Scott, though wearied with the intrusions of their spurious brethren.

The progression of the age requires something better than this imitation;—requires that the above-mentioned suggestion should be used. If an author of equal genius with Scott were to arise to-morrow, he would not meet with an equal reception; not only because novelty is worn off, but because the serious temper of the times requires a new direction of the genius of the age. Under the pressure of difficulty, in the prospect of extensive change, armed with expectations or filled with determination as the general mind now is, it has not leisure or disposition to receive even its amusement unmixed with what is solid and has a bearing upon its engrossing interests. There may still be the thoughtless and indolent, to whom mere fiction is necessary as a pastime; but these are not they who can guarantee an author's influence, or secure his popularity. The bulk of the reading public, whether or not on the scent of utility, cannot be interested without a larger share of philosophy, or a graver purpose in fiction, than formerly; and the writer who would effect most for himself and others in this department must take his heroes and heroines from a different class than any which has yet been adequately represented. This difference of character implies, under the hands of a good artist, a difference of scenery and incident; for the incidents of a fiction are worth nothing, unless they arise out of the characters; and the scenery, both natural and moral, has no charm unless it be harmonious with both. Instead of tales of knightly love and glory, of chivalrous loyalty, of the ambition of ancient courts, and the bygone superstitions of a half-savage state, we must have, in a new novelist, the graver themes—not the less picturesque, perhaps, for their reality—which the present condition of society suggests. We have had enough of ambitious intrigues; why not now take the magnificent subject, the birth of political principle, whose advent has been heralded so long? What can afford finer moral scenery than the transition state in which society now is! Where are nobler heroes to be found than those who sustain society in the struggle; and what catastrophe so grand as the downfall of bad institutions, and the issues of a process of renovation? Heroism may now be found, not cased in helm and cuirass, but strengthening itself in the cabinet of the statesman, guiding the movements of the unarmed multitude, and patiently bearing up against hardship, in the hope of its peaceful removal. Love may now be truly represented as sanctified by generosity and self-denial in many of the sad majority of cases where its course runs not smooth. All the virtues which have graced fictitious delineations, are still at the service of the novelist; but their exercise and discipline should be represented as different from what they were. The same passions still sway human hearts; but they must be shown to be intensified or redressed by the new impulses which a new state of things affords. Fiction must not be allowed to expire with Scott, or to retain only that languid existence which is manifest merely in imitations of his works: we must hope,—not, alas! for powers and copiousness like his,—but for an enlightened application of his means of achievement to new aims: the higher quality of which may in some measure compensate for the inferiority of power and richness which it is only reasonable to anticipate.

It appears, then, from the inquiry we have pursued, that the services for which society has to be eternally grateful to Walter Scott are of three distinct kinds. He has vindicated the character of genius by the healthiness of his own. He has achieved marvels in the province of art, and stupendous benefits in that of morals. He has indicated, by his own achievements, the way to larger and higher achievements.—What a lot for a man,—to be thus a threefold benefactor to his race! to unite in himself the functions of moralist, constructor, and discoverer! What a possession for society to have had! and to retain for purposes of amelioration, incitement, and guidance! He can never be lost to us, whatever rival or kindred spirit may be destined to arise, or whether he is to be the last of his class. If the latter supposition should prove true,—which, however, appears to us impossible,—he will stand a fadeless apparition on the structure of his own achievements, distanced, but not impaired, by time: if the former, his spirit will migrate into his successors, and communicate once more with us through them. In either case, we shall have him with us still.

But, it will be said, the services here attributed to Scott were, for the most part, rendered unconsciously. True; and why should not the common methods of Providence have place here as in all other instances? Scott did voluntarily all that he could; and that he was destined to do yet more involuntarily, is so much the greater honor, instead of derogating, from his merit. That some of this extra service was of a nature which he might have declined if offered a choice, is only an additional proof that the designs of men are over-ruled, and their weakness not only compensated for by divine direction, but made its instruments. Great things are done by spontaneous human action: yet greater things are done by every man without his concurrence or suspicion; all which tends, not to degrade the character of human effort, but to exemplify the purposes of Providence. Scott is no new instance of this, nor deserves less honor in proportion to his spontaneous efforts than the sages of Greece, or the historians of Rome, and the benefactors of every age, who have been destined to effect more as illustrators than even as teachers and recorders. He was happy and humbly complacent in his creative office; it is so much pure blessing that we can regard him with additional and higher complacency as a vindicator of genius, and an unconscious prophet of its future achievements.

SOURCE

Tait's 2 (December 1832); reprinted in *Miscellanies* (London, 1836).

SELECTED SECONDARY READING

Hunter, Shelagh. *Harriet Martineau: The Poetics of Moralism.* Aldershot: Scholar Press, 1995.

Martineau, Harriet. *Autobiography, with Memorials by Maria Weston Chapman.* 3 vols. Boston: Osgood, 1877.

Peterson, Linda H. "Harriet Martineau: Masculine Discourse, Female Sage." *Victorian Sages and Cultural Discourse: Renegotiating Gender and Power.* Ed. Thaïs E. Morgan. New Brunswick: Rutgers University Press, 1990.

Pichanick, Valerie Kossew. *Harriet Martineau: The Woman and Her Work.* Ann Arbor: University of Michigan Press, 1980.

Webb, R.K. *Harriet Martineau: A Radical Victorian.* New York: Columbia University Press, 1960.

REVIEW OF *VANITY FAIR* AND *JANE EYRE*
(DECEMBER 1848)

Elizabeth Rigby Eastlake

ELIZABETH RIGBY (1809–93) was born in Norwich, the daughter of a physician and his second wife. She studied art, literature, and languages at home and in Germany, and early evinced a talent for drawing. In 1836 she published her first review, an attack on Goethe, in the *Foreign Quarterly Review*, and in 1841 she published her first book, *A Residence on the Shores of the Baltic*, based on a series of letters she had written while visiting a sister in Russia. Her book was admired by J.G. Lockhart, editor of the conservative *Quarterly Review*, and she soon became the first—and for a long time, only—woman to write regularly for the prestigious review.

In 1849 she married Sir Charles Eastlake, a well-known painter and later director of the National Gallery. Both as individuals and as collaborators, the Eastlakes travelled extensively and published widely in art history and criticism. Eastlake's individual reputation was such that, after Anna Jameson's death in 1860, she was asked to complete the final volume of Jameson's *History of Our Lord as Exemplified in Works of Art*. Following her husband's death in 1865, Eastlake continued to write and publish both aesthetic criticism and cultural studies. In 1883 she published a collection of essays on *Five Great Painters*, in part because of her dislike of the D.G. Rossetti exhibit then running in London. After her death, her nephew issued her *Journals and Correspondence* (1895).

In literary criticism, Eastlake's best-known (perhaps infamous) work is her review of Thackeray's *Vanity Fair* and Charlotte Brontë's *Jane Eyre*, which is excerpted here. While Eastlake takes exception to aspects of both novels, *Jane Eyre* is singled out for particular attack, primarily because of the heroine's rebellious nature. While *Vanity Fair*'s Becky Sharp is presented as a kind of diabolic satire, Jane Eyre is presented as all too human, and her resentment of her position in life contradicts conservative Christian notions of humility. Like other conservative critics of the time, Eastlake sees in *Jane Eyre* a challenge not only to traditional notions of fiction and fictional representations of women, but also to the whole organization of society: in her estimation, the novel evinces that "tone of the mind and thought which has overthrown authority and violated every code human and divine abroad, and fostered Chartism and rebellion at home." While Jane is a powerful and compelling character, she is nevertheless "one whom we should not care for as an acquaintance, whom we should not seek as a friend, whom we should not desire for a relation, and whom we should scrupulously avoid as a governess."

A REMARKABLE NOVEL is a great event for English society. It is a kind of common friend, about whom people can speak the truth without fear of being compromised, and confess their emotions without being ashamed. We are a particularly shy and reserved people, and set about nothing so awkwardly as the simple art of getting really acquainted with each other. We meet over and over again in what is conventionally called "easy society," with the tacit understanding to go so far and no farther; to be as polite as we ought to be, and as intellectual as we can; but mutually and honourably to forbear lifting those veils which each spreads over his inner sentiments and sympathies. For this purpose a host of devices have been contrived by which all the forms of friendship may be gone through, without committing ourselves to one spark of the spirit. We fly with eagerness to some common ground in which each can take the liveliest interest, without taking the slightest in the world in his companion. Our various fashionable manias, for charity one season, for science the next, are only so many clever contrivances for keeping our neighbour at arm's length. We can attend committees, and canvas for subscribers, and archaeologise, and geologise, and take ether with our fellow Christians for a twelvemonth, as we might sit cross-legged and smoke the pipe of fraternity with a Turk for the same period—and know at the end of the time as little of the real feelings of the one as we should about the domestic relations of the other. But there are ways and means for lifting the veil which equally favour our national idiosyncrasy; and a new and remarkable novel is one of them—especially the nearer it comes to real life. We invite our neighbour to a walk with the deliberate and malicious object of getting thoroughly acquainted with him. We ask no impertinent questions—we proffer no indiscreet confidences—we do not even sound him, ever so delicately, as to his opinion of a common friend, for he would be sure not to say, lest we should go and tell; but we simply discuss Becky Sharp, or Jane Eyre, and our object is answered at once.

There is something about these two new and noticeable characters which especially compels everybody to speak out. They are not to be dismissed with a few commonplace moralities and sentimentalities. They do not fit any ready-made criticism. They give the most stupid something to think of, and the most reserved something to say; the most charitable too are betrayed into home comparisons which they usually condemn, and the most ingenious stumble into paradoxes which they can hardly defend. Becky and Jane also stand well side by side both in their analogies and their contrasts. Both the ladies are governesses, and both make the same move in society; the one, in Jane Eyre phraseology, marrying her "master," and the other her master's son. Neither starts in life with more than a moderate capital of good looks—Jane Eyre with hardly that—for it is the fashion now-a-days with novelists to give no encouragement to the insolence of mere beauty, but rather to prove to all whom it may concern how little a sensible woman requires to get on with in the world. Both have also an elfish kind of nature, with which they divine the secrets of other hearts, and conceal those of their own; and both rejoice in that peculiarity of feature which Mademoiselle de Luzy has not contributed to render popular, viz., green eyes. Beyond this, however, there is no similarity either in the minds, manners, or fortunes of the two heroines. They think and act upon diametrically opposite principles—at least so the author of *Jane Eyre* intends us to believe—and each, were they to meet, which we should of all things enjoy to see them do, would cordially despise and abominate the other. Which of the two, however, would most successfully *dupe* the other is a different question, and one not so easy to decide; though we have our own ideas upon the subject.

We must discuss *Vanity Fair* first, which, much as we were entitled to expect from its author's pen, has fairly taken us by surprise. We were perfectly aware that Mr. Thackeray had of old assumed the jester's habit, in order the more unrestrainedly to indulge the privilege of speaking the truth;—we had traced his clever progress through *Fraser's Magazine* and the ever-improving pages of *Punch*—which wonder of the time has been infinitely obliged to him—but still we were little prepared for the keen observation, the deep wisdom, and the consummate art which he has interwoven in the slight texture and whimsical pattern of *Vanity Fair*. Everybody, it is to be supposed, has read the volume by this time; and even for those who have not, it is not necessary to describe the order of the story. It is not a novel, in the common acceptation of the word, with a plot purposely contrived to bring about certain scenes, and develop certain characters, but simply a history of those average sufferings, pleasures, penalties, and rewards to which various classes of mankind gravitate as naturally and certainly in this world as the sparks fly upward. It is only the same game of life which every player sooner or later makes for himself—were he to have a hundred chances, and shuffle the cards of circumstance every time. It is only the same busy, involved drama which may be seen at any time by any one, who is not engrossed with the magnified minutiae of his own petty part, but with composed curiosity looks on to the stage where his fellow men and women are the actors; and that not even heightened by the conventional colouring which Madame de Staël[1]

---

[1] Germaine de Staël (1766–1816), French-Swiss essayist and novelist.

philosophically declares that fiction always wants in order to make up for its not being truth. Indeed, so far from taking any advantage of this novelist's licence, Mr. Thackeray has hardly availed himself of the natural average of remarkable events that really do occur in this life. The battle of Waterloo, it is true, is introduced; but, as far as regards the story, it brings about only one death and one bankruptcy, which might either of them have happened in a hundred other ways. Otherwise the tale runs on, with little exception, in that humdrum course of daily monotony, out of which some people coin materials to act, and others excuses to doze, just as their dispositions may be.

It is this reality which is at once the charm and the misery here. With all these unpretending materials it is one of the most amusing, but also one of the most distressing books we have read for many a long year. We almost long for a little exaggeration and improbability to relieve us of that sense of dead truthfulness which weighs down our hearts, not for the Amelias and Georges of the story, but for poor kindred human nature. In one light this truthfulness is even an objection. With few exceptions the personages are too like our every-day selves and neighbours to draw any distinct moral from. We cannot see our way clearly. Palliations of the bad and disappointments in the good are perpetually obstructing our judgment, by bringing what should decide it too close to that common standard of experience in which our only rule of opinion is charity. For it is only in fictitious characters which are highly coloured for one definite object, or in notorious personages viewed from a distance, that the course of the true moral can be seen to run straight—once bring the individual with his life and circumstances closely before you, and it is lost to the mental eye in the thousand pleas and witnesses, unseen and unheard before, which rise up to overshadow it. And what are all these personages in *Vanity Fair* but feigned names for our own beloved friends and acquaintances, seen under such a puzzling cross-light of good in evil and evil in good, of sins and sinnings against, of little to be praised virtues, and much to be excused vices, that we cannot presume to moralise upon them—not even to judge them,—content to exclaim sorrowfully with the old prophet, "Alas! my brother!" Every actor on the crowded stage of *Vanity Fair* represents some type of that perverse mixture of humanity in which there is ever something not wholly to approve or to condemn. There is the desperate devotion of a fond heart to a false object, which we cannot respect; there is the vain, weak man, half good and half bad, who is more despicable in our eyes than the decided villain. There are the irretrievably wretched education, and the unquenchably manly instincts, both contending in the confirmed *roué*, which melt us to the tenderest pity. There is the self-ishness and self-will which the possessor of great wealth and fawning relations can hardly avoid. There is the vanity and fear of the world, which assist mysteriously with pious principles in keeping a man respectable; there are combinations of this kind of every imaginable human form and colour, redeemed but feebly by the steady excel-lence of an awkward man, and the genuine heart of a vulgar woman, till we feel inclined to tax Mr. Thackeray with an under estimate of our nature, forgetting that Madame de Staël is right after all, and that without a little conventional rouge no human complexion can stand the stage-lights of fiction.

But if these performers give us pain, we are not ashamed to own, as we are speaking openly, that the chief actress herself gives us none at all. For there is of course a principal pilgrim in *Vanity Fair*, as much in its emblematical original, Bunyan's *Progress*;[1] only unfortunately this one is travelling the wrong way. And we say "unfortunately" merely by way of courtesy, for in reality we care little about the matter. No, Becky—our hearts neither bleed for you, nor cry out against you. You are wonderfully clever, and amusing, and accomplished, and intelligent, and the Soho *ateliers* were not the best nurseries for a moral training; and you were married early in life to a regular black-leg, and you have had to live upon your wits ever since, which is not an improving sort of maintenance; and there is much to be said for and against; but still you are not one of us, and there is an end to our sympathies and censures. People who allow their feelings to be lacer-ated by such a character and career as yours, are doing both you and themselves great injustice. No author could have openly introduced

---

[1] Vanity Fair is a location in John Bunyan's (1628–88) allegory *The Pilgrim's Progress* (1678).

a near connexion of Satan's into the best London society, nor would the moral end intended have been answered by it; but really and honestly, considering Becky in her human character, we know of none which so thoroughly satisfies our highest *beau ideal* of feminine wickedness, with so slight a shock to our feelings and proprieties. It is very dreadful, doubtless, that Becky neither loved the husband who loved her, nor the child of her own flesh and blood, nor indeed any body but herself; but, as far as she is concerned we cannot pretend to be scandalized—for how could she without a heart? It is very shocking of course that she committed all sorts of dirty tricks, and jockeyed her neighbours, and never cared what she trampled under foot if it happened to obstruct her step; but how could she be expected to do otherwise without a conscience? The poor little woman was most tryingly placed; she came into the world without the customary letters of credit upon those two great bankers of humanity, "Heart and Conscience," and it was no fault of hers if they dishonoured all her bills. All she could do in this dilemma was to establish the firmest connexion with the inferior commercial branches of "Sense and Tact," who secretly do much business in the name of the head concern, and with whom her "fine frontal development" gave her unlimited credit. She saw that selfishness was the metal which the stamp of heart was suborned to pass; that hypocrisy was the homage that vice rendered to virtue; that honesty was, at all events, acted, because it was the best policy; and so she practiced the arts of selfishness and hypocrisy like anybody else in *Vanity Fair*, only with this difference, that she brought them to their highest possible pitch of perfection. For why is it that, looking round in this world, we find plenty of characters to compare with her up to a certain pitch, but none which reach her actual standard? Why is it that, speaking of this friend or that, we say in the tender mercies of our hearts, "No, she is not *quite* so bad as Becky?" We fear not only because she has more heart and conscience, but also because she has less cleverness.

No; let us give Becky her due. There is enough in this world of ours, as we all know, to provoke a saint, far more a poor little devil like her. She had none of those fellow-feelings which make us wondrous kind. She saw people around her cowards in vice, and simpletons in virtue, and she had no patience with either, for she was as little the one as the other herself. She saw women who loved their husbands and yet teazed them, and ruining their children although they doated upon them, and she sneered at their utter inconsistency. Wickedness or goodness, unless coupled with strength, were alike worthless to her. That weakness which is the blessed pledge of our humanity was to her only the despicable badge of our imperfection. She thought, it might be, of her master's words, "Fallen cherub! to be weak is to be miserable!" and wondered how we could be such fools as first to sin and then to be sorry. Becky's light was defective, but she acted up to it. Her goodness goes as far as good temper, and her principles as far as shrewd sense, and we may thank her consistency for showing us what they are both worth.

It is another thing to pretend to settle whether such a character be *primâ facie* impossible, though devotion to the better sex might well demand the assertion. There are mysteries of iniquity, under the semblance of man and woman, read of in history, or met with in the unchronicled sufferings of private life, which would almost make us believe that the powers of Darkness occasionally made use of this earth for a Foundling Hospital, and sent their imps to us, already provided with a return-ticket. We shall not decide on the lawfulness or otherwise of any attempt to depict such importations; we can only rest perfectly satisfied that, granting the author's premises, it is impossible to imagine them carried out with more felicitous skill and more exquisite consistency than in the heroine of *Vanity Fair*. At all events, the infernal regions have no reason to be ashamed of little Becky,nor the ladies either: she has, at least, all the cleverness of the sex.

The great charm, therefore, and comfort of Becky is, that we may study her without any compunctions. The misery of this life is not the evil that we see, but the good and the evil which are so inextricably twisted together. It is that perpetual memento ever meeting one—

How in this vile world below
Noblest things find vilest using,[1]

---

[1] Lines from "Palm Sunday" in John Keble's (1792–1866) 1827 book of devotional verse, *The Christian Year.*

that is so very distressing to those who have hearts as well as eyes. But Becky relieves them of all this pain—at least in her own person. Pity would be thrown away upon one who has not heart enough for it to ache even for herself. Becky is perfectly happy, as all must be who excel in what they love best. Her life is one exertion of successful power. Shame never visits her, for "'Tis conscience that makes cowards of us all"—and she has none. She realizes that *ne plus ultra*[1] of sublunary comfort which it was reserved for a Frenchman to define—the blessed combination of "*le bon estomac et le mauvais coeur*":[2] for Becky adds to her other good qualities that of an excellent digestion.

Upon the whole, we are not afraid to own that we rather enjoy her *ignis fatuus* course, dragging the weak and the vain and the selfish, through mud and mire, after her, and acting all parts, from the modest rushlight to the gracious star, just as it suits her. Clever little imp that she is! What exquisite tact she shows!—what unflagging good humour!—what ready self-possession! Becky never disappoints us; she never even makes us tremble. We know that her answer will come exactly suiting her one particular object, and frequently three or four more in prospect. What respect, too, she has for those decencies which more virtuous, but more stupid humanity, often disdains! What detection of all that is false and mean! What instinct for all that is true and great! She is her master's true pupil in that: she knows what is really divine as well as he, and bows before it. She honours Dobbin in spite of his big feet: she respects her husband more than ever she did before, perhaps for the first time, at the very moment when he is stripping not only her jewels, but name, honour, and comfort off her.

We are not so sure either whether we are justified in calling her "*le mauvais coeur.*" Becky does not pursue any one vindictively; she never does gratuitous mischief. The fountain is more dry than poisoned. She is even generous—when she can afford it. Witness that burst of plain speaking in Dobbin's favour to the little dolt Amelia, for which we forgive her many a sin. 'Tis true she wanted to get rid of her; but

---

[1] Height, pinnacle.
[2] Good stomach (digestion) and bad heart.

REVIEW OF *VANITY FAIR* AND *JANE EYRE*

let that pass. Becky was a thrifty dame, and liked to despatch two birds with one stone. And she was honest, too, after a fashion. The part of wife she acts at first as well, and better than most; but as for that of mother, there she fails from the beginning. She knew that maternal love was no business of hers—that a fine frontal development could give her no help there—and puts so little spirit into her imitation that no one could be taken in for a moment. She felt that that bill, of all others, would be sure to be dishonoured, and it went against her conscience—we mean her sense—to send it in.

In short, the only respect in which Becky's course gives us pain is when it locks itself into that of another, and more genuine child of this earth. No one can regret those being entangled in her nets whose vanity and meanness of spirit alone led them into its meshes—such are rightly served: but we do grudge her that real sacred thing called *love*, even of a Rawdon Crawley, who has more of that self-forgetting, all-purifying feeling for his little evil spirit than many a better man has for a good woman. We do grudge Becky *a heart*, though it belong only to a swindler. Poor, sinned against, vile, degraded, but still true-hearted Rawdon!—you stand next in our affections and sympathies to honest Dobbin himself. It was the instinct of a good nature which made the Major feel that the stamp of the Evil One was upon Becky; and it was the stupidity of a good nature which made the Colonel never suspect it. He was a cheat, a black-leg, an unprincipled dog; but still "Rawdon *is* a man, and be hanged to him," as the Rector says. We follow him through the illustrations, which are, in many instances, a delightful enhancement to the text—as he stands there, with his gentle eyelid, coarse moustache, and foolish chin, bringing up Becky's coffee-cup with a kind of dumb fidelity; or looking down at little Rawdon with a more than paternal tenderness. All Amelia's philoprogenitive idolatries do not touch us like one fond instinct of "stupid Rawdon."

Dobbin sheds a halo over all the long-necked, loose-jointed, Scotch-looking gentlemen of our acquaintance. Flat feet and flap ears seem henceforth incompatible with evil. He reminds us of one of the sweetest creations that have appeared from any modern pen—that plain, awkward, loveable "Long Walter," in Lady Georgina Fullerton's beautiful novel of *Grantley Manor*.[1] Like him, too, in his proper self-respect; for Dobbin—lumbering, heavy, shy, and absurdly over-modest as the ugly fellow is—is yet true to himself. At one time he seems to be sinking into the mere abject dangler after Amelia; but he breaks his chains like a man, and resumes them again like a man, too, although half disenchanted of his amiable delusion.

But to return for a moment to Becky. The only criticism we would offer is one which the author has almost disarmed by making her mother a Frenchwoman. The construction of this little clever monster is diabolically French. Such a *lusus naturae*[2] as a woman without a heart and conscience would, in England, be a mere brutal savage, and poison half a village. France is the land for the real Syren, with the woman's face and the dragon's claws. The genus of Pigeon and Laffarge[3] claims her for its own—only that our heroine takes a far higher class by not requiring the vulgar matter of fact of crime to develop her full powers. It is an affront to Becky's tactics to believe that she could ever be reduced to so low a resource, or, that if she were, anybody would find it out. We, therefore, cannot sufficiently applaud the extreme discretion with which Mr. Thackeray has hinted at the possibly assistant circumstances of Joseph Sedley's dissolution. A less delicacy of handling would have marred the harmony of the whole design. Such a casualty as that suggested to our imagination was not intended for the light net of *Vanity Fair* to draw on shore; it would have torn it to pieces. Besides it is not wanted. Poor little Becky is bad enough to satisfy the most ardent student of "good books." Wickedness, beyond a certain pitch, gives no increase of gratification even to the sternest moralist; and one of Mr. Thackeray's excellences is the sparing quantity he consumes. The whole *use*, too, of the work—that of generously measuring one another by this standard—is lost, the moment you convict Becky of a capital crime. Who can, with any face, liken a dear friend to a murderess? Whereas now there are no little symptoms of fascinating ruthlessness, graceful ingratitude, or

---

[1] Novel published in 1847 by Lady Georgina Fullerton (1812–85).
[2] Freak of nature.
[3] Notorious French women. Marie Cappelle Laffarge was accused of poisoning her husband and became the subject of an 1840 play.

ladylike selfishness, observable among our charming acquaintance, that we may not immediately detect to an inch, and more effectually intimidate by the simple application of the Becky gauge than by the most vehement use of all ten commandments. Thanks to Mr. Thackeray, the world is now provided with an *idea*, which, if we mistake not, will be the skeleton in the corner of every ball-room and boudoir, for a long time to come. Let us leave it intact in its unique point and freshness—a Becky, and nothing more. We should, therefore, advise our readers to cut out that picture of our heroine's "Second Appearance as Clytemnestra,"[1] which casts so uncomfortable a glare over the latter part of the volume, and, disregarding all hints and inuendoes, simply to let the changes and chances of this mortal life have due weight in their minds. Jos had been much in India. His was a bad life; he ate and drank most imprudently, and his digestion was not to be compared with Becky's. No respectable office would have ensured "Waterloo Sedley."

Vanity Fair is pre-eminently a novel of the day—not in the vulgar sense, of which there are too many, but as a literal photograph of the manners and habits of the nineteenth century, thrown on to paper by the light of a powerful mind; and one also of the most artistic effect. Mr. Thackeray has a peculiar adroitness in leading on the fancy, or rather memory of his reader from one set of circumstances to another by the seeming chances and coincidences of common life, as an artist leads the spectator's eye through the subject of his picture by a skilful repetition of colour. This is why it is impossible to quote from his book with any justice to it. The whole growth of the narrative is so matted and inter-woven together with tendril-like links and bindings, that there is no detaching a flower with sufficient length of stalk to exhibit it to advantage. There is that mutual dependence in his characters which is the first requisite in painting every-day life: no one is stuck on a separate pedestal—no one is sitting for his portrait. There may be one exception—we mean Sir Pitt Crawley, senior: it is possible, nay, we hardly doubt, that this baronet was closer drawn

---

[1] Thackeray's own illustration with this title shows Becky behind a curtain, menacing Jos Sedley with a knife.

from individual life than anybody else in the book; but granting that fact, the animal was so unique an exception, that we wonder so shrewd an artist could stick him into a gallery so full of our familiars. The scenes in Germany, we can believe, will seem to many readers of an English book hardly less extravagantly absurd—grossly and gratuitously overdrawn; but the initiated will value them as containing some of the keenest strokes of truth and humour that *Vanity Fair* exhibits, and not enjoy them the less for being at our neighbour's expense. For the thorough appreciation of the chief character they are quite indispensable too. The whole course of the work may be viewed as the *Wander-Jahre* of a far cleverer female *Wilhelm Meister*.[1] We have watched her in the ups-and-downs of life—among the humble, the fashionable, the great, and the pious—and found her ever new, yet ever the same; but still Becky among the students was requisite to complete the full measure of our admiration.

Jane Eyre, as a work, and one of equal popularity, is, in almost every respect, a total contrast to *Vanity Fair*. The characters and events, though some of them masterly in conception, are coined expressly for the purpose of bringing out great effects. The hero and heroine are beings both so singularly unattractive that the reader feels they can have no vocation in the novel but to be brought together; and they do things which, though not impossible, lie utterly beyond the bounds of probability. On this account a short sketch of the plan seems requisite; not but what it is a plan familiar enough to all readers of novels—especially those of the old school and those of the lowest school of our own day. For Jane Eyre is merely another Pamela,[2] who, by the force of her character and the strength of her principles, is carried victoriously through great trials and temptations from the man she loves. Nor is she even a Pamela adapted and refined to modern notions; for though the story is conducted without those derelictions of decorum which we are to believe had their excuse in the manners of Richardson's time, yet it is stamped with a coarseness

---

[1] Johann Wolfgang von Goethe's (1749–1842) 1822 bildungsroman. The second section is entitled "*Wander-Jahre*," a year of wanderings and discovery.

[2] Servant-girl heroine in Samuel Richardson's 1740–41 novel by that name.

of language and laxity of tone which have certainly no excuse in ours. It is a very remarkable book: we have no remembrance of another combining such genuine power with such horrid taste. Both together have equally assisted to gain the great popularity it has enjoyed; for in these days of extravagant adoration of all that bears the stamp of novelty and originality, sheer rudeness and vulgarity have come in for a most mistaken worship.

The story is written in the first person. Jane begins with her earliest recollections, and at once takes possession of the reader's intensest interest by the masterly picture of a strange and oppressed child she raises up in a few strokes before him. She is an orphan, and a dependant in the house of a selfish, hard-hearted aunt, against whom the disposition of the little Jane chafes itself in natural antipathy, till she contrives to make the unequal struggle as intolerable to her oppressor as it is to herself. She is therefore, at eight years of age, got rid of to a sort of Dothegirls Hall,[1] where she continues to enlist our sympathies for a time with her little pinched fingers, cropped hair, and empty stomach. But things improve: the abuses of the institution are looked into. The Puritan patron, who holds that young orphan girls are only safely brought up upon the rules of La Trappe,[2] is superceded by an enlightened committee—the school assumes a sound English character—Jane progresses from scholar to teacher, and passes ten profitable and not unhappy years at Lowood. Then she advertises for a situation as a governess, and obtains one immediately in one of the midland counties. We see her, therefore, as she leaves Lowood, to enter upon a new life—a small, plain, odd creature, who has been brought up dry upon school learning, and somewhat stunted accordingly in mind and body, and who is now thrown upon the world as ignorant of its ways, and as destitute of its friendships, as a shipwrecked mariner upon a strange coast.

Thornfield Hall is the property of Mr. Rochester—a bachelor addicted to travelling. She finds it at first in all the peaceful prestige

---

[1] Play on "Dotheboys Hall," the sadistic boarding school in Dickens's *Nicholas Nickleby* (1838–39).

[2] Trappists or Cistercians, order of monks noted for their strict discipline.

of an English gentleman's seat when "nobody is at the hall." The companions are an old decayed gentlewoman housekeeper—a far away cousin of the squire's—and a young French child, Jane's pupil, Mr. Rochester's ward and reputed daughter. There is a pleasing monotony in the summer solitude of the old country house, with its comfort, respectability, and dulness, which Jane paints to the life; but there is one circumstance which varies the sameness and casts a mysterious feeling over the scene. A strange laugh is heard from time to time in a distant part of the house—a laugh which grates discordantly upon Jane's ear. She listens, watches, and inquires, but can discover nothing but a plain matter of fact woman, who sits sewing somewhere in the attics, and goes up and down stairs peaceably to and from her dinner with the servants. But a mystery there is, though nothing betrays it, and it comes in with marvellous effect from the monotonous reality of all around. After awhile Mr. Rochester comes to Thornfield, and sends for the child and her governess occasionally to bear him company. He is a dark, strange-looking man—strong and large—of the brigand stamp, with fine eyes and lowering brows—blunt and sarcastic in his manners, with a kind of misanthropical frankness, which seems based upon utter contempt for his fellow creatures, and a surly truthfulness which is more rudeness than honesty. With his arrival disappears all the prestige of country innocence that had invested Thornfield Hall. He brings the taint of the world upon him, and none of its illusions. The queer little governess is something new to him. He talks to her at one time imperiously as to a servant, and at another recklessly as to a man. He pours into her ears disgraceful tales of his past life, connected with the birth of little Adèle, which any man with common respect for a woman, and that a mere girl of eighteen, would have spared her; but which eighteen in this case listens to as if it were nothing new, and certainly nothing distasteful. He is captious and Turk-like—she is one day his confidant, and another his unnoticed dependant. In short, by her account, Mr. Rochester is a strange brute, somewhat in the Squire Western style of absolute and capricious eccentricity, though redeemed in him by signs of a cultivated intellect, and gleams of a certain fierce justice of heart. He has a *mind*, and when he opens it at all, he opens it freely to her. Jane becomes attached to her "master," as Pamela-like she calls him, and it is not difficult to see that solitude and propinquity are taking effect upon him also. An odd circumstance heightens the dawning romance. Jane is awoke one night by that strange discordant laugh close to her ear—then a noise as if hands feeling along the wall. She rises—opens her door, finds the passage full of smoke, is guided by it to her master's room, whose bed she discovers enveloped in flames, and by her timely aid saves his life. After this they meet no more for ten days, when Mr. Rochester returns from a visit to a neighbouring family, bringing with him a housefull of distinguished guests; at the head of whom is Miss Blanche Ingram, a haughty beauty of high birth, and evidently the especial object of the Squire's attentions—upon which tumultuous irruption Miss Eyre slips back into her naturally humble position.

Our little governess is now summoned away to attend her aunt's death-bed, who is visited by some compunctions towards her, and she is absent a month. When she returns Thornfield Hall is quit of all its guests, and Mr. Rochester and she resume their former life of captious cordiality on the one side, and diplomatic humility on the other. At the same time the bugbear of Miss Ingram and of Mr. Rochester's engagement with her is kept up, though it is easy to see that this and all concerning that lady is only a stratagem to try Jane's character and affection upon the most approved Griselda precedent. Accordingly an opportunity for explanation ere long offers itself, where Mr. Rochester has only to take it. Miss Eyre is desired to walk with him in shady alleys, and to sit with him on the roots of an old chestnut-tree towards the close of evening, and of course she cannot disobey her "master"— whereupon there ensues a scene which as far as we remember, is new equally in art or nature; in which Miss Eyre confesses her love—where-upon Mr. Rochester drops not only his cigar (which she seems to be in the habit of lighting for him) but his mask, and finally offers not only heart, but hand. The wedding-day is soon fixed, but strange misgivings and presentiments haunt the young lady's mind. The night but one before, her bed-room is entered by a horrid phantom, who tries on the wedding veil, sends Jane into a swoon of terror, and defeats all the favourite refuge of a bad dream by leaving the veil in two pieces. But all is ready. The bride has no friends to assist—the couple walk to church—only the clergyman and the clerk are there—but Jane's quick eye has seen two figures lingering among the tombstones, and these two follow them into church. The ceremony commences, when at the due charge which summons any man to come forward and show just cause why they should not be joined together, a voice interposes to forbid the marriage. There is an impediment, and a serious one. The bridegroom has a wife not only living, but living under the very roof of Thornfield Hall.

Hers was that discordant laugh which had so often caught Jane's ear; she it was who in her malice had tried to burn Mr. Rochester in his bed—who had visited Jane by night and torn her veil, and whose attendant was that same pretended sew-woman who had so strongly excited Jane's curiosity. For Mr. Rochester's wife is a creature, half fiend, half maniac, whom he had married in a distant part of the world, and whom now, in his self-constituted code of morality, he had thought it his right, and even his duty, to supersede by a more agreeable companion. Now follow scenes of a truly tragic power. This is the grand crisis in Jane's life. Her whole soul is wrapt up in Mr. Rochester. He has broken her trust, but not diminished her love. He entreats her to accept all that he still can give, his heart and his home; he pleads with the agony not only of a man who has never known what it was to conquer a passion, but of one who, by that same self-constituted code, now burns to atone for a disappointed crime. There is no one to help her against him or against herself. Jane had no friends to stand by her at the altar, and she has none to support her now she is plucked away from it. There is no one to be offended or disgraced at her following him to the sunny land of Italy, as he proposes, till the maniac should die. There is no duty to any one but to herself, and this feeble reed quivers and trembles beneath the overwhelming weight of love and sophistry opposed to it. But Jane triumphs; in the middle of the night she rises—glides out of her room—takes off her shoes as she passes Mr. Rochester's chamber;—leaves the house, and casts herself upon a world more desert than ever to her—

Without a shilling and without a friend,

Thus the great deed of self-conquest is accomplished; Jane has passed through the fire of temptation from without and from within; her character is stamped from that day; we need therefore follow her no further into wanderings and sufferings which, though not unmixed with plunder from Minerva-lane,[1] occupy some of, on the whole, the most striking chapters in the book. Virtue of course finds her reward. The maniac wife sets fire to Thornfield Hall, and perishes herself in the flames. Mr. Rochester, in endeavouring to save her, loses the sight of his eyes. Jane rejoins her blind master; they are married, after which of course the happy man recovers his sight.

Such is the outline of a tale in which, combined with great materials for power and feeling, the reader may trace gross inconsistencies and improbabilities, and chief and foremost that highest moral offence a novel writer can commit, that of making an unworthy character interesting in the eyes of the reader. Mr. Rochester is a man who deliberately and secretly seeks to violate the laws both of God and man, and yet we will be bound half our lady readers are enchanted with him for a model of generosity and honour. We would have thought that such a hero had no chance, in the purer taste of the present day; but the popularity of *Jane Eyre* is a proof how deeply the love for illegitimate romance is implanted in our nature. Not that the author is strictly responsible for this. Mr. Rochester's character is tolerably consistent. He is made as coarse and as brutal as can in all conscience be required to keep our sympathies at a distance. In point of literary consistency the hero is at all events impugnable, though we cannot say as much for the heroine.

As to Jane's character—there is none of that harmonious unity about it which made little Becky so grateful a subject of analysis—nor are the discrepancies of that kind which have their excuse and their response in our nature. The inconsistencies of Jane's character lie mainly not in her own imperfections, though of course she has her share, but in the author's. There is that confusion in the relations between cause and effect, which is not so much untrue to human

---

[1] The Minerva Press (1790–1820) published lowbrow, popular fiction, much of it romance or gothic.

nature as to human art. The error in Jane Eyre is, not that her character is this or that, but that she is made one thing in the eyes of her imaginary companions, and another in that of the actual reader. There is a perpetual disparity between the account she herself gives of the effect she produces, and the means shown us by which she brings that effect about. We hear nothing but self-eulogiums on the perfect tact and wondrous penetration with which she is gifted, and yet almost every word she utters offends us, not only with the absence of these qualities, but with the positive contrasts of them, in either her pedantry, stupidity, or gross vulgarity. She is one of those ladies who put us in the unpleasant predicament of undervaluing their very virtues for dislike of the person in whom they are represented. One feels provoked as Jane Eyre stands before us—for in the wonderful reality of her thoughts and descriptions, she seems accountable for all done in her name—with principles you must approve in the main, and yet with language and manners that offend you in every particular. Even in that *chef-d'oeuvre* of brilliant retrospective sketching, the description of her early life, it is the childhood and not the child that interests you. The little Jane, with her sharp eyes and dogmatic speeches, is a being you neither could fondle nor love. There is a hardness in her infantine earnestness, and a spiteful precocity in her reasoning, which repulses all our sympathy. One sees that she is of a nature to dwell upon and treasure up every slight and unkindness, real or fancied, and such natures we know are surer than any others to meet with plenty of this sort of thing. As the child, so also the woman—an uninteresting, sententious, pedantic thing; with no experience of the world, and yet with no simplicity or freshness in its stead. What are her first answers to Mr. Rochester but such as would have quenched all interest, even for a prettier woman, in any man of common knowledge of what was nature—and especially in a *blasé* monster like him? A more affected governessy effusion we never read. The question is à propos of *cadeaux*.

"Who talks of cadeaux?" said he gruffly: "did you expect a present, Miss Eyre? Are you fond of presents?" and he searched my face with eyes that I saw were dark, irate, and piercing.

"I hardly know, Sir; I have little experience of them; they are generally thought pleasant things."

"Generally thought! But what do *you* think?"

"I should be obliged to take time, Sir, before I could give you an answer worthy of your acceptance: a present has many faces to it, has it not? and one should consider all before pronouncing an opinion as to its nature."

"Miss Eyre, you are not so unsophisticated as Adèle: she demands a cadeau clamorously the moment she sees me; you beat about the bush."

"Because I have less confidence in my deserts than Adèle has; she can prefer the right of old acquaintance and the right too of custom; for she says you have always been in the habit of giving her playthings; but if I had to make out a case I should be puzzled, since I am a stranger, and have done nothing to entitle me to an acknowledgment."

"Oh! don't fall back on over modesty! I have examined Adèle, and find you have taken great pains with her: she is not bright—she has no talent, yet in a short time she has made much improvement."

"Sir, you have now given me my cadeau; I am obliged to you: it is the meed teachers most covet; praise of their pupil's progress."

"Humph!" said Mr. Rochester.—vol. i, p. 234.

Let us take a specimen of her again when Mr. Rochester brings home his guests to Thornfield. The fine ladies of this world are a new study to Jane, and capitally she describes her first impression of them as they leave the dinner table and return to the drawing-room—nothing can be more gracefully graphic than this.

There were but eight of them, yet somehow as they flocked in, they gave the impression of a much larger number. Some of them were very tall, and all had a sweeping amplitude of array that seemed to magnify their persons as a mist magnifies the moon. I rose and curtseyed to them: one or two bent their heads in return; the others only stared at me.

They dispersed about the room, reminding me, by the lightness and buoyancy of their movements, of a flock of white plumy birds. Some of them threw themselves in half-reclining positions on the sofa and ottomans; some bent over the tables and examined the flowers and books; the rest gathered in a group round the fire: all talked in a low but clear tone which seemed habitual to them.—vol. ii. p. 38.

But now for the reverse. The moment Jane Eyre sets these graceful creatures conversing, she falls into mistakes which display not so much a total ignorance of the habits of society, as a vulgarity of mind inherent in herself. They talked together by her account like *parvenues* trying to show off. They discuss the subject of governesses before her very face, in what Jane affects to consider the exact tone of fashionable contempt. They bully the servants in language no lady would dream of using to her own—far less to those of her host and entertainer—though certainly the "Sam" of Jane Eyre's is not precisely the head servant one is accustomed to meet with in houses of the Thornfield class. For instance this is a conversation which occurs in her hearing. An old gypsy has come to the Hall, and the servants can't get rid of her—

"What does she want?" asked Mrs. Eshton.

"To tell the gentry their fortunes, she says, Ma'am: and she swears she must and will do it."

"What is she like?" inquired the Misses Eshton in a breath.

"A shocking ugly old creature, Miss; almost as black as a crock."

"Why she's a real sorceress," cried Frederick Lynn. "Let us have her in of course."

"My dear boys, what are you thinking about?" exclaimed Lady Lynn.

"I cannot possibly countenance any such inconsistent proceedings," chimed in the Dowager Ingram.

"Indeed, Mama, but you can—and will," pronounced the haughty voice of Blanche, as she turned round on the pianostool, where till now she had sat silent, apparently examining sundry sheets of music. "I have a curiosity to hear my fortune told: therefore, Sam, order the beldame forward."

"My darling Blanche! recollect—"

"I do—I recollect all you can suggest; and I must have my will—quick, Sam!"

"Yes—yes—yes," cried all the juveniles, both ladies and gentlemen. "Let her come, it will be excellent sport!"

The footman still lingered. "She looks such a rough one," said he.

"Go!" ejaculated Miss Ingram, and the man went.

Excitement instantly seized the whole party; a running fire of raillery and jests was proceeding when Sam returned.

"She won't come now," said he. "She says it is not her mission to appear before the 'vulgar herd' (them's her words). I must show her into a room by herself, and them who wish to consult her must go to her one by one."

"You see now, my queenly Blanche," began Lady Ingram, "she encroaches. Be advised my angel girl—and—"

"Show her into the library of course," cut in the "angel girl." "It is not my mission to listen to her before the vulgar herd either; I mean to have her all to myself. Is there a fire in the library?"

"Yes, Ma'am, but she looks such a tinkler."

"Cease that chatter, blockhead! and do my bidding!"—vol. ii., p. 82.

The old gypsy woman, by the way, turns out to be Mr. Rochester—whom Jane of course alone recognises—as silly an incident as can well be contrived. But the crowning scene is the offer—governesses are said to be sly on such occasions, but Jane out-governesses them all—little Becky would have blushed for her. They are sitting together at the foot of the old chestnut tree, as we have already mentioned, towards the close of evening, and Mr. Rochester is informing her, with his usual delicacy of language, that he is engaged to Miss Ingram—"a strapper! Jane, a real strapper!"—and that as soon as he brings home his bride to Thornfield, she, the governess, must "trot forthwith"—but that he shall make it his duty to look out for employment and an asylum for her—indeed, that he has already heard of a charming situation in the depths of Ireland—all with a brutal jocoseness which most women of spirit, unless grievously despairing of any other lover, would have resented, and any woman of sense would have seen through. But Jane, that profound reader of the human heart, and especially of Mr. Rochester's, does neither. She meekly hopes she may be allowed to stay where she is till she has found another shelter to betake herself to—she does not fancy going to Ireland—Why?

> "It is a long way off, Sir." "No matter—a girl of your sense will not object to the voyage or the distance." "Not the voyage, but the distance, Sir; and then the sea is a barrier—" "From what, Jane?" "From England, and from Thornfield; and—" "Well?" "From *you*, sir."—vol. ii., p. 205

and then the lady bursts into tears in the most approved fashion.

Although so clever in giving hints, how wonderfully slow she is in taking them! Even when, tired of his cat's play, Mr. Rochester proceeds to rather indubitable demonstrations of affection—"enclosing me in his arms, gathering me to his breast, pressing his lips on my lips"—Jane has no idea what he can mean. Some ladies would have thought it high time to leave the Squire alone with his chestnut tree; or, at all events, unnecessary to keep up that tone of high-souled feminine obtusity which they are quite justified in adopting if gentlemen will not speak out—but Jane again does neither. Not that we say she was wrong, but quite the reverse, considering the circumstances of the case—Mr. Rochester was her master, and "Duchess or nothing" was her first duty—only she was not quite so artless as the author would have us suppose.

But if the manner in which she secures the prize be not inadmissible according to the rules of the art, that in which she manages it when caught, is quite without authority or precedent, except perhaps in the servants' hall. Most lover's play is wearisome and nonsensical to the lookers on—but the part Jane assumes is one which could only be efficiently sustained by the substitution of Sam for her master. Coarse as Mr. Rochester is, one winces for him under the infliction of this housemaid *beau idéal* of the arts of coquetry. A little more, and we should have flung the book aside to lie for ever among the trumpery with which such scenes ally it; but it were a pity to have halted here, for wonderful things lie beyond—scenes of suppressed feeling, more fearful to witness than the most violent tornados of passion—struggles with such intense sorrow and suffering as it is sufficient misery to know that any one should have conceived, far less passed through; and yet with that stamp of truth which takes precedence in the human heart before actual experience. The flippant, fifth-rate, plebeian actress has vanished, and only a noble, high-souled woman, bound to us by the reality of her sorrow, and yet raised above us by the strength of her will, stands in actual life before us. If this be Jane Eyre, the author has done her injustice hitherto, not we. Let us look at her in the first recognition of her sorrow after the discomfiture of the marriage. True, it is not the attitude of a Christian, who knows that all things work together for good to those who love God, but it is a splendidly drawn picture of a natural heart, of high power, intense feeling, and fine religious instinct, falling prostrate, but not grovelling, before the tremendous blast of sudden affliction. The house is cleared of those who had come between her and a disgraceful happiness.[1]

• • •

We have said that this was the picture of a natural heart. This, to our view, is the great and crying mischief of the book. Jane Eyre is throughout the personification of an unregenerate and undisciplined spirit, the more dangerous to exhibit from that prestige of principle and self-control which is liable to dazzle the eye too much for it to observe the inefficient and unsound foundation on which it rests. It is true Jane does right, and exerts great moral strength, but it is the strength of a mere heathen mind which is a law unto itself. No Christian grace is perceptible upon her. She has inherited in fullest measure the worst sin of our fallen nature—the sin of pride. Jane Eyre is proud, and therefore she is

---

[1] Eastlake here quotes a long passage from the conclusion of volume 2 (chapter 26) of *Jane Eyre*.

ungrateful too. It pleased God to make her an orphan, friendless, and penniless—yet she thanks nobody, and least of all Him, for the food and raiment, the friends, companions, and instructors of her helpless youth—for the care and education vouchsafed to her till she was capable in mind as fitted in years to provide for herself. On the contrary, she looks upon all that has been done for her not only as her undoubted right, but as falling far short of it. The doctrine of humility is not more foreign to her mind than it is repudiated by her heart. It is by her own talents, virtues, and courage that she is made to attain the summit of human happiness, and, as far as Jane Eyre's own statement is concerned, no one would think that she owed anything either to God above or to man below. She flees from Mr. Rochester, and has not a being to turn to. Why was this? The excellence of the present institution at Casterton, which succeeded that of Cowan Bridge near Kirkby Lonsdale—these being distinctly, as we hear, the original and the reformed Lowoods of the book—is pretty generally known. Jane had lived there for eight years with 110 girls and fifteen teachers. Why had she formed no friendships among them? Other orphans have left the same and similar institutions, furnished with friends for life, and puzzled with homes to choose from. How comes it that Jane had acquired neither? Among that number of associates there were surely some exceptions to what she so presumptuously stigmatises as "the society of inferior minds." Of course it suited the author's end to represent the heroine as utterly destitute of the common means of assistance, in order to exhibit both her trials and her powers of self-support—the whole book rests on this assumption—but it is one which, under the circumstances, is very unnatural and very unjust.

Altogether the auto-biography of Jane Eyre is pre-eminently an anti-Christian composition. There is throughout it a murmuring against the comforts of the rich and against the privations of the poor, which, as far as each individual is concerned, is a murmuring against God's appointment—there is a proud and perpetual assertion of the rights of man, for which we find no authority either in God's word or in God's providence—there is that pervading tone of ungodly discontent which is at once the most prominent and the most subtle evil which the law and the pulpit, which all civilized society in fact has at the present day to contend with. We do not hesitate to say, that the tone of mind and thought which has overthrown authority and violated every code human and divine abroad, and fostered Chartism and rebellion at home, is the same which has also written *Jane Eyre*.

Still we say again this is a very remarkable book. We are painfully alive to the moral, religious, and literary deficiencies of the picture, and such passages of beauty and power as we have quoted cannot redeem it, but it is impossible not to be spellbound with the freedom of the touch. It would be mere hackneyed courtesy to call it "fine writing." It bears no impress of being written at all, but is poured out rather in the heat and hurry of an instinct, which flows ungovernably on to its object, indifferent by what means it reaches it, and unconscious too. As regards the author's chief object, however, it is a failure—that, namely, of making a plain, odd woman, destitute of all the conventional features of feminine attraction, interesting in our sight. We deny that he has succeeded in this. Jane Eyre, in spite of some grand things about her, is a being totally uncongenial to our feelings from beginning to end. We acknowledge her firmness—we respect her determination—we feel for her struggles; but, for all that, and setting aside higher considerations, the impression she leaves on our mind is that of a decidedly vulgar-minded woman—one whom we should not care for as an acquaintance, whom we should not seek as a friend, whom we should not desire for a relation, and whom we should scrupulously avoid for a governess.

There seems to have arisen in the novel-reading world some doubts as to who really wrote this book; and various rumours, more or less romantic, have been current in Mayfair, the metropolis of gossip, as to the authorship. For example, *Jane Eyre* is sentimentally assumed to have proceeded from the pen of Mr. Thackeray's governess, whom he had himself chosen as his model of Becky, and who, in mingled love and revenge, personified him in return as Mr. Rochester. In this case, it is evident that the author of *Vanity Fair*, whose own pencil makes him grey-haired, has had the best of it, though his children may have had the worst, having, at all events, succeeded in hitting that vulnerable point in the Becky bosom, which it is our firm belief no man born of woman, from her Soho to her Ostend days, had ever so much as grazed. To this ingenious rumour the coincidence of the second edition of *Jane Eyre* being dedicated to Mr. Thackeray has probably given rise. For our parts, we see no great interest in the question at all. The first edition of *Jane Eyre* purports to be edited by Currer Bell, on of a trio of brothers, or sisters, or cousins, by names Currer, Acton, and Ellis Bell, already known as the joint-authors of a volume of poems. The second edition the same—dedicated, however, by the author to Mr. Thackeray; and the dedication (itself an indubitable *chip* of Jane Eyre) signed Currer Bell. Author and editor therefore are one, and we are as much satisfied to accept this double individual under the name of "Currer Bell," as under any other, more or less euphonious. Whoever it be, it is a person who, with great mental powers, combines a total ignorance of the habits of society, a great coarseness of taste, and a heathenish doctrine of religion. And as these characteristics appear more or less in the writings of all three, Currer, Acton, and Ellis alike, for their poems differ less in degree of power than in kind, we are ready to accept the fact of their identity or of their relationship with equal satisfaction. At all events there can be no interest attached to the writer of *Wuthering Heights*—a novel succeeding *Jane Eyre*, and purporting to be written by Ellis Bell—unless it were for the sake of more individual reprobation. For though there is a decided family like-ness between the two, yet the aspect of the Jane and Rochester animals in their native state, as Catherine and Heathfield,[1] is too odiously and abominably pagan to be palatable even to the most vitiated class of English readers. With all the unscrupulousness of the French school of novels it combines that repulsive vulgarity in the choice of its vice which supplies its own antidote. The question of authorship, there-fore, can deserve a moment's curiosity only as far as *Jane Eyre* is concerned, and though we cannot pronounce that it appertains to a real Mr. Currer Bell and to no other, yet that it pertains to a man, and not, as many assert, to a woman, we are strongly inclined to affirm. Without entering into the question whether the power of the writing be above her, or the vulgarity below her, there are, we believe, minu-tiae of circumstantial evidence which at once acquit the feminine hand. No woman—a lady friend, whom we are always happy to consult,

---

[1] Heathcliff.

assures us—makes mistakes in her own *métier*—no woman *trusses game* and garnishes dessert-dishes with the same hands, or talks of so doing in the same breath. Above all, no woman attires another in such fancy dresses as Jane's ladies assume—Miss Ingram coming down, irresistible, "in a *morning* robe of sky-blue crape, a gauze azure scarf twisted in her hair!!" No lady, we understand, when suddenly routed in the night, would think of hurrying on "*a frock*." They have garments more convenient for such occasions, and more becoming too. This evidence seems incontrovertible. Even granting that these incongruities were purposely assumed, for the sake of disguising the female pen, there is nothing gained; for if we ascribe the book to a woman at all, we have no alternative but to ascribe it to one who has, for some sufficient reason, long forfeited the society of her own sex.

And if by no woman, it is certainly also by no artist. The Thackeray eye has had no part there. There is not more disparity between the art of drawing Jane assumes and her evident total ignorance of its first principles, than between the report she gives of her own character and the conclusions we form for ourselves. Not but what, in another sense, the author may be classed as an artist of very high grade. Let him describe the simplest things in nature—a rainy landscape, a cloudy sky, or a bare moorside, and he shows the hand of a master; but the moment he talks of the art itself, it is obvious that he is a complete ignoramus.[1]

SOURCE

Quarterly Review 84 (December 1848).

SELECTED SECONDARY READING

Lochhead, Marion. *Elizabeth Rigby, Lady Eastlake.* London: Murray, 1961.

---

[1] In the last section of this review, Eastlake discusses the plight of actual governesses, as described in the 1847 report of the Governesses Benevolent Institution. Suggesting that many families have hired governesses (at paltry wages) merely out of laziness or for show, she urges women either to pay their governesses better wages and pensions, or to educate their daughters themselves.

PEOPLE WHO DO NOT LIKE POETRY
(MAY 1849)

Eliza Cook

ELIZA COOK (1818–89) was born in London to a family of
the artisan class and grew up in the Sussex countryside. Largely
self-educated, she began to write poetry very early. Her mother,
who had encouraged her gifts, died when Eliza was 15, and the
loss motivated some of Cook's best-known lyrics, including "The
Old Arm-Chair." Cook published her first volume of poems,
Lays of a Wild Harp (1835), when she was only 17 and thereafter
published in popular periodicals like the *New Monthly Magazine*,
winning both popular and critical acclaim for her simple and
direct lyrics and for her great sympathy with the unfortunate or
marginalized. She eventually published two more volumes of
poetry, *Melaia and Other Poems* (1838) and *New Echoes and Other
Poems* (1864), as well as collected editions of her work. While
much of her early poetry is extremely sentimental, her more
mature poetry frequently sounds political notes and evinces a
rousing command of language. Some of her later work was
published in the radical paper *The North Star*.

By the mid-1840s, Cook had moved to London, where
both her literary reputation and her unconventional, unfem-
inine dress drew attention. From 1845 to about 1849, she was
the companion of the American actress Charlotte Cushman,
to whom she addressed a number of passionate poems. The
relationship seems to have foundered both because Cook was
unwilling to travel and because of Cushman's budding relationship with journalist and actress Matilda ("Max") Hays.

In 1849, Cook launched a weekly magazine, *Eliza Cook's Journal.* Directed primarily at women, the *Journal* published a mix of poetry, housekeeping tips, children's features, and informational essays. Cook's politics were outspokenly progressive, and *Eliza Cook's Journal* consistently called for expanded vocational opportunities for women and the working classes, the opening of public libraries and museums, and a general democratization of British society. Cook directed the *Journal* until 1854, when ill-health forced her to retire. In 1863, she was granted a Civil List pension, and she seems to have lived as a semi-recluse until her death.

While contributors to *Eliza Cook's Journal* such as Samuel Smiles, author of *Self-Help,* stressed hard work and self-denial as the keys to self-improvement, Cook herself heralded the importance of the arts, especially poetry, in elevating the human spirit. The following piece is typical of Cook's lighter criticism. Originally published in 1849 in *Eliza Cook's Journal,* and republished in Cook's 1860 essay anthology *Jottings from My Journal,* "People Who Do Not Like Poetry" gently satirizes the pragmatic, utilitarian mindset that Dickens savaged in the opening chapters of *Hard Times.* People who do not like poetry, Cook asserts, lack an essential element of romance: they "have no ear for music in a 'babbling brook,' without the said brook turns a very profitable mill." But worse, this lack of romance signals an absence of essential human sympathy: "they see nothing in the attachment between a poor man and his cur dog, but a crime worthy the imprisonment of one, and the hanging of the other." In Cook's analysis, those who maintained a poetic imagination even without reading "a line of printed cadence" were to be admired—the others to be avoided at all costs.

WE HAVE OFTEN HEARD POETRY spoken of by certain shallow-hearted, hammer-headed people, as an infinite something of meretricious nothingness, if one may use an Irishism. They look upon poetry as a sort of fantastic, gossamer cobweb, woven by the hand of unrecognized insanity, and wonder it should be permitted to flit about the highways of the world; they flout it as a trumpery and contemptible production of no earthly *use*, and of course their practical statistics never descend to the question of *ornament*. They are totally ignorant that Poetry is identified and incorporated in the primitive elements of all that makes God visible and man glorious; they know not that poetry is co-existent with a flourishing state and a great people; they know not that it is poetic instinct which prompts a Washington to free his country, and calls the tear of repentance into the felon's eye, as he wakes from a dream of green fields and his mother. They only comprehend there is something arranged in syllables, that this something is unprofitable and ridiculous, composed of imaginary trash, and called poetry. It is "stuff," "rubbish," "nonsense," and in the arrogance of their self-sufficiency, we have heard those people rash enough to assert, that they could see no great use in Shakspere's plays. To listen to the arguments, or rather, declarations, of those dealers in hardware, one would think the Creator had sadly wasted his might and ingenuity in scattering the profusions of exquisite matter about us, which we have yet been unable to convert into tangible utility or mercenary profit. One would be induced to fancy that the myriads of sweet-bosomed, bright-headed flowers, flung on the untrodden valleys and mountain-sides, should be exterminated from the land, since they cannot be packed into bales of merchandize, nor cast up in day-books. We should begin to interrogate the wisdom of sending unnumbered nightingales and thrushes, for the express purpose of whistling away with all their might in the green boughs, and yet yielding nothing in the great "commercial account." Be it understood, that by "people who do not like poetry," we have no intention of alluding to those who may have no special devotion to measured feet and gentle rhythm. We advert not to the myriads who go about their business in everyday sobriety; who live, die, woo, wed, make fortunes, or become bankrupts, and fill up the ranks of life without the slightest knowledge of poetry in its tangible and professed sense.

Such heads may be totally unacquainted with the classical existence of a Helicon.[1] They may never dream deliciously in the fairy-land of a Spencer, and even be unfamiliar with the voice of a Goldsmith.[2] Yet we see hundreds of these people, with the spirit of poetry playing about them in revelling gambols, at every opportunity the chances of fate may offer. The most exquisite love of the ideal, and the most ardent glow of enthusiasm, often abide in the bosom that knows not the name of its residents; and many a rough-hewn denizen of earth goes from his cradle to his grave, full of rich, sweet poetry, without even a suspicion of the "divinity that stirs within him." No! it is not these people we anathematize, for these are the mysterious and ceaseless echoings of the first great Voice that pronounced all things good and beautiful. These unconsciously pour forth the perfumed incense of immortality, purifying the foul vapours that gather so chokingly in God's Great temple. No! it is not these we denounce, for we worship and honour the untold numbers who think and feel poetry in its noblest essence, yet never breathe, and seldom read, a line of printed cadence.

It is the flinty, crude mass of "utilitarianism," the hard, unbending unit of creation, standing in upright, frozen selfishness, entertaining no speculation but that depending on a thriving railway, and respecting no laws but those of Blackstone and Coke; those who depreciate all knowledge, save that denominated "worldly"; a knowledge too frequently testified by conduct that would bear the less equivocal term of "craft"; those who sneer at a sentiment, and despise a feeling that may go an inch beyond the very commonest of sense; it is such we most heartily pray to be delivered from during our sojourn here below. They may be useful and necessary—so may the cholera; but in honest simplicity, we desire to keep clear of both inflictions.

These people have no ear for music in a "babbling brook," without the said brook turns a very profitable mill. They find no "sermons in stones," beyond those preached by the walls of a Royal Exchange. They see nothing in a mob of ragged urchins loitering about the

---

[1] In Greek mythology, the home of the nine Muses, and thus the source of poetic inspiration.

[2] Edmund Spenser (1552–99), English poet, whose best-known work is his *Faerie Queene* (1590); Oliver Goldsmith (1730–74), Irish poet.

streets in a spring twilight, busy over a handful of buttercups and daisies, lugged with anxious care from Putney or Clapham—they see nothing but a tribe of tiresome children who deserve, and sometimes get, a box on the ears for "being in the way." They see nothing in the attachment between a poor man and his cur dog, but a crime worthy the imprisonment of one, and the hanging of the other. Indeed, we have remarked that these "people who do not like poetry" seldom have sympathy for mendacity of any description. If a sick woman with a sicklier child, or an old man with palsied limbs, solicit a halfpenny, these people have a stereotyped knack of parading the comforts of the "Union,"[1] and the audacity of "going about begging." If an orphan boy of Seven Dials' genealogy is recommended by some benevolent idiot to clean boots and shoes, "they will have no such young scamp about them."—"But he has not yet done anything dishonest," says the pleader for poverty. "No matter," is the reply; "I shan't take him, and there's an end of it." Ah! these people are doubt-less "wise in their generation." It is too true that imposition and ingratitude are stalking about us everywhere; the pale woman and the trembling man may not be quite so wretched as they seem, and the offspring of ignorance and misery may not prove a moral Crichton;[2] yet, with a "day of judgment" in the Christian's distance, we have a prejudice in favour of giving an odd penny now and then, without too strict inquiry as to whether the applicant's cup of sorrow is brimfull; and we have a prejudice equally strong, that it is not contrary to human philosophy to endeavour to "snatch a brand from the burn-ing,"[3] and give the chance of honest pursuits to the children of infamy, even though they have "no character" to begin with.

"People who do not like poetry" have rarely much participation in the elasticities of our moral lot. Eating, drinking, sleeping, and "look-ing to the main chance," generally form their whole consecutive occu-pations; but, if any occasional development of humour and cheerfulness occur in the genus, we have observed that it usually tends

---

[1] Poorhouse or workhouse.

[2] Possible allusion to Dr. James Crichton (1765–1823), founder of a mental hospital offer-ing the "moral treatment" of patients, a scheme based on kindness and individualized care.

[3] Proverbial saying, from Zechariah 3:2.

to "practical joking and coarse badinage." This is the lowest, and apparently, the only grade of wit they are capable of exercising with any facility; but with the utmost touchiness, at the same time, if any responsive liberty be taken with their own respected person. The spirit of poetry at least instils the justice of bearing that which we are eager to award; but our utilitarians have no notion of this. Some of them even advocate the strong practical joke of killing off the superfluous population, but we never find their own names on the superabundant list.

"People who do not like poetry" are invariably the most revengeful in their animosities. They hold malice with strong tenacity; forgiving and forgetting are not in their creed; and their bosoms seem charged with an ascetic vengeance, that is never neutralized by the weak, ridiculous, humanizing spirit of poetry.

"People who do not like poetry" are the worst possible companions, in any shape. Take them on a tour through a lovely country, and they see nothing at all in the tumbling waterfall or Elysian valley, but are eternally breaking in on your rapt admiration, with some abrupt and common-place jargon, that raises a strong desire to serve them as Crooked Richard did his nephews.[1] Have them at a social dinner-party, and they strenuously seek to limit the conversation to "dry and dusty business" of some kind or other; party politics, state of dividends, joint-stock companies, the cotton market, or some such themes, are all they can dilate on; and with loud and pertinacious determination they "stick to their last," to the exclusion of general and polite interchange of discussions and opinions. Walk with them into an exhibition of paintings, and, most likely, you will have to blush up to your ears, for they treat all things connected with "Fine Arts" as mere trumpery, and, of course, make very audible and very ignorant remarks on matters, concerning which, the slightest poetical delicacy would make them silent. Meet them when you are attired in a new garb of deep mourning, and their first question will be, "Who have you lost?" Let a child cry in their presence, and they instantly express an impatient disgust, that would warrant one in supposing that they

---

[1]   Richard III (1452–85) was suspected of having had his nephews put to death to protect his own claim to the throne.

had passed through infancy without a single kick or scream. Let an old horse, that has worked twenty years in their service, be pronounced unfit for his duty, and they coolly take forty shillings and consign the worn-out beast to cruelty, starvation, and "a sand-cart," without a ghost of conscience.

Oh! these "people who do not like poetry" are sad thorns in the side of refined humanity. We repeat, they may be useful; but we honestly confess, if we have one prejudice stronger than another, it exists against those animated fossils who "do not like poetry."

SOURCE

Eliza Cook's Journal (May 1849); reprinted in *Jottings from My Journal* (London, 1860).

SELECTED SECONDARY READING

"Eliza Cook." *Notable Women of Our Own Times: A Collection of Biographies of Royal and Other Ladies Celebrated in Literature, Art, and Society.* London: Ward, Lock, [1883].

Merrill, Lisa. *When Romeo Was a Woman: Charlotte Cushman and Her Circle of Female Spectators.* Ann Arbor: University of Michigan Press, 1999.

Robinson, Solveig C. "Of 'Haymakers' and 'City Artisans': The Chartist Poetics of Eliza Cook's Songs of Labor." *Victorian Poetry* 39.2 (2001): 229–53.

EDITOR'S PREFACE TO THE NEW EDITION OF *WUTHERING HEIGHTS*
(1850)

Charlotte Brontë

CHARLOTTE BRONTË (1816–55) was born in Yorkshire, the third of six children of a clergyman and his wife. The family was early struck by tragedy: a few years after their mother died of cancer, Charlotte's two older sisters sickened and died. The surviving children, thrown frequently upon their own resources, paired off—Charlotte with her brother Branwell (born 1817), and the younger sisters Emily (born 1818) and Anne (born 1820)—and created imaginary worlds that were to serve as the inspiration for their more mature poetry and fiction.

Aware that they would need to be self-supporting, Charlotte aFnd her sisters sought educational opportunities to train themselves for governessing or, ideally, to run their own school. All three attended the Roe Head school (Emily for less than a year), where Charlotte remained to teach. Charlotte and Emily also studied languages in Brussels. The dream of opening their own school was never realized, but in 1845 Charlotte convinced her sisters to attempt a literary career. Their joint volume of verse appeared in 1846 and introduced the androgynous pseudonyms they were to employ during their brief careers: Acton (Anne), Ellis (Emily), and Currer (Charlotte) Bell. The following year, Anne's and Emily's first novels, *Agnes Grey* and *Wuthering Heights*, were accepted for publication, but Charlotte's was not. Undaunted, Charlotte began a new novel which was accepted and published immediately. *Jane Eyre* (1847), with its plain and rebellious heroine, marked a watershed in English fiction.

The tragedy that had shadowed her family's early years returned during a terrible eight-month period in 1848 to 1849, during which time Branwell, Emily, and Anne died. The necessity of sorting out for posterity the authorship of her own and her sisters' works prompted Charlotte to agree to write introductory prefaces for the reissues of Emily's and Anne's novels. In her Preface to *Wuthering Heights,* Charlotte creates an origin myth to respond to critics' charges that her sister's novel is "coarse" and its author unladylike. Painting Emily as an unschooled child of nature, Charlotte depicts the novel as the work of relative immaturity. "Had she but lived," she declares, Emily's mind would have grown like a tree, "loftier, straighter, wider-spreading, and its matured fruits would have attained a mellower ripeness and sunnier bloom." Nevertheless, *Wuthering Heights* itself is described as a work of monumental weight and impact, one that will permanently loom over the literary landscape.

I HAVE JUST READ OVER *Wuthering Heights,* and, for the first time, have obtained a clear glimpse of what are termed (and, perhaps, really are) its faults; have gained a definite notion of how it appears to other people—to strangers who knew nothing of the author; who are unacquainted with the locality where the scenes of the story are laid; to whom the inhabitants, the customs, the natural characteristics of the outlying hills and hamlets in the West-Riding of Yorkshire are things alien and unfamiliar.

To all such *Wuthering Heights* must appear a rude and strange production. The wild moors of the north of England can for them have no interest; the language, the manners, the very dwellings and household customs of the scattered inhabitants of those districts, must be to such readers in a great measure unintelligible, and—where intelligible—repulsive. Men and women who, perhaps, naturally very calm, and with feelings moderate in degree, and little marked in kind, have been trained from their cradle to observe the utmost evenness of manner and guardedness of language, will hardly know what to make of the rough, strong utterance, the harshly manifested passions, the unbridled aversions, and headlong partialities of unlettered moorland hinds and rugged moorland squires, who have grown up untaught and unchecked, except by mentors as harsh as themselves. A large class of readers, likewise, will suffer greatly from the introduction into the pages of this work of words printed with all their letters, which it has become the custom to represent by the initial and final letter only—a blank line filling the interval. I may as well say at once that, for this circumstance, it is out of my power to apologize; deeming it, myself, a rational plan to write words at full length. The practice of hinting by single letters those expletives with which profane and violent persons are wont to garnish their discourse, strikes me as a proceeding which, however well meant, is weak and futile. I cannot tell what good it does—what feeling it spares—what horror it conceals.

With regard to the rusticity of *Wuthering Heights*, I admit the charge, for I feel the quality. It is rustic all through. It is moorish, and wild, and knotty as a root of heath. Nor was it natural that it should be otherwise; the author being herself a native and nursling of the moors. Doubtless, had her lot been cast in a town, her writings, if she had written at all, would have possessed another character. Even had chance or taste led her to choose a similar subject, she would have treated it otherwise. Had Ellis Bell been a lady or a gentleman accustomed to what is called "the world," her view of a remote and unreclaimed region, as well as of the dwellers therein, would have differed greatly from that actually taken by the homebred country girl. Doubtless it would have been wider—more comprehensive; whether it would have been more original or more truthful is not so certain. As far as the scenery and locality are concerned, it could scarcely have been so sympathetic: Ellis Bell did not describe as one whose eye and taste alone found pleasure in the prospect; her native hills were far more to her than a spectacle; they were what she lived in, and by, as much as the wild birds, their tenants, or as the heather, their produce. Her descriptions, then, of natural scenery, are what they should be, and all they should be.

Where delineation of human character is concerned, the case is different. I am bound to avow that she had scarcely more practical knowledge of the peasantry amongst whom she lived, than a nun has of the country people who sometimes pass her convent gates. My sister's disposition was not naturally gregarious; circumstances favoured and fostered her tendency to seclusion; except to go to church or take a walk on the hills, she rarely crossed the threshold of home. Though her feeling for the people round was benevolent, intercourse with them she never sought; nor, with very few exceptions, ever experienced. And yet she knew them: knew their ways, their language, their family histories; she could hear of them with interest and talk of them with detail, minute, graphic, and accurate; but *with* them, she rarely exchanged a word. Hence it ensued that what her mind had gathered of the real concerning them, was too exclusively confined to those tragic and terrible traits of which, in listening to the secret annals of every rude vicinage, the memory is sometimes compelled to receive the impress. Her imagination, which was a spirit more sombre than sunny, more powerful than sportive, found in such traits material whence it wrought creations like Heathcliff, like Earnshaw, like Catherine. Having formed these beings, she did not know what she had done. If the auditor of her work when read in manuscript, shuddered under the grinding influence of natures so relentless and implacable, of spirits so lost and fallen; if it was complained that the mere hearing of certain vivid and fearful scenes banished sleep by night, and disturbed mental peace by day, Ellis Bell would wonder what was meant, and suspect the complainant of affectation. Had she but lived, her mind would of itself have grown like a strong tree, loftier, straighter, wider-spreading, and its matured fruits would have attained a mellower ripeness and sunnier bloom; but on that mind time and experience alone could work: to the influence of other intellects, it was not amenable.

Having avowed that over much of *Wuthering Heights* there broods "a horror of great darkness";[1] that, in its storm-heated and electrical atmosphere, we seem at times to breathe lightning, let me point to those spots where clouded daylight and the eclipsed sun still attest

---

[1] See Genesis 15:12.

their existence. For a specimen of true benevolence, and homely fidelity, look at the character of Nelly Dean; for an example of constancy and tenderness, remark that of Edgar Linton. (Some people will think these qualities do not shine so well incarnate in a man as they would do in a woman, but Ellis Bell could never be brought to comprehend this notion: nothing moved her more than any insinuation that the faithfulness and clemency, the long-suffering and loving-kindness which are esteemed virtues in the daughters of Eve, become foibles in the sons of Adam. She held that mercy and forgiveness are the divinest attributes of the Great Being who made both man and woman, and that what clothes the Godhead in glory, can disgrace no form of feeble humanity.) There is a dry saturnine humour in the delineation of old Joseph, and some glimpses of grace and gaiety animate the younger Catherine. Nor is even the first heroine of the name destitute of a certain strange beauty in her fierceness, or of honesty in the midst of perverted passion and passionate perversity.

Heathcliff, indeed, stands unredeemed; never once swerving in his arrow-straight course to perdition, from the time when "the little black-haired, swarthy thing, as dark as if it came from the Devil," was first unrolled out of the bundle and set on its feet in the farm-house kitchen, to the hour when Nelly Dean found the grim, stalwart corpse laid on its back in the panel-enclosed bed, with wide-gazing eyes that seemed "to sneer at her attempt to close them, and parted lips and sharp white teeth that sneered too."

Heathcliff betrays one solitary human feeling, and that is *not* his love for Catherine; which is a sentiment fierce and inhuman: a passion such as might boil and glow in the bad essence of some evil genius; a fire that might form the tormented centre—the ever-suffering soul of a magnate of the infernal world: and by its quenchless and ceaseless ravage effect the execution of the decree which dooms him to carry Hell with him wherever he wanders. No; the single link that connects Heathcliff with humanity is his rudely confessed regard for Hareton Earnshaw—the young man whom he has ruined; and then his half-implied esteem for Nelly Dean. These solitary traits omitted, we should say he was child neither of Lascar nor gipsy, but a man's shape animated by demon life—a Ghoul—an Afreet.

Whether it is right or advisable to create beings like Heathcliff, I do not know: I scarcely think it is. But this I know; the writer who possesses the creative gift owns something of which he is not always master—something that at times strangely wills and works for itself. He may lay down rules and devise principles, and to rules and principles it will perhaps for years lie in subjection; and then, haply without any warning of revolt, there comes a time when it will no longer consent "to harrow the vallies or be bound with a band in the furrow"—when it "laughs at the multitude of the city, and regards not the crying of the driver"[1]—when, refusing absolutely to make ropes out of sea-sand any longer, it sets to work on statue-hewing, and you have a Pluto or a Jove, a Tisiphone[2] or a Psyche, a Mermaid or a Madonna, as Fate or Inspiration direct. Be the work grim or glorious, dread or divine, you have little choice left but quiescent adoption. As for you—the nominal artist—your share in it has been to work passively under dictates you neither delivered nor could question— that would not be uttered at your prayer, nor suppressed nor changed at your caprice. If the result be attractive, the world will praise you, who little deserve praise; if it be repulsive, the same World will blame you, who almost as little deserve blame.

Wuthering Heights was hewn in a wild workshop, with simple tools out of homely materials. The statuary found a granite block on solitary moor: gazing thereon, he saw how from the crag might be elicited a head, savage swart, sinister; a form moulded with at least one element of grandeur—power. He wrought with a rude chisel, and from no model but the vision of his meditations. With time and labour, the crag took human shape; and there it stands colossal, dark and frowning, half statue, half rock: in the former sense, terrible and goblin-like; in the latter, almost beautiful, for its colouring is of mellow grey, and moorland moss clothes it; and heath, with its blooming bells and balmy fragrance, grows faithfully close to the giant's foot.

---

[1] See Job 39.
[2] In Greek mythology, Tisiphone is an Erinye, an avenger of murder.

EDITOR'S PREFACE TO THE NEW EDITION OF *WUTHERING HEIGHTS*

SOURCE

Wuthering Heights (London, 1850).

SELECTED SECONDARY READING

Allott, Miriam F., ed. *The Brontës: The Critical Heritage*. London: Routledge, 1974.

Barker, Juliet. *The Brontës*. New York: St. Martin's Press, 1994.

Gaskell, Elizabeth. *The Life of Charlotte Brontë*. 1857. Harmondsworth: Penguin, 1981.

SILLY NOVELS BY LADY NOVELISTS
(OCTOBER 1856)

George Eliot

MARY ANN (LATER MARIAN) EVANS (1819–80) was
the youngest child of a county estate manager and his second
wife. Educated at boarding schools in Attleborough,
Nuneaton, and Coventry, Evans showed promise as a student,
particularly in the subjects of music and French. After her
mother's death and her elder sister's marriage, Evans kept
house for her father, pursuing her own studies in languages,
philosophy, and literature. When her father retired in 1841
to the outskirts of Coventry, Evans joined an important circle
of friends, the Hennells and Brays, freethinkers and journalists who inspired both Evans's break with the evangelical religion of her youth and her literary ambitions.

In 1844 she began her first professional work, a translation
of David Friedrich Strauss's *Life of Jesus* (1846). After her
father's death in 1849, which left her with a small legacy, she
travelled to Europe and then settled in London. The
publisher of her Strauss translation, John Chapman, invited
her first to review and then to work as the (unpaid) editor of
the prestigious *Westminster Review*. From 1852 to 1854 Evans
performed the substantive editorial work of the journal, a
position that gave her an opportunity to meet some of the
most important liberal intellectuals then in London, including Herbert Spencer and George Henry Lewes.

In 1854, having put the finishing touches on another
translation, Ludwig Feuerbach's *Essence of Christianity*, the

only published work she signed with her own name, she eloped to Europe with the married Lewes, who was unable to divorce after having previously condoned his wife's adultery. Despite the initial scandal and the enduring disapproval of Evans's brother, Evans and Lewes enjoyed a happy and mutually supportive literary life until Lewes's death in 1878. During this period she published the books for which she is renowned: the stories *Scenes of Clerical Life* (1858) and the six novels—*Adam Bede* (1859), *The Mill on the Floss* (1860), *Silas Marner* (1861), *Romola* (1863), *Felix Holt, the Radical* (1866), *Middlemarch* (1871–72), and *Daniel Deronda* (1876)—that make up the works of "George Eliot." The popular and critical acclaim for these novels, masterpieces of the realist tradition, established her reputation as one of the most important writers of her age and did much to efface the scandal of her private life. Two years after Lewes's death, her marriage to the much younger John Walter Cross effected a reconciliation with her family shortly before she herself died.

Published in the *Westminster Review* in 1856, shortly before she began writing her own fiction, "Silly Novels by Lady Novelists" has many of the hallmarks of what would become George Eliot's defining style. Witty and irreverent, the review essay takes exception to the critical double standard. While "Silly Novels" is usually read as an indictment of the kind of fiction Eliot herself would *not* write, the essay is more ambitious. Eliot intertwines the lack of alternative vocational options for women with her categories of silly novels, so that the target of her attack is not merely the vain and untalented writers themselves, but the society that has presented them with no other viable—and more appropriate—outlets for their ambitions. Eliot protests vehemently against chivalrous criticism that begins with the "extremely false impression that to write *at all* is a proof of superiority in a woman." "Fiction is a department of literature in which women can, after their kind, fully equal men," she concludes, and the best service that can be rendered to fiction and to writers is to judge all literary efforts by the same exacting standards.

SILLY NOVELS BY LADY NOVELISTS are a genus with many species, determined by the particular quality of silliness that predominates in them—the frothy, the prosy, the pious, or the pedantic. But it is a mixture of all these—a composite order of feminine fatuity, that produces the largest class of such novels, which we shall distinguish as the *mind-and-millinery* species. The heroine is usually an heiress, probably a peeress in her own right, with perhaps a vicious baronet, an amiable duke, and an irresistible younger son of a marquis as lovers in the foreground, a clergyman and a poet sighing for her in the middle distance, and a crowd of undefined adorers dimly indicated beyond. Her eyes and her wit are both dazzling; her nose and her morals are alike free from any tendency to irregularity; she has a superb *contralto* and a superb intellect; she is perfectly well-dressed and perfectly religious; she dances like a sylph, and reads the Bible in the original tongues. Or it may be that the heroine is not an heiress—that rank and wealth are the only things in which she is deficient; but she infallibly gets into high society, she has the triumph of refusing many matches and securing the best, and she wears some family jewels or other as a sort of crown of righteousness at the end. Rakish men either bite their lips in impotent confusion at her repartees, or are touched to penitence by her reproofs, which, on appropriate occasions, rise to a lofty strain of rhetoric; indeed, there is a general propensity in her to make speeches, and to rhapsodize at some length when she retires to her bedroom. In her recorded conversations she is amazingly eloquent, and in her unrecorded conversations, amazingly witty. She is understood to have a depth of insight that looks through and through the shallow theories of philosophers, and her superior instincts are a sort of dial by which men have only to set their clocks and watches, and all will go well. The men play a very subordinate part by her side. You are consoled now and then by a hint that they have affairs,[1] which keeps you

---

[1] Business affairs.

in mind that the working-day business of the world is somehow being carried on, but ostensibly the final cause of their existence is that they may accompany the heroine on her "starring" expedition through life. They see her at a ball, and are dazzled; at a flower-show, and they are fascinated; on a riding excursion, and they are witched by her noble horsemanship; at church, and they are awed by the sweet solemnity of her demeanour. She is the ideal woman in feelings, faculties, and flounces. For all this, she as often as not marries the wrong person to begin with, and she suffers terribly from the plots and intrigues of the vicious baronet; but even death has a soft place in his heart for such a paragon, and remedies all mistakes for her just at the right moment. The vicious baronet is sure to be killed in a duel, and the tedious husband dies in his bed, requesting his wife, as a particular favour to him, to marry the man she loves best, and having already dispatched a note to the lover informing him of the comfortable arrangement. Before matters arrive at this desirable issue our feelings are tried by seeing the noble, lovely, and gifted heroine pass through many *mauvais moments*,[1] but we have the satisfaction of knowing that her sorrows are wept into embroidered pocket-handkerchiefs, that her fainting form reclines on the very best upholstery, and that whatever vicissitudes she may undergo, from being dashed out of her carriage to having her head shaved in a fever, she comes out of them all with a complexion more blooming and locks more redundant than ever.

We may remark, by the way, that we have been relieved from a serious scruple by discovering that silly novels by lady novelists rarely introduce us into any other than very lofty and fashionable society. We had imagined that destitute women turned novelists, as they turned governesses, because they had no other "lady-like" means of getting their bread. On this supposition, vacillating syntax and improbable incident had a certain pathos for us, like the extremely supererogatory pincushions and ill-devised nightcaps that are offered for sale by a blind man. We felt the commodity to be a nuisance, but we were glad to think that the money went to relieve the necessitous, and we pictured to ourselves lonely women struggling for a maintenance, or wives and daughters

---

[1] Unfortunate circumstances.

devoting themselves to the production of "copy" out of pure heroism,—perhaps to pay their husband's debts, or to purchase luxuries for a sick father. Under these impressions we shrank from criticizing a lady's novel: her English might be faulty, but, we said to ourselves, her motives are irreproachable; her imagination may be uninventive, but her patience is untiring. Empty writing was excused by an empty stomach, and twaddle was consecrated by tears. But no! This theory of ours, like many other pretty theories, has had to give way before observation. Women's silly novels, we are now convinced, are written under totally different circumstances. The fair writers have evidently never talked to a tradesman except from a carriage window; they have no notion of the working classes except as "dependants"; they think £500 a year a miserable pittance; Belgravia[1] and "baronial halls" are their primary truths; and they have no idea of feeling interest in any man who is not at least a great landed proprietor, if not a prime minister. It is clear that they write in elegant boudoirs, with violet-coloured ink and a ruby pen; that they must be entirely indifferent to publishers' accounts, and inexperienced in every form of poverty except poverty of brains. It is true that we are constantly struck with the want of verisimilitude in their representations of the high society in which they seem to live; but then they betray no closer acquaintance with any other form of life. If their peers and peeresses are improbable, their literary men, tradespeople, and cottagers are impossible; and their intellect seems to have the peculiar impartiality of reproducing both what they have seen and heard, and what they have not seen and heard, with equal unfaithfulness.

There are few women, we suppose, who have not seen something of children under five years of age, yet in *Compensation*,[2] a recent novel of the mind-and-millinery species, which calls itself a "story of real life," we have a child of four and a half years old talking in this Ossianic fashion—

> "Oh, I am so happy, dear gran'mamma;—I have seen,—I have seen such a delightful person: he is like everything beautiful,—

---

1   Fashionable section of London.
2   By Henrietta Lascelles, Lady Chatterton (1806–76).

like the smell of sweet flowers, and the view from Ben Lomond;—
or no, *better than that*—he is like what I think of and see when I
am very, very happy; and he is really like mamma, too, when she
sings; and his forehead is like *that distant sea*," she continued,
pointing to the blue Mediterranean; "there seems no end—no
end; or like the clusters of stars I like best to look at on a warm
fine night ... Don't look so ... your forehead is like Loch Lomond,
when the wind is blowing and the sun is gone in; I like the
sunshine best when the lake is smooth ... So now—I like it better
than ever ... it is more beautiful still from the dark cloud that has
gone over it, *when the sun suddenly lights up all the colours of the forests
and shining purple rocks, and it is all reflected in the waters below.*"

We are not surprised to learn that the mother of this infant phenomenon, who exhibits symptoms so alarmingly like those of adolescence
repressed by gin, is herself a phoenix. We are assured, again and again,
that she had a remarkably original mind, that she was a genius, and
"conscious of her originality," and she was fortunate enough to have a
lover who was also a genius, and a man of "most original mind."

This lover, we read, though "wonderfully similar" to her "in powers
and capacity," was "infinitely superior to her in faith and development," and she saw in him the "'Agape'—so rare to find—of which
she had read and admired the meaning in her Greek Testament;
having, *from her great facility in learning languages,* read the Scriptures
in their original tongues." Of course! Greek and Hebrew are mere
play to a heroine; Sanscrit is no more than *a b c* to her; and she can
talk with perfect correctness in any language except English. She is a
polking polyglot, a Creuzer in crinoline.[1] Poor men! There are so few
of you who know even Hebrew; you think it something to boast of if,
like Bolingbroke, you only "understand that sort of learning, and
what is writ about it";[2] and you are perhaps adoring women who can
think slightingly of you in all the Semitic languages successively. But,

---

[1] Reference to Georg Friedrich Creuzer (1771–1858), eminent German philologist.
[2] Poet Alexander Pope's (1688–1744) tribute to philosopher Henry Bolingbroke (1678–1751).

then, as we are almost invariably told, that a heroine has a "beautifully small head," and as her intellect has probably been early invigorated by an attention to costume and deportment, we may conclude that she can pick up the Oriental tongues, to say nothing of their dialects, with the same aerial facility that the butterfly sips nectar. Besides, there can be no difficulty in conceiving the depth of the heroine's erudition, when that of the authoress is so evident.

In Laura Gay,[1] another novel of the same school, the heroine seems less at home in Greek and Hebrew, but she makes up for the deficiency by a quite playful familiarity with the Latin classics—with "dear old Virgil," "the graceful Horace, the humane Cicero and the pleasant Livy";[2] indeed it is such a matter of course with her to quote Latin, that she does it at a picnic in a very mixed company of ladies and gentlemen, having, we are told, "no conception that the nobler sex were capable of jealousy on this subject. And if, indeed," continues the biographer of Laura Gay, "the wisest and noblest portion of that sex were in the majority, no such sentiment would exist; but while Miss Wyndhams and Mr. Redfords abound, great sacrifices must be made to their existence." Such sacrifices, we presume, as abstaining from Latin quotations, of extremely moderate interest and applicability, which the wise and noble minority of the other sex would be quite as willing to dispense with, as the foolish and ignoble majority. It is as little the custom of well-bred men as of well-bred women to quote Latin in mixed parties; they can contain their familiarity with "the humane Cicero" without allowing it to boil over in ordinary conversation, and even references to "the pleasant Livy" are not absolutely irrepressible. But Ciceronian Latin is the mildest form of Miss Gay's conversational power. Being on the Palatine with a party of sight-seers, she falls into the following vein of well-rounded remark:—

> Truth can only be pure objectively, for even in the creeds where
> it predominates, being subjective, and parceled out into portions,
> each of these necessarily receives a hue of idiosyncrasy, that is, a

---

[1] Published anonymously.
[2] Standard classical authors.

taint of superstition more or less strong; while in such creeds as
the Roman Catholic, ignorance, interest, the bias of ancient idolatries, and the force of authority, have gradually accumulated on
the pure truth, and transformed it, at last, into a mass of superstition for the majority of its votaries; and how few are there, alas!
whose zeal, courage, and intellectual energy are equal to the
analysis of this accumulation, and to the discovery of the pearl of
great price which lies hidden beneath this heap of rubbish.

We have often met with women much more novel and profound in their
observations than Laura Gay, but rarely with any so inopportunely long-
winded. A clerical lord, who is half in love with her, is alarmed by the
daring remarks just quoted, and begins to suspect that she is inclined to
free-thinking. But he is mistaken; when in a moment of sorrow he delicately begs leave to "recall to her memory, a *dépôt*[1] of strength and consolation under affliction, which, until we are hard pressed by the trials of
life, we are too apt to forget," we learn that she really has "recurrence to
that sacred dépôt, together with the tea-pot. There is a certain flavour
of orthodoxy mixed with the parade of fortunes and fine carriages in
Laura Gay, but it is an orthodoxy mitigated by study of "the humane
Cicero," and by an "intellectual disposition to analyse."

Compensation is much more heavily dosed with doctrine, but then it
has a treble amount of snobbish worldliness and absurd incident to
tickle the palate of pious frivolity. Linda, the heroine, is still more speculative and spiritual than Laura Gay, but she has been "presented,"
and has more, and far grander, lovers; very wicked and fascinating
women are introduced—even a French *lionne*;[2] and no expense is
spared to get up as exciting a story as you will find in the most immoral
novels. In fact it is a wonderful pot pourri of Almack's, Scotch second-
sight, Mr. Rogers's breakfasts,[3] Italian brigands, death-bed conversions,
superior authoresses, Italian mistresses, and attempts at poisoning old
ladies, the whole served up with a garnish of talk about "faith and

---

[1] Deposit.
[2] Literary lion; a writer who is currently much admired.
[3] Almack's was a fashionable assembly room in London; Samuel Rogers (1763–1855)
hosted literary and society breakfasts.

development," and "most original minds." Even Miss Susan Barton, the superior authoress, whose pen moves in a "quick decided manner when she is composing," declines the finest opportunities of marriage; and though old enough to be Linda's mother (since we are told that she refused Linda's father), has her hand sought by a young earl, the heroine's rejected lover. Of course, genius and morality must be backed by eligible offers, or they would seem rather a dull affair; and piety, like other things, in order to be *comme il faut*,[1] must be in "society," and have admittance to the best circles.

Rank and Beauty[2] is a more frothy and less religious variety of the mind-and-millinery species. The heroine, we are told, "if she inherited her father's pride of birth and her mother's beauty of person, had in herself a tone of enthusiastic feeling that perhaps belongs to her age even in the lowly born, but which is refined into the high spirit of wild romance only in the far descended, who feel that it is their best inheritance." This enthusiastic young lady, by dint of reading the newspaper to her father, falls in love with the *prime minister*, who, through the medium of leading articles and "the *resumé*[3] of the debates," shines upon her imagination as a bright particular star, which has no parallax for her, living in the country as simple Miss Wyndham. But she forthwith becomes Baroness Umfraville in her own right, astonishes the world with her beauty and accomplishments when, she bursts upon it from her mansion in Spring Gardens, and, as you foresee, will presently come into contact with the unseen *objet aimé*.[4] Perhaps the words "prime minister" suggest to you a wrinkled or obese sexagenarian; but pray dismiss the image. Lord Rupert Conway has been "called while still almost a youth to the first situation which a subject can hold in the *universe*," and even leading articles and a *resumé* of the debates have not conjured up a dream that surpasses the fact.

> The door opened again, and Lord Rupert Conway entered.
> Evelyn gave one glance. It was enough; she was not disappointed.

---

1   Well-bred.
2   Published anonymously.
3   Summary.
4   Beloved.

It seemed as if a picture on which she had long gazed was suddenly instinct with life, and had stepped from its frame before her. His tall figure, the distinguished simplicity of his air—it was a living Vandyke,[1] a cavalier, one of his noble cavalier ancestors, or one to whom her fancy had always likened him, who long of yore had, with an Umfraville, fought the Paynim far beyond sea. Was this reality?

Very little like it, certainly.

By and by, it becomes evident that the ministerial heart is touched. Lady Umfraville is on a visit to the Queen at Windsor, and,—

> The last evening of her stay, when they returned from riding, Mr. Wyndham took her and a large party to the top of the Keep, to see the view. She was leaning on the battlements, gazing from that "stately height" at the prospect beneath her, when Lord Rupert was by her side. "What an unrivalled view!" exclaimed she.
>
> "Yes, it would have been wrong to go without having been up here. You are pleased with your visit?"
>
> "Enchanted! 'A Queen to live and die under,' to live and die for!"
>
> "Ha!" cried he, with sudden emotion, and with a *eureka* expression of countenance, as if he had *indeed found a heart in unison with his own.*

The "*eureka* expression of countenance," you see at once to be prophetic of marriage at the end of the third volume; but before that desirable consummation, there are very complicated misunderstandings, arising chiefly from the vindictive plotting of Sir Luttrell Wycherley, who is a genius, a poet, and in every way a most remarkable character indeed. He is not only a romantic poet, but a hardened rake and a cynical wit; yet his deep passion for Lady Umfraville has so impoverished his epigrammatic talent, that he cuts an extremely poor figure in conversation. When she rejects him, he rushes into the shrubbery, and rolls himself in the dirt; and on recovering, devotes

---

[1] Portrait by painter Antoon van Dyck (1599–1641).

himself to the most diabolical and laborious schemes of vengeance, in the course of which he disguises himself as a quack physician, and enters into general practice, foreseeing that Evelyn will fall ill, and that he shall be called in to attend her. At last, when all his schemes are frustrated, he takes leave of her in a long letter, written, as you will perceive from the following passage, entirely in the style of an eminent literary man:—

> Oh, lady, nursed in pomp and pleasure, will you ever cast one thought upon the miserable being who addresses you? Will you ever, as your gilded galley is floating down the unruffled stream of prosperity, will you ever, while lulled by the sweetest music— thine own praises,—hear the far-off sigh from that world to which I am going?

On the whole, however, frothy as it is, we rather prefer *Rank and Beauty* to the two other novels we have mentioned. The dialogue is more natural and spirited; there is some frank ignorance, and no pedantry; and you are allowed to take the heroine's astounding intellect upon trust, without being called on to read her conversational refutations of sceptics and philosophers, or her rhetorical solutions of the mysteries of the universe.

Writers of the mind-and-millinery school are remarkably unanimous in their choice of diction. In their novels, there is usually a lady or gentleman who is more or less of a upas tree: the lover has a manly breast; minds are redolent of various things; hearts are hollow; events are utilized; friends are consigned to the tomb; infancy is an engaging period; the sun is a luminary that goes to his western couch, or gathers the rain-drops into his refulgent bosom; life is a melancholy boon; Albion and Scotia are conversational epithets. There is a striking resemblance, too, in the character of their moral comments, such, for instance, as that "It is a fact, no less true than melancholy, that all people, more or less, richer or poorer, are swayed by bad example"; that "Books, however trivial, contain some subjects from which useful information may be drawn"; that "Vice can too often borrow the language of virtue"; that "Merit and nobility of nature must exist, to be accepted, for clamour and pretension cannot impose upon those too well read in human nature to be easily deceived"; and that, "In order to forgive, we must have been injured." There is, doubtless, a class of readers to whom these remarks appear peculiarly pointed and pungent; for we often find them doubly and trebly scored with the pencil, and delicate hands giving in their determined adhesion to these hardy novelties by a distinct *très vrai*,[1] emphasized by many notes of exclamation. The colloquial style of these novels is often marked by much ingenious inversion, and a careful avoidance of such cheap phraseology as can be heard every day. Angry young gentlemen exclaim—"'Tis ever thus, methinks"; and in the half hour before dinner a young lady informs her next neighbour that the first day she read Shakspeare she "stole away into the park, and beneath the shadow of the greenwood tree, devoured with rapture the inspired page of the great magician." But the most remarkable efforts of the mind-and-millinery writers lie in their philosophic reflections. The authoress of *Laura Gay*, for example, having married her hero and heroine, improves the event by observing that "if those sceptics, whose eyes have so long gazed on matter that they can no longer see aught else in man, could once enter with the heart and soul into such bliss as this, they would come to say that the soul of man and the polypus[2] are not of common origin, or of the same texture." Lady novelists, it appears, can see something else besides matter; they are not limited to phenomena, but can relieve their eyesight by occasional glimpses of the *noumenon*,[3] and are, therefore, naturally better able than any one else to confound sceptics, even of that remarkable, but to us unknown school, which maintains that the soul of man is of the same texture as the polypus.

The most pitiable of all silly novels by lady novelists are what we may call the *oracular* species—novels intended to expound the writer's religious, philosophical, or moral theories. There seems to be a notion abroad among women, rather akin to the superstition that the speech and actions of idiots are inspired, and that the human being most

---

[1] Very true.
[2] Octopus.
[3] Philosophical concept; an object that exists independently of perception by the senses.

entirely exhausted of common sense is the fittest vehicle of revelation. To judge from their writings, there are certain ladies who think that an amazing ignorance, both of science and of life, is the best possible qualification for forming an opinion on the knottiest moral and speculative questions. Apparently, their recipe for solving all such difficulties is something like this:—Take a woman's head, stuff it with a smattering of philosophy and literature chopped small, and with false notions of society baked hard, let it hang over a desk a few hours every day and serve up hot in feeble English, when not required. You will rarely meet with a lady novelist of the oracular class who is diffident of her ability to decide on theological questions,—who has any suspicion that she is not capable of discriminating with the nicest accuracy between the good and evil in all church parties,—who does not see precisely how it is that men have gone wrong hitherto,—and pity philosophers in general that they have not had the opportunity of consulting her. Great writers, who have modestly contented themselves with putting their experience into fiction, and have thought it quite a sufficient task to exhibit men and things as they are, she sighs over as deplorably deficient in the application of their powers. "They have solved no great questions"—and she is ready to remedy their omission by setting before you a complete theory of life and manual of divinity, in a love story, where ladies and gentlemen of good family go through genteel vicissitudes, to the utter confusion of Deists, Puseyites, and ultra-Protestants,[1] and to the perfect establishment of that particular view of Christianity which either condenses itself into a sentence of small caps, or explodes into a cluster of stars on the three hundred and thirtieth page. It is true, the ladies and gentlemen will probably seem to you remarkably little like any you have had the fortune or misfortune to meet with, for, as a general rule, the ability of a lady novelist to describe actual life and her fellow-men, is in inverse proportion to her confident eloquence about God and the other world, and the means by which she usually chooses to conduct you to true ideas of the invisible is a totally false picture of the visible.

---

[1]   Different religious sects. Edward Pusey (1800–82) was a leader of the Oxford Movement.

As typical a novel of the oracular kind as we can hope to meet with, is *The Enigma: A Leaf from the Chronicles of Wolchorley House.*[1] The "enigma" which this novel is to solve, is certainly one that demands powers no less gigantic than those of a lady novelist, being neither more nor less than the existence of evil. The problem is stated, and the answer dimly foreshadowed on the very first page. The spirited young lady, with raven hair, says, "All life is an inextricable confusion"; and the meek young lady, with auburn hair, looks at the picture of the Madonna which she is copying, and—"*There* seemed the solution of that mighty enigma." The style of this novel is quite as lofty as its purpose; indeed, some passages on which we have spent much patient study are quite beyond our reach, in spite of the illustrative aid of italics and small caps; and we must await further "development" in order to understand them. Of Ernest, the model young clergyman, who sets every one right on all occasions, we read, that "he held not of marriage in the marketable kind, after a social desecration"; that, on one eventful night, "sleep had not visited his divided heart, where tumultuated, in varied type and combination, the aggregate feelings of grief and joy"; and that, "for the *marketable* human article he had no toleration, be it of what sort, or set for what value it might, whether for worship or class, his upright soul abhorred it, whose ultimatum, the self-deceiver, was to him THE *great spiritual lie*, 'living in a vain show, deceiving and being deceived'; since he did not suppose the phylactery and enlarged border on the garment to be *merely* a social trick." (The italics and small caps are the author's, and we hope they assist the reader's comprehension.) Of Sir Lionel, the model old gentleman, we are told that "the simple ideal of the middle age, apart from its anarchy and decadence, in him most truly seemed to live again, when the ties which knit men together were of heroic cast. The first-born colours of pristine faith and truth engraven on the common soul of man, and blent into the wide arch of brotherhood, where the primaeval law of *order* grew and multiplied, each perfect after his kind, and mutually independent." You see clearly, of course, how colours are first engraven on a soul, and then blent into a wide arch, on which arch of colours—apparently a rainbow—the law

---

[1] Published anonymously.

of order grew and multiplied, each—apparently the arch and the law—perfect after his kind? If, after this, you can possibly want any further aid towards knowing what Sir Lionel was, we can tell you, that in his soul "the scientific combinations of thought could educe no fuller harmonies of the good and the true, than lay in the primaeval pulses which floated as an atmosphere around it!" and that, when he was sealing a letter, "Lo! the responsive throb in that good man's bosom echoed back in simple truth the honest witness of a heart that condemned him not, as his eye, bedewed with love, rested, too, with something of ancestral pride, on the undimmed motto of the family —Loiauté."[1]

The slightest matters have their vulgarity fumigated out of them by the same elevated style. Commonplace people would say that a copy of Shakspeare lay on a drawing-room table; but the authoress of *The Enigma*, bent on edifying periphrasis, tells you that there lay on the table, "that fund of human thought and feeling, which teaches the heart through the little name, 'Shakspeare.'" A watchman sees a light burning in an upper window rather longer than usual, and thinks that people are foolish to sit up late when they have an opportunity of going to bed; but, lest this fact should seem too low and common, it is presented to us in the following striking and metaphysical manner: "He marvelled—as man *will* think for others in a necessarily separate personality, consequently (though disallowing it) in false mental premise,—how differently *he* should act, how gladly *he* should prize the rest so lightly held of within." A footman—an ordinary Jeames, with large calves and aspirated vowels—answers the door-bell, and the opportunity is seized to tell you that he was a "type of the large class of pampered menials, who follow the curse of Cain—'vagabonds' on the face of the earth, and whose estimate of the human class varies in the graduated scale of money and expenditure ... These, and such as these, O England, be the false lights of thy morbid civilization!" We have heard of various "false lights," from Dr. Cumming to Robert Owen, from Dr. Pusey to the Spirit-rappers,[2] but we never before heard of the false light that emanates from plush and powder.

---

[1] Loyalty.

[2] Theorists of different religious views. Dr. John Cumming (1807–81), leader in the Scottish National Church; Robert Owen (1771–1858), Welsh early socialist thinker.

In the same way very ordinary events of civilized life are exalted into the most awful crises, and ladies in full skirts and *manches à la chinoise*,[1] conduct themselves not unlike the heroines of sanguinary melodramas. Mrs. Percy, a shallow woman of the world, wishes her son Horace to marry the auburn-haired Grace, she being an heiress; but he, after the manner of sons, falls in love with the raven-haired Kate, the heiress's portionless cousin; and, moreover, Grace herself shows every symptom of perfect indifference to Horace. In such cases, sons are often sulky or fiery, mothers are alternately manoeuvering and waspish, and the portionless young lady often lies awake at night and cries a good deal. We are getting used to these things now, just as we are used to eclipses of the moon, which no longer set us howling and beating tin kettles. We never heard of a lady in a fashionable "front"[2] behaving like Mrs. Percy under these circumstances. Happening one day to see Horace talking to Grace at a window, without in the least knowing what they are talking about, or having the least reason to believe that Grace, who is mistress of the house and a person of dignity, would accept her son if he were to offer himself, she suddenly rushes up to them and clasps them both, saying, "with a flushed countenance and in an excited manner"—"This is indeed happiness; for, may I not call you so, Grace?—my Grace—my Horace's Grace!—my dear children!" Her son tells her she is mistaken, and that he is engaged to Kate, whereupon we have the following scene and tableau:—

Gathering herself up to an unprecedented height,(!) her eyes lightning forth the fire of her anger:—

"Wretched boy!" she said, hoarsely and scornfully, and clenching her hand. "Take then the doom of your own choice! Bow down your miserable head and let a mother's—"

"Curse not!" spake a deep low voice from behind, and Mrs. Percy started, scared, as though she had seen a heavenly visitant appear, to break upon her in the midst of her sin.

---

[1] Broad, full sleeves, in a Chinese style.
[2] Hair style.

Meantime, Horace had fallen on his knees at her feet, and hid his face in his hands.

Who, then, is she—who! Truly his "guardian spirit" has stepped between him and the fearful words, which, however unmerited, must have hung as a pall over his future existence; a spell which could not be unbound—which could not be unsaid.

Of an earthly paleness, but calm with the still, iron-bound calmness of death—the only calm one there,—Katherine stood; and her words smote on the ear in tones whose appallingly slow and separate intonation rung on the heart like the chill, isolated tolling of some fatal knell.

"He would have plighted me his faith, but I did not accept it; you cannot, therefore—you *dare* not curse him. And here," she continued, raising her hand to heaven, whither her large dark eyes also rose with a chastened glow, which, for the first time *suffering* had lighted in those passionate orbs,—"here I promise, come weal, come woe, that Horace Wolchorley and I do never interchange vows without his mother's sanction—without his mother's blessing!"

Here, and throughout the story, we see that confusion of purpose which is so characteristic of silly novels written by women. It is a story of quite modern drawing-room society—a society in which polkas are played and Puseyism discussed; yet we have characters and incidents, and traits of manner introduced, which are mere shreds from the most heterogeneous romances. We have a blind Irish harper "relic of the picturesque bards of yore," startling us at a Sunday-school festival of tea and cake in an English village; we have a crazy gypsy, in a scarlet cloak, singing snatches of romantic song, and revealing a secret on her death-bed which, with the testimony of a dwarfish miserly merchant, who salutes strangers with a curse and a devilish laugh, goes to prove that Ernest, the model young clergyman, is Kate's brother; and we have an ultra-virtuous Irish Barney, discovering that a document is forged, by comparing the date of the paper with the date of the alleged signature, although the same document has passed through a court of law, and occasioned a fatal decision. The "Hall" in which Sir Lionel lives is the venerable country-seat of an old family, and this, we suppose, sets the imagination of the authoress flying to donjons and battlements, where "lo! the warder blows his horn"; for, as the inhabitants are in their bedrooms on a night certainly within the recollection of Pleaceman X., and a breeze springs up, which we are at first told was faint, and then that it made the old cedars bow their branches to the greensward, she falls in to this mediae-val vein of description (the italics are ours): "The banner *unfurled it* at the sound, and shook its guardian wing above, while the startled owl *flapped her* in the ivy; the firmament looking down through her 'argus eyes'—

Ministers of heaven's mute melodies.

And lo! two strokes tolled out the warder tower, and 'Two o'clock' re-echoed its interpreter below."

Such stories as this of *The Enigma* remind us of the pictures clever chil-dren sometimes draw "out of their own head," where you will see a modern villa on the right, two knights in helmets fighting in the fore-ground, and a tiger grinning in a jungle on the left, the several objects being brought together because the artist thinks each pretty, and perhaps still more because he remembers seeing them in other pictures.

But we like the authoress much better on her mediaeval stilts than on her oracular ones,—when she talks of the *Ich* and of "subjective" and "objective," and lays down the exact line of Christian verity, between "right-hand excesses and left-hand declensions."[1] Persons who deviate from this line are introduced with a patronizing air of charity. Of a certain Miss Inshquine she informs us, with all the lucidity of italics and small caps, that "*function*, not *form*, as THE INEVITABLE OUTER EXPRESSION OF THE SPIRIT IN THIS TABERNACLED AGE, weakly engrossed her." And *à propos* of Miss Mayjar, an evangelical lady who is a little too apt to talk of her visits to sick women and the state of their souls, we are told that the model clergyman is "not one to disallow, through the *super* crust, the under-current towards good in the *subject*, or the positive benefits, neverthe-less, to the *object*." We imagine the double-refined accent and protrusion of chin which are feebly represented by the italics in this lady's

---

[1]   Terms from contemporary German philosophy.

sentences. We abstain from quoting any of her oracular doctrinal passages, because they refer to matters too serious for our pages just now.

The epithet "silly" may seem impertinent, applied to a novel which indicates so much reading and intellectual activity as *The Enigma*; but we use this epithet advisedly. If, as the world has long agreed, a very great amount of instruction will not make a wise man, still less will a very mediocre amount of instruction make a wise woman. And the most mischievous form of feminine silliness is the literary form, because it tends to confirm the popular prejudice against the more solid education of women. When men see girls wasting their time in consultations about bonnets and ball dresses, and in giggling or senti- mental love-confidences, or middle-aged women mismanaging their children, and solacing themselves with acrid gossip, they can hardly help saying, "For Heaven's sake, let girls be better educated; let them have some better objects of thought—some more solid occupations." But after a few hours' conversation with an oracular literary woman, or a few hours' reading of her books, they are likely enough to say, "After all, when a woman gets some knowledge, see what use she makes of it! Her knowledge remains acquisition, instead of passing into culture; instead of being subdued into modesty and simplicity by a larger acquaintance with thought and fact, she has a feverish consciousness of her attainments; she keeps a sort of mental pocket- mirror, and is continually looking in it at her own 'intellectuality'; she spoils the taste of one's muffin by questions of metaphysics; 'puts down' men at a dinner-table with her superior information; and seizes the opportunity of a *soirée* to catechize us on the vital question of the relation between mind and matter. And then, look at her writings! She mistakes vagueness for depth, bombast for eloquence, and affec- tation for originality; she struts on one page, rolls her eyes on another, grimaces in a third, and is hysterical in a fourth. She may have read many writings of great men, and a few writings of great women; but she is as unable to discern the difference between her own style and theirs as a Yorkshireman is to discern the difference between his own English and a Londoner's: rhodomontade is the native accent of her intellect. No—the average nature of women is too shallow and feeble a soil to bear much tillage; it is only fit for the very lightest crops."

It is true that the men who come to such a decision on such very superficial and imperfect observation may not be among the wisest in the world; but we have not now to contest their opinion—we are only pointing out how it is unconsciously encouraged by many women who have volunteered themselves as representatives of the feminine intellect. We do not believe that a man was ever strengthened in such an opinion by associating with a woman of true culture, whose mind had absorbed her knowledge instead of being absorbed by it. A really cultured woman, like a really cultured man, is all the simpler and less obtrusive for her knowledge; it has made her see herself and her opinions in something like just proportions; she does not make it a pedestal from which she flatters herself that she commands a complete view of men and things, but makes it a point of observation from which to form a right estimate of herself. She neither spouts poetry nor quotes Cicero on slight provocation; not because she thinks that a sacrifice must be made to the prejudices of men, but because that mode of exhibiting her memory and Latinity does not present itself to her as edifying or graceful. She does not write books to confound philosophers, perhaps because she is able to write books that delight them. In conversation she is the least formidable of women, because she understands you, without wanting to make you aware that you *can't* understand her. She does not give you information, which is the raw material of culture,— she gives you sympathy, which is its subtlest essence.

A more numerous class of silly novels than the oracular (which are generally inspired by some form of High Church, or transcendental Christianity), is what we may call the *white neck-cloth* species, which represent the tone of thought and feeling in the Evangelical party. This species is a kind of genteel tract on a large scale, intended as a sort of medicinal sweetmeat for Low Church young ladies; an Evangelical substitute for the fashionable novel, as the May Meetings[1] are a substitute for the Opera. Even Quaker children, one would think, can hardly have been denied the indulgence of a doll; but it must be a doll dressed in a drab gown and a coal-scuttle bonnet—not a worldly doll, in gauze and spangles. And there are no young ladies, we imagine,—unless they

---

[1] Missionary Society's annual meetings in London.

belong to the Church of the United Brethren,[1] in which people are married without any love-making—who can dispense with love stories. Thus, for Evangelical young ladies there are Evangelical love stories, in which the vicissitudes of the tender passion are sanctified by saving views of Regeneration and the Atonement. These novels differ from the oracular ones, as a Low Churchwoman often differs from a High Churchwoman: they are a little less supercilious, and a great deal more ignorant, a little less correct in their syntax, and a great deal more vulgar.

The Orlando[2] of Evangelical literature is the young curate, looked at from the point of view of the middle class, where cambric bands are understood to have as thrilling an effect on the hearts of young ladies as epaulettes have in the classes above and below it. In the ordinary type of these novels, the hero is almost sure to be a young curate, frowned upon, perhaps, by worldly mammas, but carrying captive the hearts of their daughters, who can "never forget *that* sermon"; tender glances are seized from the pulpit stairs instead of the opera-box; *tête-à-têtes* are seasoned with quotations from Scripture, instead of quotations from the poets; and questions as to the state of the heroine's affections are mingled with anxieties as to the state of her soul. The young curate always has a background of well-dressed and wealthy, if not fashionable society;—for Evangelical silliness is as snobbish as any other kind of silliness; and the Evangelical lady novelist, while she explains to you the type of the scapegoat on one page, is ambitious on another to represent the manners and conversation of aristocratic people. Her pictures of fashionable society are often curious studies considered as efforts of the Evangelical imagination; but in one particular the novels of the White Neck-cloth School are meritoriously realistic,—their favourite hero, the Evangelical young curate, is always rather an insipid personage.

The most recent novel of this species that we happen to have before us, is *The Old Grey Church*.[3] It is utterly tame and feeble; there is no one set of objects on which the writer seems to have a stronger

---

[1] Protestant sect.

[2] Hero.

[3] By Lady Caroline Lucy Scott (1784–1857).

grasp than on any other; and we should be entirely at a loss to conjec-
ture among what phases of life her experience has been gained, but
for certain vulgarisms of style which sufficiently indicate that she has
had the advantage, though she has been unable to use it, of mingling
chiefly with men and women whose manners and characters have not
had all their bosses and angles rubbed down by refined conventionalism. It is less excusable in an Evangelical novelist, than in any other,
gratuitously to seek her subjects among titles and carriages. The real
drama of Evangelicalism—and it has abundance of fine drama for any
one who has genius enough to discern and reproduce it—lies among
the middle and lower classes; and are not Evangelical opinions understood to give an especial interest in the weak things of the earth,
rather than in the mighty? Why then, cannot our Evangelical lady
novelists show us the operation of their religious views among people
(there really are many such in the world) who keep no carriage, "not
so much as a brass-bound gig," who even manage to eat their dinner
without a silver fork, and in whose mouths the authoress's question-
able English would be strictly consistent? Why can we not have
pictures of religious life among the industrial classes in England, as
interesting as Mrs. Stowe's pictures of religious life among the
negroes?[1] Instead of this, pious ladies nauseate us with novels which
remind us of what we sometimes see in a worldly woman recently
"converted";—she is as fond of a fine dinner table as before, but she
invites clergymen instead of beaux; she thinks as much of her dress
as before, but she adopts a more sober choice of colours and patterns;
her conversation is as trivial as before, but the triviality is flavoured
with Gospel instead of gossip. In *The Old Grey Church*, we have the
same sort of Evangelical travesty of the fashionable novel, and of
course the vicious, intriguing baronet is not wanting. It is worth while
to give a sample of the style of conversation attributed to this high-
born rake—a style that in its profuse italics and palpable innuendoes,
is worthy of Miss Squeers.[2] In an evening visit to the ruins of the

---

[1] Reference to Harriet Beecher Stowe's (1811–96) novel *Dred*, which Eliot reviewed in
the same issue of the *Westminster Review*.
[2] Character in Dickens's *Nicholas Nickleby*.

Colosseum, Eustace, the young clergyman, has been withdrawing the heroine, Miss Lushington, from the rest of the party, for the sake of a *tête-à-tête*. The baronet is jealous, and vents his pique in this way:—

> There they are, and Miss Lushington, no doubt, quite safe; for she is under the holy guidance of Pope Eustace the First, who has, of course, been delivering to her an edifying homily on the wickedness of the heathens of yore, who, as tradition tells us, in this very place let loose the wild *beasties* on poor Saint Paul!—Oh, no! by the bye, I believe I am wrong, and betraying my want of clergy, and that it was not at all Saint Paul, nor was it here. But no matter, it would equally serve as a text to preach from, and from which to diverge to the degenerate *heathen* Christians of the present day, and all their naughty practices, and so end with an exhortation to "come out from among them, and be separate";—and I am sure, Miss Lushington, you have most scrupulously conformed to that injunction this evening, for we have seen nothing of you since our arrival. But every one seems agreed it has been a *charming party of pleasure*, and I am sure we all feel *much indebted* to Mr. Grey for having *suggested* it; and as he seems so capital a cicerone, I hope he will think of something else equally agreeable to *all*.

This drivelling kind of dialogue, and equally drivelling narrative, which, like a bad drawing, represents nothing, and barely indicates what is meant to be represented, runs through the book; and we have no doubt is considered by the amiable authoress to constitute an improving novel, which Christian mothers will do well to put into the hands of their daughters. But everything is relative; we have met with American vegetarians whose normal diet was dry meal, and who, when their appetite wanted stimulating, tickled it with *wet* meal; and so, we can imagine that there are Evangelical circles in which *The Old Grey Church* is devoured as a powerful and interesting fiction.

But, perhaps, the least readable of silly women's novels, are the *modern-antique* species, which unfold to us the domestic life of Jannes and Jambres, the private love affairs of Sennacherib, or the mental struggles and ultimate conversion of Demetrius the silversmith.[1] From most silly novels we can at least extract a laugh; but those of the modern-antique school have a ponderous, a leaden kind of fatuity, under which we groan. What can be more demonstrative of the inability of literary women to measure their own powers, than their frequent assumption of a task which can only be justified by the rarest concurrence of acquirement with genius? The finest effort to reanimate the past is of course only approximative—is always more or less an infusion of the modern spirit into the ancient form,—

Was ihr den Geist der Zeiten heisst,
Das ist im Grund der Herren eigner Geist,
In dem die Zeiten sich bespiegeln.[2]

Admitting that genius which has familiarized itself with all the relics of an ancient period can sometimes, by the force of its sympathetic divination, restore the missing notes in the "music of humanity," and reconstruct the fragments into a whole which will really bring the remote past nearer to us, and interpret it to our duller apprehension,—this form of imaginative power must always be among the very rarest, because it demands as much accurate and minute knowledge as creative vigour. Yet we find ladies constantly choosing to make their mental mediocrity more conspicuous, by clothing it in a masquerade of ancient names; by putting their feeble sentimentality into the mouths of Roman vestals or Egyptian princesses, and attributing their rhetorical arguments to Jewish high-priests and Greek philosophers. A recent example of this heavy imbecility is *Adonijah, a Tale of the Jewish Dispersion*,[3] which forms part of a series, "uniting," we are told, "taste, humour, and sound principles." *Adonijah*, we presume exemplifies the tale of "sound principles"; the taste and humour are to be found in

---

[1] Jannes and Jambres were magicians in ancient Egypt (see 2 Timothy 3:8); Sennacherib (705–681 BC) was king of Assyria; Demetrius appears in Acts 19.

[2] Lines from German poet and dramatist Johann von Goethe's (1749–1832) *Faust*: "What you call the 'Spirit of the Age' is really the critic's spirit, in whose pages the times are reflected."

[3] By Jane Margaret Stickland (1800–88).

other members of the series. We are told on the cover, that the incidents of this tale are "fraught with unusual interest," and the preface winds up thus: "To those who feel interested in the dispersed of Israel and Judea, these pages may afford, perhaps, information on an important subject, as well as amusement." Since the "important subject" on which this book is to afford information is not specified, it may possibly lie in some esoteric meaning to which we have no key; but if it has relation to the dispersed of Israel and Judea at any period of their history, we believe a tolerably well-informed school-girl already knows much more of it than she will find in this "Tale of the Jewish Dispersion." *Adonijah* is simply the feeblest kind of love story, supposed to be instructive, we presume, because the hero is a Jewish captive, and the heroine a Roman vestal; because they and their friends are converted to Christianity after the shortest and easiest method approved by the "Society for Promoting the Conversion of the Jews"; and because, instead of being written in plain language, it is adorned with that peculiar style of grandiloquence which is held by some lady novelists to give an antique colouring; and which we recognize at once in such phrases as these:—"the splendid regnal talents undoubtedly possessed by the Emperor Nero"—"the expiring scion of a lofty stem"—"the virtuous partner of his couch"—"ah, by Vesta!"—and "I tell thee, Roman." Among the quotations which serve at once for instruction and ornament on the cover of this volume, there is one from Miss Sinclair,[1] which informs us that "Works of imagination are *avowedly* read by men of science, wisdom, and piety"; from which we suppose the reader is to gather the cheering influence that Dr. Daubeny, Mr. Mill, or Mr. Maurice,[2] may openly indulge himself with the perusal of *Adonijah*, without being obliged to secrete it among the sofa cushions, or read it by snatches under the dinner-table.

"Be not a baker if your head be made of butter," says a homely proverb, which, being interpreted, may mean, let no woman rush into print who is not prepared for the consequences. We are aware that

---

[1] Catherine Sinclair (1800–64), Scottish novelist.
[2] Charles Giles Daubeny (1795–1867), chemist; J.S. Mill (1800–73), philosopher; F.D. Maurice (1805–72), theologian.

our remarks are in a very different tone from that of the reviewers who, with a perennial recurrence of precisely similar emotions, only paralleled, we imagine, in the experience of monthly nurses, tell one lady novelist after another that they "hail" her productions "with delight." We are aware that the ladies at whom our criticism is pointed are accustomed to be told, in the choicest phraseology of puffery, that their pictures of life are brilliant, their characters well-drawn, their style fascinating, and their sentiments lofty. But if they are inclined to resent our plainness of speech, we ask them to reflect for a moment on the chary praise, and often captious blame, which their panegyrists give to writers whose works are on the way to become classics. No sooner does a woman show that she has genius or effective talent, than she receives the tribute of being moderately praised and severely criticized. By a peculiar thermometric adjustment, when a woman's talent is at zero, journalistic approbation is at the boiling pitch; when she attains mediocrity, it is already at no more than summer heat; and if ever she reaches excellence, critical enthusiasm drops to the freezing point. Harriet Martineau, Currer Bell, and Mrs. Gaskell have been treated as cavalierly as if they had been men. And every critic who forms a high estimate of the share women may ultimately take in literature, will, on principle, abstain from any exceptional indulgence towards the productions of literary women. For it must be plain to every one who looks impartially and extensively into feminine literature, that its greatest deficiencies are due hardly more to the want of intellectual power than to the want of those moral qualities that contribute to literary excellence—patient diligence, a sense of the responsibility involved in publication, and an appreciation of the sacredness of the writer's art. In the majority of women's books you see that kind of facility which springs from the absence of any high standard; that fertility in imbecile combination or feeble imitation which a little self-criticism would check and reduce to barrenness; just as with a total want of musical ear people will sing out of tune, while a degree more melodic sensibility would suffice to render them silent. The foolish vanity of wishing to appear in print, instead of being counterbalanced by any consciousness of the intellectual or moral derogation implied in futile authorship seems to be encouraged by the extremely false impression that to write *at all* is a proof of superiority in a woman. On this ground, we believe that the average intellect of women is unfairly represented by the mass of feminine literature, and that while the few women who write well are very far above the ordinary intellectual level of their sex, the many women who write ill are very far below it. So that, after all, the severer critics are fulfilling a chivalrous duty in depriving the mere fact of feminine authorship of any false prestige which may give it a delusive attraction, and in recommending women of mediocre faculties—as at least a negative service they can render their sex—to abstain from writing.

The standing apology for women who become writers without any special qualification is, that society shuts them out from other spheres of occupation. Society is a very culpable entity, and has to answer for the manufacture of many unwholesome commodities, from bad pickles to bad poetry. But society, like "matter," and Her Majesty's Government, and other lofty abstractions, has its share of excessive blame as well as excessive praise. Where there is one woman who writes from necessity, we believe there are three who write from vanity; and, besides there is something so antiseptic in the mere healthy fact of working for one's bread, that the most trashy and rotten kind of feminine literature is not likely to have been produced under such circumstances. "In all labour there is profit";[1] but ladies' silly novels, we imagine, are less the result of labour than of busy idleness.

Happily, we are not dependent on argument to prove that Fiction is a department of literature in which women can, after their kind, fully equal men. A cluster of great names, both living and dead, rush to our memories in evidence that women can produce novels not only fine, but among the very finest;—novels, too, that have a precious speciality, lying quite apart from masculine aptitudes and experience. No educational restrictions can shut women out from the materials of fiction, and there is no species of art which is so free from rigid requirements. Like crystalline masses, it make take any form, and yet be beautiful; we have only to pour in the right elements—genuine observation, humour, and passion. But it is precisely this absence of

---

[1] See Proverbs 14:23.

rigid requirement which constitutes the fatal seduction of novel-writing to incompetent women. Ladies are not wont to be very grossly deceived as to their power of playing on the piano; here certain positive difficulties of execution have to be conquered, and incompetence inevitably breaks down. Every art which has its absolute *technique* is, to a certain extent, guarded from the intrusions of mere left-handed imbecility. But in novel-writing there are no barriers for incapacity to stumble against, no external criteria to prevent a writer from mistaking foolish facility for mastery. And so we have again and again the old story of La Fontaine's ass, who puts his nose to the flute, and, finding that he elicits some sound, exclaims, "Moi, aussi, je joue de la flute";[1]—a fable which we commend, at parting, to the consideration of any feminine reader who is in danger of adding to the number of "silly novels by lady novelists."

SOURCE

Westminster Review 66 (October 1856).

SELECTED SECONDARY READING

Ashton, Rosemary. *George Eliot: A Life.* New York: Penguin, 1997.
Haight, Gordon. *George Eliot: A Biography.* New York: Penguin, 1968.
Rush, Susan Rowland. *George Eliot and the Conventions of Popular Women's Fiction: A Serious Literary Response to the "Silly Novels by Lady Novelists."* New York: Peter Lang, 1993.

---

[1] "I, too, am playing the flute!" This story does not actually appear in the *Fables of Jean de la Fontaine* (1621–95).

TO NOVELISTS—AND A NOVELIST
(APRIL 1861)

Dinah Mulock Craik

DINAH MULOCK (1826–87) was born in Stoke-on-Trent, the eldest child of a rather unstable Irish dissenting minister and a schoolteacher. After Mulock's father lost his chapel, the family moved first to Newcastle under Lyme and eventually to London, where Mulock's parents separated. As a young girl, Dinah helped her mother teach school, and after her mother's death in 1845, she supported herself and her younger brothers by writing, publishing fiction, poetry, and essays in a variety of popular periodicals, including *Chambers's Edinburgh Journal*, *Fraser's*, *Macmillan's*, *Household Words*, *Good Words*, and the *Cornhill Magazine*. Her first three novels were fairly well received, but it was her fourth, *John Halifax, Gentleman* (1856), which established both her popular and critical reputations.

In 1865, Mulock married a somewhat younger man, George Lillie Craik, who was then an editor for, and later a partner in, *Macmillan's*. The couple adopted a daughter from a parish workhouse in 1869. Both partners continued their literary work throughout their marriage. When Mulock died of sudden heart failure in 1887, her standing was such that her memorial was planned by such luminaries as Tennyson, Browning, Matthew Arnold, and Millais.

Mulock's fiction is frequently concerned with the struggles of individuals against the rigidities of Victorian society. In *John Halifax*, an orphan rises from tanner's apprentice to become proprietor of his own business and to see his daughter courted by an aristocrat; in *Olive* (1850), an orphan supports herself and her half-sister by painting and eventually marries happily; in *A Life for a Life* (1859), the narrative follows the efforts of a murderer and a fallen woman to redeem themselves; in her children's tale *The Little Lame Prince* (1875), the young prince overcomes loneliness and disability to become a much-loved, successful king. Similar ideals are upheld in Mulock's essays, notably *A Woman's Thoughts about Women* (1858), which encourages women of all classes and conditions to work together and mutually support one another.

Given her propensity to show earnest young people overcoming adversity and finding happiness, it is no wonder Mulock protested against the ending of George Eliot's *The Mill on the Floss* (1861), despite her great admiration for Eliot's talent as a novelist. *The Mill on the Floss*, she declares, "is as perfect as the novel can well be made" and even "one of the finest imaginative works in our language." However, Mulock maintains that because novelists exert an influence over readers that persists "long after we have come to that age, if we ever reach it, which all good angels forbid! when we 'don't read novels,'" it behooves them to offer uplifting fare. And when she asks whether the story of *The Mill on the Floss* "will lighten any burdened heart, help any perplexed spirit, comfort the sorrowful, succour the tempted, or bring back the erring into the way of peace"—and particularly whether it will inspire any of "the hundreds of clever girls" to persevere in the face of difficulties and setbacks—Mulock sadly has to answer "No."

To justify the ways of God to men.—Milton[1]

THE HISTORY OF A HUMAN LIFE is a strange thing. It is also a somewhat serious thing—to the individual: who often feels himself,

---

[1] Line from the opening of Milton's *Paradise Lost.*

or appears to others, not unlike the elder-pith figure of an electrical experimentor—vibrating ridiculously and helplessly between influences alike invisible and incomprehensible. What *is* Life—and what is the heart of its mystery? We know not; and through Death only can we learn. Nevertheless, nothing but the blindest obtuseness of bigotry, the maddest indifference of epicureanism—two states not so opposite as they at first seem—can stifle those

> Obstinate questionings
> Of sense and outward things,
> Fallings from us, vanishings,
> Blank misgivings of a creature
> Moving about in worlds not realized.[1]

And continually in our passage through these "worlds not realized"—either the world of passion, or intellect, or beauty—do we lift up our heads from the chaos, straining our eyes to discern, if possible, where we are, why we are there, what we are doing, or what is being done with us, and by whom. Then if we think we have caught even the fag end of a truth or a belief, how eagerly do we sit down and write about it, or mount pulpits and preach about it, or get on a platform and harangue about it! We feel so sure that we have something to say; something which it must benefit the world to hear. Harmless delusion! Yet not ignoble, for it is a form of that eternal aspiration after perfect good, without which the whole fabric of existence, mortal and immortal, natural and supernatural, slides from us, and there remains nothing worth living for, nothing worth dying for; since the smallest animalcule in a drop of water—the meanest created organism which boasts the principle of life—is as noble a being as we.

Now there is something in us which *will not* "say Amen to that." We will not die—and die for ever: we will not while any good remains in us, cease to believe in a God, who is all we know or can conceive of goodness made perfect. As utterly as we refuse to regard Him as a mere Spirit of Nature, unto whom our individuality is indifferent and

---

[1] Lines from Wordsworth's "Ode: Intimations of Immortality."

unknown, do we refuse to see in Him a Being omniscient as omnipotent, who puts us into this awful world without our volition, leaves us to struggle through it as we can, and, if we fail, finally to drop out of it into hell-fire or annihilation. Is it blasphemy to assert that on such a scheme of existence, the latter only could be consistent with His deity?

No, human as we are, we must have something divine to aspire to. It is curious to trace this instinct through all the clouded wisdoms of the wise; how the materialist, who conscientiously believes that he believes in nothing, will on parting bid you "good bye and God bless you!" as if there were really a God to bless, and that He could bless, and that He would take the trouble to bless *you*. Stand with the most confirmed infidel by the coffin of one he loved, or any coffin, and you will hear him sigh that he would give his whole mortal life, with all its delights, and powers, and possibilities, if he could only see clearly some hope of attaining the life immortal.

What do these facts imply? That the instinct which prompts us to seek in every way to unriddle the riddle of life, or as Milton puts it,

> To justify the ways of God to men,

is as irrepressible as universal. It is at the root of all the creeds and all the philosophies, of the solid literature which discourses on life, and the imaginative literature which attempts to pourtray it.

It were idle to reason how the thing has come about; but, undeniably, the modern novel is one of the most important moral agents of the community. The essayist may write for his hundreds; the preacher preach to his thousands; but the novelist counts his audience by millions. His power is threefold—over heart, reason, and fancy. The orator we hear eagerly, but as his voice fades from us its lessons depart: the moral philosopher we read and digest, by degrees, in a serious, ponderous way: but the really good writer of fiction takes us altogether by storm. Young and old, grave and gay, learned or imaginative, who of us is safe from his influence? He creeps innocently on our family-table in the shapes of those three well-thumbed library volumes—sits for days after, invisibly at our fireside, a provocative of incessant discussion: slowly but surely, either by admiration or aversion, his opinions, ideas, feelings, impress themselves upon us, which impression remains long after we have come to that age, if we ever reach it, which all good angels forbid! when we "don't read novels."

The amount of new thoughts scattered broadcast over society within one month of the appearance of a really popular novel, the innumerable discussions it creates, and the general influence which it exercises in the public mind, form one of the most remarkable facts of our day. For the novelist has ceased to be a mere story-teller or romancist. He—we use the superior pronoun in a general sense, even as an author should be dealt with as a neutral being, to be judged solely by "its" work,—he buckles to his task in solemn earnest. For what is it to "write a novel"? Something which the multitude of young contributors to magazines, or young people who happen to have nothing to do but weave stories, little dream of. If they did, how they would shrink from the awfulness of what they have taken into their innocent, foolish hands; even a piece out of the tremendous web of human life, so wonderful in its pattern, so mysterious in its convolutions, and of which—most solemn thought of all—warp, woof and loom, are in the hands of the Maker of the universe alone.

Yet this the true novel-writer essays to do, and he has a right to do it. He is justified in weaving his imaginary web side by side with that which he sees perpetually and invisibly woven around him, of which he has deeply studied the apparent plan, so as to see the under threads that guide the pattern, keener perhaps than other men. He has learned to deduce motives from actions, and to evolve actions from motives: he has seen that from certain characters (and in a less degree certain circumstances) such and such results, which appear accidental, become in reality as inevitable as the laws which govern the world. Laws physical and moral, with which no *Deus ex machinâ* can interfere, else the whole working of the Universe would be disturbed.

Enough has been said, we trust, to indicate the serious position held by what used to be thought "a mere writer of fiction." Fiction forsooth! It is at the core of all the truths of this world; for it is the truth of life itself. He who dares to reproduce it is a Prometheus who has stolen celestial fire: let him beware that he uses it for the benefit of his fellow-mortals.[1] Otherwise one can imagine no vulture fiercer than the remorse which would gnaw the heart of such a writer, on the clear-visioned mountain-top of life's ending, if he began to suspect he had written a book which would live after him to the irremediable injury of the world.

We do not refer to impure or immoral books. There can be but one opinion concerning *them*—away with them to the Gehenna[2] from which they come. We speak of those works, blameless in plan and execution, yet which fall short—as great works only can—of the highest ideal, for which, beyond intellectual perfection, a great author ought to strive. For he is not like other men, or other writers. His very power makes him the more dangerous. His uncertainties, however small, shake to their ruin hundreds of lesser minds, and

> When he falls, he falls like Lucifer,
> Never to rise again.[3]

If a mountebank at a fair mouths his antics of folly or foulness, we laugh, or pass by—he is but a mountebank: he can do little harm: but when a hierophant connives at a false miracle, or an eloquent sincere apostle goes about preaching a bewildering lie, we shrink, we grieve, we tremble. By and by, we take courage openly to denounce, not the teacher but the teaching. "You are an earnest man—doubtless, a true man—but your doctrine is not true. We, who cannot speak, but only feel—we *feel* that it is not true. You are treading dangerous ground. You have raised a ghost you cannot lay, you have thrown down a city which you cannot rebuild. You are the very Prometheus, carrying the stolen fire. See that it does not slip from your unwary hands, and go devastating the world."

Thoughts somewhat like these must have passed through the mind of many a reader of a novel, the readers of which have been millions. Probably the whole history of fiction does not present an instance of

---

[1]   In Greek mythology, the Titan Prometheus took pity on human beings and stole fire from heaven to help them.
[2]   Hell.
[3]   Lines from Shakespeare's *Henry VIII.*

two such remarkable books, following one another within so short a time as *Adam Bede*, and *The Mill on the Floss*. All the world has read them; and though some may prefer one, and some the other, and, in a moral point of view, some may admire and some condemn—all the world grants their wonderful intellectual power, and is so familiar with the details of them that literary analysis becomes unnecessary.

Nor do we desire to attempt it. The question which these books, and especially the latter, have suggested, is quite a different thing. It is a question with which literary merit has nothing to do. Nor, in one sense, literary morality,—the external morality which, thank heaven, our modern reading public both expects and exacts, and here undoubtedly finds. Ours is more an appeal than a criticism—an appeal which any one of an audience has a right to make, if he thinks he sees what the speaker, in the midst of all his eloquence, does not see—

> The little pitted speck in garnered fruit,
> That, rotting inward, slowly moulders all.[1]

Of *The Mill on the Floss*, in a literary point of view, there can be but one opinion—that, as a work of art, it is as perfect as the novel can well be made: superior even, to *Adam Bede*. For the impression it gives of *power*, evenly cultivated and clear sighted,—the power of creation, amalgamating real materials into a fore-planned ideal scheme; the power of selection, able to distinguish at once the fit and the unfit, choosing the one and rejecting the other, so as to make every part not only complete as to itself, but as to its relation with a well-balanced whole—the *Mill on the Floss* is one of the finest imaginative works in our language. In its diction, too: how magnificently rolls on that noble Saxon English—terse and clear, yet infinitely harmonious, keeping in its most simple common-place flow a certain majesty and solemnity which reminds one involuntarily of the deep waters of the Floss. The fatal Floss, which runs through the whole story like a Greek fate or a Gothic destiny—ay, from the very second chapter, when

---

[1] Lines from Tennyson's "All in All."

"Maggie, Maggie," continued the mother, in a tone of half-coax-ing fretfulness, as this small mistake of nature entered the room, "where's the use o' my telling you to keep away from the water? You'll tumble in and be drownded some day, an' then you'll be sorry you didn't do as mother told you."

This is a mere chance specimen of the care over small things—the exquisite polish of each part, that yet never interferes with the breadth of the whole—which marks this writer as one of the truest *artists*, in the highest sense, of our or any other age.

Another impression made strongly by the first work of "George Eliot," and repeated by "his" (we prefer to respect the pseudonym) second, is the earnestness, sincerity, and heart-nobility of the author. Though few books are freer from that morbid intrusion of self in which many writers of fiction indulge, no one can lay down *The Mill on the Floss* without a feeling of having held commune with a mind of rare individuality, with a judgment active and clear, and with a moral nature, conscientious, generous, religious, and pure. It is to this moral nature, this noblest half of all literary perfectness, in our author, as in all other authors, that we now make appeal.

"George Eliot," or any other conscientious novelist, needs not to be told that he who appropriates this strange phantasmagoria of human life, to repaint and rearrange by the light of his own imagi-nation, takes materials not his own, nor yet his reader's. He deals with mysteries which, in their entirety, belong alone to the Maker of the universe. By the force of his intellect, the quick sympathies of his heart, he may pierce into them a little way—farther, perhaps, than most people—but at best only a little way. He will be continually stopped by things he cannot understand—matters too hard for him, which make him feel, the more deeply and humbly as he grows more wise, how we are, at best,

Like infants crying in the dark
And with no language but a cry.[1]

---

[1] Lines from Tennyson's *In Memoriam*.

If by his dimly-beheld, one-sided, fragmentary representations, which mimic untruly the great picture of life, this cry, either in his own voice, or in the involuntary utterance of his readers, rises into an accusation against God, how awful is his responsibility, how tremendous the evil that he may originate!

We doubt not, the author of the *Mill on the Floss* would shudder at the suspicion of this sort of involuntary blasphemy, and yet such is the tendency of the book and its story.

A very simple story. A girl of remarkable, gifts—mentally, physically, and morally; born, like thousands more, of parents far inferior to herself—struggles through a repressed childhood, a hopeless youth: brought suddenly out of this darkness into the glow of a first passion for a man who, ignoble as he may be, is passionately in earnest with regard to her: she is tempted to treachery, and sinks into a great error, her extrication out of which, without involving certain misery and certain wrong to most or all around her, is simply an impossibility. The author cuts the Gordian knot by creating a flood on the Floss, which wafts this poor child out of her troubles and difficulties into the other world.

Artistically speaking, this end is very fine. Towards it the tale has gradually climaxed. From such a childhood as that of Tom and Maggie Tulliver, nothing could have come but the youth Tom and the girl Maggie, as we find them throughout that marvellous third volume: changed indeed, but still keeping the childish images of little Tom, and little Maggie, of Dorlcote Mill. Ay, even to the hour, when with that sense of the terrible exalted into the sublime, which only genius can make us feel—we see them go down to the deeps of the Floss "in an embrace never to be parted: living through again, in one supreme moment, the days when they had clasped their little hands in love, and roamed through the daisied fields together."

So far as exquisite literary skill, informed and vivified by the highest order of imaginative power, can go, this story is perfect. But take it from another point of view. Ask, what good will it do?—whether it will lighten any burdened heart, help any perplexed spirit, comfort the sorrowful, succour the tempted, or bring back the erring into the way of peace; and what is the answer? Silence.

Let us reconsider the story, not artistically, but morally.

Here is a human being, placed during her whole brief life—her hapless nineteen years—under circumstances the hardest and most fatal that could befal one of her temperament. She has all the involuntary egotism and selfishness of a nature that, while eagerly craving for love, loves ardently and imaginatively rather than devotedly; and the only love that might have at once humbled and raised her, by showing her how far nobler it was than her own—Philip's—is taken from her in early girlhood. Her instincts of right, true as they are, have never risen into principles; her temptations to vanity, and many other faults, are wild and fierce; yet no human help ever comes near her to strengthen one or subdue the other. This *may* be true to nature, and yet we think it is not. Few of us, calmly reviewing our past, can feel that we have ever been left so long and so utterly without either outward aid, or the inner voice—never silent in a heart like poor Maggie's. It is, in any case, a perilous doctrine to preach—the doctrine of overpowering circumstances.

Again, notwithstanding the author's evident yearning over Maggie, and disdain for Tom, we cannot but feel that if people are to be judged by the only fair human judgment, of how far they act up to what they believe in, Tom, so far as his light goes, is a finer character than his sister. He alone has the self-denial to do what he does not like, for the sake of doing right: he alone has the self-command to smother his hopeless love, and live on, a brave, hard-working life; he, except in his injustice to poor Maggie, has at least the merit of having made no one else miserable. Perfectly true is what he says, though he says it in a Pharisaical way, "Yes, *I* have had feelings to struggle with, but I conquered them. I have had a harder life than you have had, but I have found *my* comfort in doing my duty." Nay, though perhaps scarcely intended, Bob Jakin's picture of the solitary lad, "as close as an iron biler," who "sits by himself so glumpish, a-knittin' his brow, an' a-lookin' at the fire of a night," is in its way as pathetic as Maggie's helpless cry to Dr. Kenn, at the bazaar, "Oh, I must go."

In the whole history of this fascinating Maggie there is a picturesque piteousness which somehow confuses one's sense of right and wrong. Yet what—we cannot help asking—what is to become of the hundreds of clever girls, born of uncongenial parents, hemmed in with unsympathising kindred of the Dodson sort, blest with no lover on whom to bestow their strong affections, no friend to whom to cling for guidance and support? They must fight their way, heaven help them! alone and unaided through cloud and darkness, to the light. And, thank heaven, hundreds of them do, and live to hold out a helping hand afterwards to thousands more. "The middle-aged" (says "George Eliot," in this very book), "who have lived through their strongest emotions, but are yet in the time when memory is still half-passionate and not merely contemplative, should surely be a sort of natural priesthood, whom life has disciplined and consecrated to be the refuge and rescue of early stumblers and victims of self-despair."

Will it help these—such a picture as Maggie, who, with all her high aspirations and generous qualities, is, throughout her poor young life, a stay and comfort to no human being, but, on the contrary, a source of grief and injury to every one connected with her? If we are to judge character by results—not by grand imperfect essays, but by humbler fulfilments—of how much more use in the world were even fond, shallow Lucy, and narrow-minded Tom, than this poor Maggie, who seems only just to have caught hold of the true meaning and beauty of existence in that last pathetic prayer, "If my life is to be long, let me live to bless and comfort," when she is swept away out of our sight and love for ever.

True this is, as we have said, a magnificent ending for the book; but is it for the life—the one human life which this author has created so vividly and powerfully, that we argue concerning it as if we had actually known it? Will it influence for good any other real lives—this passionately written presentment of temptation never conquered, or just so far that we see its worst struggle as but beginning; of sorrows which teach nothing, or teach only bitterness; of love in its most delicious, most deadly phase; love blind, selfish, paramount, seeing no future but possession, and, that hope gone, no alternative but death—death, welcomed as the solution of all difficulties, the escape from all pain?

Is this right? Is it a creed worthy of an author who has preeminently what all novelists should have, "the brain of a man and the heart of a woman," united with what we may call a sexless intelligence, clear and calm, able to observe, and reason, and guide mortal passions, as those may, who have come out of the turmoil of flesh into the region of ministering spirits, "αγγελοι,"[1] messengers between God and man? What if the messenger testify falsely? What if the celestial trumpet give forth an uncertain sound?

Yet let us be just. There are those who argue that this—perhaps the finest ending, artistically, of any modern novel, is equally fine in a moral sense: that the death of Maggie and Tom is a glorious Euthanasia, showing that when even at the eleventh hour, temptation is conquered, error atoned, and love reconciled, the life is complete: its lesson has been learnt, its work done; there is nothing more needed but the *vade in pacem*[2] to an immediate heaven. This, if the author so meant it, was an idea grand, noble, Christian: as Christian (be it said with reverence) as the doctrine preached by the Divine Pardoner of all sinners to the sinner beside whom He died—"To-day shalt thou be with me in paradise."[3] But the conception ought to have been worked out so plainly that no reader could mistake it. We should not have been left to feel, as we do feel, undecided whether this death was a translation or an escape: whether if they had not died, Maggie would not have been again the same Maggie, always sinning and always repenting; and Tom the same Tom, hard and narrow-minded, though the least ray of love and happiness cast over his gloomy life might have softened and made a thoroughly good man of him. The author ought to have satisfied us entirely as to the radical change in both; else we fall back upon the same dreary creed of overpowering circumstances: of human beings struggling for ever in a great quagmire of unconquerable temptations, inevitable and hopeless woe. A creed more fatal to every noble effort, and brave self-restraint—above all to that humble faith in the superior Will which alone should govern ours—can hardly be conceived. It is true that there occur sometimes in life positions so complex and overwhelming, that plain right and wrong become confused; until the most righteous and religious man is hardly able to judge clearly or act fairly. But to meet such positions is one thing, to *invent* them is another. It becomes a serious question whether any author—who, great as his genius may be, sees

[1] Angels.
[2] Depart in peace; a benediction.
[3] Luke 23:43.

no farther than mortal intelligence can—is justified in leading his readers into a labyrinth, the way out of which he does not, first, see clearly himself, and next, is able to make clear to them, so as to leave them mentally and morally at rest, free from all perplexity and uncertainty.

Now, uncertainty is the prevailing impression with which we close the *Mill on the Floss*. We are never quite satisfied in our detestation of the Dodson family, the more odious because so dreadfully natural that we feel we all are haunted by some of the race, could name them among our own connections, perhaps have even received kindnesses from a Mrs. Pullet, a Mrs. Glegg, or a Mrs. Tulliver. We are vexed with ourselves for being so angry with stern, honest, upright, business-like Tom—so contemptuously indifferent to gentle unsuspicious Lucy, with her universal kindness, extending from "the more familiar rodents" to her silly aunt Tulliver. We question much whether such a generous girl as Maggie would have fallen in love with Stephen at all; whether she would not from the first have regarded him simply as her cousin's lover, and if his passion won anything from her, it would but have been the half-angry half-sorrowful disdain which a high-minded woman could not help feeling towards a man who forgot duty and honour in selfish love, even though the love were for herself. And, last and chief perplexity of all, we feel that, granting the case as our author puts it, the mischief done, the mutual passion mutually confessed, Stephen's piteous arguments have some justice on their side. The wrong done to him in Maggie's forsaking him was almost as great as the wrong previously done to Philip and Lucy:—whom no self-sacrifice on her part or Stephen's could ever have made happy again.

And, to test the matter, what reader will not confess, with a vague sensation of uneasy surprise, to have taken far less interest in all the good injured personages of the story, than in this mad Stephen and treacherous Maggie? Who that is capable of understanding—as a thing which has been or is, or may one day be—the master-passion that furnishes the key to so many lives, will not start to find how vividly this book revives it, or wakens it, or places it before him as a future possibility? Who does not think with a horribly delicious feeling, of such a crisis, when right and wrong, bliss and bale, justice and conscience, seem swept from their boundaries, and a whole existence of Dodsons, Lucys, and Tom Tullivers, appears worth nothing compared to the ecstasy of that "one kiss—the last" between Stephen and Maggie in the lane?

Is this right? The spell once broken—broken with the closing of the book—every high and pure and religious instinct within us answers unhesitatingly—"No."

It is *not* right to paint Maggie only, as she is in her strong, unsatisfied, erring youth—and leave her there, her doubts unresolved, her passions unregulated, her faults unatoned and unforgiven: to cut her off ignobly and accidentally, leaving two acts, one her recoil with regard to Stephen, and the other her instinctive self-devotion in going to rescue Tom, as the sole noble landmarks of a life that had in it every capability for good with which a woman could be blessed. It is *not* right to carry us on through these three marvellous volumes, and leave us at the last standing by the grave of the brother and sister, ready to lift up an accusatory cry, less to beneficent Deity than to the humanly-invented Arimanes[1] of the universe.—"Why should such things be? Why hast Thou made us thus?"

But it may be urged, that fiction has its counterpart, and worse, in daily truth. How many perplexing histories do we not know of young lives blighted, apparently by no fault of their own; of blameless lives dragged into irresistible temptations; of high natures so meshed in by circumstances that they, as well as we, judging them from without, can hardly distinguish right from wrong, guilt from innocence; of living and loveable beings so broken down by unmerited afflictions, that when at last they come to an end, we look on the poor dead face with a sense of thankfulness that there at least,

There is no other thing expressed:
But long disquiet merged in rest.[2]

All this is most true, *so far as we see*. But we never can see, not even the wisest and greatest of us, anything like *the whole* of even the meanest and

---

[1] In Persian mythology, Arimanes is the source of all evil.
[2] Lines from Tennyson's "The Two Voices."

briefest human life. We never can know through what fiery trial of temptation, nay, even sin,—for sin itself appears sometimes in the wonderful alchemy of the universe to be used as an agent for good,—a strong soul is being educated into a saintly minister to millions of weaker souls: coming to them with the authority of one whom suffering has taught how to heal suffering; nay, whom the very fact of having sinned once, has made more deeply to pity, so as more easily to rescue sinners. And, lastly, we never can comprehend, unless by experience, that exceeding peace—the "peace which passeth all understanding," which is oftentimes seen in those most heavily and hopelessly afflicted: those who have lost all, and gained their own souls: whereof they possess themselves in patience: waiting until the supreme moment of which our author speaks, but which is to them not an escape from the miseries of this world, but a joyful entrance into the world everlasting.

Ay, thank heaven, though the highest human intellect may fail to hear it, there are millions of human hearts yet living and throbbing, or mouldering quietly into dust, who have felt, all through the turmoil or silence of existence, though lasting for threescore years and ten, a continual still small voice, following them to the end: "Fear not: for I am thy God."[1]

Would that in some future book, as powerful as *The Mill on the Floss*, the author might become a true "αγγελοξ"[2] and teach us this!

SOURCE
Macmillan's 3 (April 1861).

SELECTED SECONDARY READING
Mitchell, Sally. *Dinah Mulock Craik*. Boston: Twayne, 1983.

---

[1] Isaiah 41:10.
[2] Angel.

THE USES AND PLEASURES OF POETRY FOR THE WORKING CLASSES
(1863)

Janet Hamilton

JANET THOMSON (1795–1873) was born in Shotts, Lanarkshire, the daughter of a shoemaker and his wife. When she was still very young, the family moved to nearby Langloan, where her parents worked for a time as field labourers. As a child, she contributed to the family's income first by spinning yarn and later by her embroidery. She also taught herself to read before she was five years old, and borrowed books from neighbours and the village library, notably Milton's *Paradise Lost*, various histories, volumes of the *Spectator* and *Rambler*, and the poetry of Robert Burns, as well as the Bible. In 1809 she married John Hamilton, who worked for her father, and they eventually had ten children, all of whom she educated at home while continuing to work as an embroiderer.

Although she had not yet learned to write, Hamilton began composing poetry in her teens, memorizing her works as she composed them. She finally taught herself to write at the age of 54, and she soon after submitted a number of essays to a contest in the penny weekly *Working-Man's Friend*. She continued to publish essays in the *Working-Man's Friend* under the byline "Janet Hamilton, a Shoemaker's Wife" until the journal folded in 1854, one of the only women to do so. She also began to write down her poetry, eventually publishing a number of volumes, including *Poems and Essays of a Miscellaneous Character* (1863), *Poems of Purpose and Sketches in Prose* (1865), *Poems and Ballads* (1868), and *Poems, Essays, and*

Sketches (1870). Her writing slowed down as her eyesight began to fail, but she remained a popular and respected figure whose work was favourably reviewed in the press. More than 400 people attended her funeral in 1873, and when sufficient money was raised to erect a memorial to her in Coatbridge a few years later, as many as 20,000 people gathered to hear the dedicatory lecture.

The following piece, which was published in *Poems and Essays*, presents Hamilton's deep commitment to education. Opening with her regret that the working classes are debarred from many opportunities for personal enrichment, Hamilton points out that access to literature nevertheless makes it possible for any one to "indulge a taste for the sublime and beautiful." The essay, though brief, is impressive in the range of its allusions, from Milton to Shakespeare to Gray, Cowper, and Campbell—all of whom Hamilton quotes from memory, giving testament to the quality of her own self-education. Notably, along with the high-culture poets, Hamilton also cites the working-class writers Robert Burns and Ebenezer Elliott, illustrating how "the gifts of God, of Nature, and of the Muses are as impartially and profusely bestowed" on the lower classes as on the upper ones.

I HAVE OFTEN THOUGHT AND FELT it to be matter of deep regret that working-men and women, in consequence of their social position, and the want of means and leisure, are to a great extent debarred from the attainment of the elegant tastes and refined perceptions acquired by those on whom the gifts of fortune, and a desire of improving and adorning their minds, have conferred the high advantages of a liberal and finished education. Still, the working-man who is a good English reader, and possessed of an intellectual cast of mind, seasoned with a dash of fancy and feeling—although he may never have offered up his personal devotions at the shrine of the Muses, nor ever essayed to "build the lofty rhyme,"[1] thanks to the facilities afforded by cheap literature!—may yet indulge a taste for the sublime and beautiful, and be quite as capable of appreciating the treasures contained in the rich and varied stores of the higher walks of the best poets, as if he had ascended through all the gradations of learning from the parish school to the finale of a classical education in the patrician halls of Oxford or Cambridge. The workman may never be able to "tread the classic shores of Italy";[2] he may never feast his eyes on the glorious monuments of antiquity which surround the eternal sunny land of Greece, "Land of the Muses and of mighty men"; nor glide with oar and sail over the gorgeous waters of the golden Horn; nor wander over "Syria's land of roses" and feel "The light wings of zephyr, oppressed with perfume," fanning his cheek amid the roses of Sharon in the Holy Land.

No; the workman, as such, will probably never see, except in dreams, these lands of song and story, nor gaze upon the glowing scenes where all that is grand and beautiful in nature and art combine to trance the soul in admiration; but still he can, when the toils of the day are ended, retire to his home, and having performed his ablutions, and solaced himself with "the cup which cheers but not inebriates,"[3] he then "when worldly crowds retire to revel or to rest," can "trim his little fire," or light his frugal taper; and while holding communion with the spirits of the mighty masters of song in their immortal pages, may feel every noble principle of his mind strengthened, every emotion of his heart warmed and purified, and every feeling refined and elevated. Does his heart beat and his pulse throb with sorrow and indignation at the wrongs and sufferings of the Magyars

> When leagued oppression, poured to Northern wars
> Her whiskered pandoors and her fierce huzzars?[4]

---

[1]   Line from Milton's *Lycidas*.

[2]   In the following passage, Hamilton quotes from classical sources, as well as from poems that celebrate Italy and Greece, such as Joseph Addison's (1672–1719) "A Letter from Italy" and Byron's "The Bride of Abydos."

[3]   In other words, tea; line from William Cowper's (1731–1800) narrative poem *The Task*.

[4]   These and the next two lines are from Scottish poet Thomas Campbell's (1777–1844) epic *The Pleasures of Hope*, about the sufferings endured by the people of Poland during its partition.

Then will he feel the full force of the sentiment expressed by the bard when he exclaimed—

> Oh! bloodiest picture in the book of Time,
> Hungaria fell, unwept, without a crime!

Or, does all the soul of man stir within him and leap out to those men who feel for, speak for, write for, nay, who spend and are spent for the cause of

> Yonder poor o'er-laboured wights,
>   So abject, mean, and vile,
> Who beg a brother of the earth
>   To give them leave to toil?[1]

Yes, to those large-hearted men who are striving to heal the sores of the beggar Lazarus, and teaching him how to obtain a nobler meal than the crumbs which fall from the rich man's table; and will not his heart respond in "thoughts that breathe, and words that burn,"[2] to the fervid rhymes launched by the muse of Elliott[3] at those who, like Dives, are "clothed in purple and fine linen, and fare sumptuously every day," and yet see unmoved their poor brother, laid down to perish at their gates?[4] And when his faith is assailed, and his ears pained by the cavillings of the Deist or the sneers of the Infidel amongst the associates of his labour, let him turn to the sublime thoughts of Young, the poet of the night, where awful truths arrayed in solemn and majestic garb, shall uncurl the lip of the scoffer and silence the cavils of the sceptic; or with Cowper he will deplore

> The quenchless thirst of ruinous inebriety,
> The stale debauch forth issuing from the styes
> Which law has licensed...

---

[1]   Lines, slightly misquoted, from Robert Burns' (1759–96) "Dirge."
[2]   Line from Thomas Gray's (1716–71) *The Progress of Poesy.*
[3]   Ebenezer Elliott (1781–1849), English working-class poet.
[4]   Reference to the parable of the rich man and the poor man (see Luke 16).

> ... While ten thousand casks,
> For ever dribbling forth their base contents,
> Touched by the Midas finger of the State,
> Bleed gold for Ministers to sport withal.[1]

And will he not at times rise on the wings of fancy, and hover enraptured over the bright world of scenic creations produced by the magic pencil of him, the great poet, painter, and worshipper of nature, glorious Shakspeare? And when he hails the return of the thrice-blessed and thrice-welcome day of sacred rest—that true well in the desert, in whose cool and sparkling waters the working-man, weary and panting from the dusty ways of life, will slake his parching thirst, and lave his flushed and throbbing temples; and then, "If summer be the tide, and sweet the hour," let him wander forth to the green woodlands, or recline on the fragrant meadow, with the Bard of Paradise for his companion, and soon the Miltonic Muse shall waft him aloft on her ethereal pinions to the Sanctuary of God, there to listen with rapt adoration to the eternal councils of peace between the Father and Son on the future salvation of man; or his heart may be attuned to the melodies of heaven, and in spirit he can join in the ecstatic and jubilant anthems of cherubim and seraphim, celebrating the triumphs of the eternal Son, when by His omnipotent right hand, armed with winged and scorching lightnings, He drove forth the apostate angels, blasted and howling—

> Down from the crystal battlements of heaven
> With sheer descent—[2]

to the burning gulf below; or the scene is changed, and, lo! before his visioned eye passes the sublime panorama of the Creation. He stands in the presence of the Deity; he sees the mystic Dove brooding over the chaos of dark and troubled waters which cover the void and formless earth; he hears the Almighty fiat, "Let there be light," and he sees the conflicting and struggling elements separated, arranged,

---

[1]   Lines from Cowper's *Task*.
[2]   Lines from Milton's *Paradise Lost*.

and organised by the word of His power into all the forms of order, utility, and beauty, so as to be most conducive to the glory of the Divine Architect and the use and accommodation of man. And now the Divine Urania will introduce him into the presence of the first human pair, fresh from the hand of God—glorious in beauty, and sinless in soul. He may roam through the groves of Paradise, and join with them in their morning and evening orisons—he may recline with them in the bowers of Eden on a couch of amaranth, and, while holding converse with angels, partake of the ambrosial fruits culled by the hand of the mother of all living.

But this is, indeed, an inexhaustible subject, and one to which my limited powers can by no means render justice; yet it is truly consoling for working-men and women to know—ay, and to feel—that on them, amidst all the toils, privations, and hardships incidental to their position in life, the gifts of God, of Nature, and of the Muses are as impartially and profusely bestowed as on that portion of the community whose highest distinctions are too often found to consist only in the accidents of birth and fortune. "Sweet are the uses of adversity,"[1] sings the poet: and "sweet are the uses of poetry," says the working-man of cultivated intellect and refined feeling—for to him there exists not a situation so irksome, a care so crushing, a trial so painful, a privation so severe, a suffering so intense, but he has felt in them all, that, next to the consolations of religion, those of Divine poesy are most potent in power to

> Minister to a mind diseased,
> And with some sweet oblivious antidote
> Cleanse the charged bosom of that perilous stuff
> That weighs upon the heart.[2]

And amidst blasted hopes and wasted aspirations he may imbibe the very spirit of courage, patience, and resignation by appropriating the sublime sentiments expressed by Campbell in those beautiful lines:—

---

[1] Line from Shakespeare's *As You Like It.*
[2] Lines from Shakespeare's *Macbeth.*

Be hushed, my dark spirit, for wisdom condemns
　　When the faint and the feeble deplore;
Be strong as the rock of the ocean that stems
　　A thousand wild waves on the shore.
Through the perils of chance and the scowl of disdain
　　May thy front be unaltered, thy courage elate!
Yea, even the name I have worshipped in vain
Shall awake not the sigh of remembrance again—
　　To bear is to conquer our fate![1]

SOURCE

Poems and Essays (Glasgow, 1863)

SELECTED SECONDARY READING

Boos, Florence. "The 'Homely Muse' in Her Diurnal Setting: The Periodical Poems of 'Marie,' Janet Hamilton, and Fanny Forrester." *Victorian Poetry* 39.2 (2001): 255–85.

Boos, Florence. "Janet Hamilton." *Victorian Women Poets.* Ed. William Thesing. Detroit: Gale Research, 1998.

Gilfillan, George. "Janet Hamilton: Her Life and Poetical Character." *Poems and Ballads.* By Janet Hamilton. Glasgow: Maclehose, 1868. ix-xxxiv.

---

[1] Verse from Campbell's "Lines," which begins "At the silence of twilight's contemplative hour."

REVIEW OF *COMETH UP AS A FLOWER*
(APRIL 1867)

Geraldine Jewsbury

GERALDINE JEWSBURY (1812–80) was born in Measham, England, the youngest child of a millowner and his wife. When their mother died in 1818, Geraldine's eldest sister Maria took over the household, and the family moved to Manchester. Maria, a poet, essayist, and regular contributor to the *Manchester Gazette*, was both mother-figure and literary inspiration for Geraldine, and her death in 1833, after moving to India with her husband, left Geraldine somewhat adrift.

Around the time of her father's death in 1840, Jewsbury began her lifelong friendship with Thomas and Jane Welsh Carlyle. The latter, with whom Jewsbury maintained a passionate and witty correspondence, provided a sounding-board when Jewsbury began to write fiction in the 1840s, and she also introduced Jewsbury to publishers and other literary figures. Jewsbury published six novels in the 1840s and 1850s, the best-known of which are *Zoe: The History of Two Lives* (1845), *The Half Sisters* (1848), and *Marian Withers* (1851). On the strength of her experience as a novelist and her connections, during this period Jewsbury also secured work as a literary critic, serving as a reviewer for the weekly literary review *The Athenaeum* from 1849 on, and also working as a manuscript reader for several publishers, especially Bentley and Son, for whom she was the primary fiction reviewer from 1858 on. As a critic, Jewsbury was astonishingly prolific: she reviewed approximately 2,300 titles for the *Athenaeum*, taking primary responsibility for the review's "New Novels" section, and as a publisher's reader for Bentley's, she advised on well over 600 works, mostly fiction, but also biography and travel-writing. Because she was positioned as a gatekeeper both at the very beginning of the publishing process and at the point that a book was first launched to its readers, Jewsbury was an extremely influential force in mid-Victorian fiction.

Jewsbury's criticism is noteworthy for its constant attention to the tastes of the typical mid-Victorian novel reader. While she always spoke on behalf of literary quality when she encountered it, she saw her primary responsibility as championing good reads. Thus, while she clearly admires the scholarship informing Charles Reade's *The Cloister and the Hearth* (1861) and George Eliot's *Romola* (1863), she warns that even patient, well-intended readers may find these historical novels somewhat pedantic and slow. By contrast, she was an early supporter of the emerging sensation novel, recognizing that the fast plotting and surprise endings would excite readers. She enthusiastically urged Bentley's to publish Ellen Price Wood's *East Lynne* (1861), and she shared the firm's disappointment when they lost the bidding war for M.E. Braddon's runaway bestsellers *Lady Audley's Secret* (1862) and *Aurora Floyd* (1863).

However, as a critic for the mainstream reviews and publishing houses, Jewsbury also had to be an upholder of middle-class morality, and novels that strayed too far from the expected formulas drew her ire. The following piece, her 1867 review of Rhoda Broughton's *Cometh Up as a Flower*, is a case in point. The previous year, Jewsbury had been instrumental in Bentley's decision not to publish Broughton's *Not Wisely but Too Well*, even after the author rewrote the ending, because of the novel's lurid plot about a young girl who falls in love with a married man who eventually kills her. Given her objections to the author's first book, Jewsbury was outraged when Bentley's published Broughton's next novel without even consulting her: in a letter to the publisher, Jewsbury demanded, "What evil angel persuaded you to accept that

coarse vulgar and very objectionable novel Cometh up as a
Flower? I felt *ashamed* as I read it." Having been unable to
prevent its publication by Bentley's, Jewsbury wreaked her
revenge in the pages of the *Athenaeum*, providing a caustic plot
summary that highlights the immorality of the two female
characters and incorporating multiple brief quotations to illus-
trate the novel's rather purple prose style. Convinced by the
unflattering portrayals of the female leads that the author had
to be a man—and one ill-acquainted with polite company—
Jewsbury calculated that the best way to convince readers that
it was a "thoroughly bad style of book" and "not redeemed by
talent" was to let the novel sink itself with its own words.

Cometh Up as a Flower professes to be the autobiography of a charming young heroine; but the reader will make much the same discovery as Slender in *The Merry Wives of Windsor*, who says, "I came yonder
at Eton to marry Mistress Anne Page, and she a great lubberly boy!"[1]
That the author is not a young woman, but a man, who, in the present story, shows himself destitute of refinement of thought or feeling,
and ignorant of all that women either are or ought to be, is evident
on every page. The style of the book is bad, and full of slang; the story
itself is not one to be put into the hands of girls with a view to what
some one calls "their beneficial amusement." There is an all-pervad-
ing coarseness of thought and expression which is startling in its free
and unrestrained utterance.

The descriptions which the young lady gives of her love-scenes would
be coarse and flippant even as the confidential narrative of a fast young
man of the order of "jolly dogs" to a kindred companion. There is a
mixture of slang and sensuality, which, setting aside all other considerations, is in the worst possible taste. Of good feeling, or ordinary good

---

[1] Characters in the subplot of Shakespeare's play. Slender is one of three contenders for
Anne Page's hand; in the end, Anne elopes with the gentleman Fenton, while Slender
and the other unsuccessful suitor each end up with a boy merely disguised as Anne.

principle, there is not a trace. There is a sensual sentimentality, self-indulgent emotion, a morbid scepticism, with dashes of equally morbid religious emotion. Of all true love or noble sentiment the story is destitute. We are sorry to see a book of this kind making its appearance among our works of fiction; it is a thoroughly bad style of book, and it is not redeemed by talent: there is no knowledge of life or character or human nature displayed. The only two phases of existence which the author, in his assumed feminine character, seems to think women recognize, are, the delight of being kissed by a man they like, and the misery of being kissed by one they don't like. These two points seem to fill up his idea of the whole duty of women.

The heroine is a young lady of nineteen, by her own account the daughter of the Rev. Sir Adrian Lestrange, who is the sole representative of an ancient family now fallen into debt and decay. At a dinner-party she meets a handsome dragoon, with yellow hair, a stalwart figure, blue eyes, and "a brow that looked like marble and smelt like myrrh." She goes "sweethearting" with him; meets him in the garden, at nine o'clock at night, three days after she has seen him for the first time, and allows him, as poor Hood sings,—

> To embrace her and to face her
> So familiar and so easy,—[1]

which is all set forth in very ardent terms. They at length "hear the gravel crunching," and some one coming. In reply to some request from her yellow-haired lover, she says, "I made the required concession with less bashfulness than might have been expected of me, and then took to my heels, panting, dishevelled, crimson, but in safety." Arrived in her own chamber, "There I sat by the open casement-window, with a box of mignonette under my nose, with my candle fast flickering in its socket, and departing this life with a grievous stink, and with the summer dawn broadening across the pearl-grey sky. I had fallen neck and crop into love." Speaking of another interview, she says, "Good God! how happy I felt, lying in his arms, and the top of my tall wreath

---

[1] Lines from an unidentified poem by Thomas Hood (1799–1845), English poet.

scratching his handsome nose!" Speaking of the surprise of a butcher on being paid his long-overdue bill, she says, "He escaped apoplexy by a near shave that time ... so he thrust a hand as big as a fillet of veal into his pocket, and counted out the change." The course of the young lady's true love is interrupted by the designs of her elder sister, who chooses she shall marry a middle-aged baronet of £12,000 a year. He was a good man, and deserved a better fate. By the aid of treachery on the part of her sister, and the pressure of debts and difficulties on her father, Nelly is induced to accept Sir Hugh Lancaster. The description of her repugnance to the marriage is very coarse. She says, "For a pair of first-class blue eyes warranted fast colour, for ditto superfine red lips, so many pounds of prime white flesh, he has paid down a handsome price on the nail without haggling." Her sister, upbraiding her with her tears, says, "You had better try to bathe the swelling and redness out of your eyes, if we are to get any money out of him; you don't look a choice morsel to bribe any man with as you are now." The baronet has some misgivings, in spite of the elder sister's lies, and offers to break the engagement in a generous and manly manner. "Nonsense," I cry; "say no more about it. I intend to be your wife, and I suppose we shall manage to scratch on pretty much as other people do." She marries him, and as her father dies almost immediately, her sacrifice is useless. She goes with her husband to his fine house, ridicules his mother, and dilates on her husband's manner to her as "horribly, needlessly, and irksomely loving." In a few weeks she discovers the deceit her sister has practised about her old lover. His regiment is ordered to India, and they have an interview, in which she says, "My hair fell in its splendid ruddy billows over his great shoulders, and my arms were flung round the stately pillar of his throat." He being a man of some principle, declines to let her run away with him. She hears of his death in India some months afterwards, and finds nothing better to do with her life than to write this autobiography and die at the age of two-and-twenty. The wicked sister becomes a viscountess, and has a train of twelve bridesmaids. "However," says the heroine, "it is rather a scratch team after all, we having been obliged to eke it out with an old maid and a child." "A bishop in very clear lawn sleeves and painfully thin legs, with two high-church clergymen," perform the service.

At every page there is some offence against good taste or good feeling; but we have quoted enough to substantiate the grave censure we have recorded against this book, which is not a desirable "flower" to come up in any *parterre*.

SOURCE

Athenaeum 2060 (April 1867).

SELECTED SECONDARY READING

Fahnestock, Jeanne Rosenmayer. "Geraldine Jewsbury: The Power of the Publisher's Reader." *Nineteenth-Century Fiction* 28.3 (1973): 253–72.

Fryckstedt, Monica Correa. *Geraldine Jewsbury's* Athenaeum *Reviews: A Mirror of Mid-Victorian Attitudes to Fiction.* Uppsala, Sweden: Acta Universitatis Upsaliensis, 1986.

Howe, Susanne. *Geraldine Jewsbury: Her Life and Errors.* London: Allen and Unwin, 1935.

NOVELS
(SEPTEMBER 1867)

Margaret Oliphant

Born in Wallyford, Scotland, near Edinburgh, to a customs official and his wife, MARGARET OLIPHANT WILSON (1828–97) claimed that she began writing because she didn't like to sew and needed a quiet occupation while sitting by her mother's sickbed. Her first novel, in a list that was to number about 100, was *Margaret Maitland* (1849). On the strength of two more novels, in 1852 she approached William Blackwood, proprietor of the prestigious Blackwood and Sons publishing house. The publication of *Katie Stewart* (1853) marked the beginning of what was to be a half-century association with the firm. Also in 1852, she married her cousin Frank Oliphant, an artist, and the young couple moved to London to establish a stained glass studio. Frank was both a rather hapless business-man and increasingly ill, and in 1859 the family moved to Italy, seeking a more congenial climate. When Frank died at the end of the year, he left the pregnant Margaret stranded with small children and considerably worse off financially than she had been led to believe. From that point until the end of her life, she wrote almost continuously, supporting with her literary earnings not only her own children, but her brothers and nieces and nephews as well. All of her children predeceased her, and her anguish over their loss is related with heartbreaking direct-ness in her posthumously published *Autobiography* (1899).

Although she wrote widely for the major periodicals and presses of the day, the relationship with Blackwood's was the defining one of her career. Oliphant not only wrote fiction for the house—most notably the series of novels that make up the Chronicles of Carlingford (1862–76)—but also biography, including the *Life of Edward Irving* (1862); history, including her *Literary History of England* (1882); and art criticism. She also wrote the authorized history of the firm, *Annals of a Publishing House* (1897). Among her 300-odd articles for *Blackwood's Edinburgh Magazine (Maga)* were numerous literary and social reviews, some of which appeared in her regular columns, "The Old Saloon" (1887–92) and "The Looker-on" (1894–96). While much of her criticism takes a relatively conservative stance, this likely reflects her catering to the tastes of *Maga*'s editors as much as her own opinions.

The following article, "Novels," is one of several influential essays on the state of English fiction published by Oliphant in *Maga* during the 1860s. In "Sensation Novels" (1862), she had warned that the spirit of the age was increasingly one of "Hectic rebellion against nature"—a rebellion symbolized by such characters as Jane Eyre and Lady Isabel in Ellen Wood's thriller *East Lynne*—and that life would begin to imitate art. By 1867, she thought her predictions were being borne out. Singling out the novels of Mary Elizabeth Braddon and of Annie Thomas (to whom she mistakenly attributed Rhoda Broughton's novel *Cometh Up as a Flower*), Oliphant objects that the picture they paint of women ruled by their passions "comes from the hands of women," but also that women readers accept the picture "as real." Applying the critical double standard, Oliphant declares that "It is a shame to women so to write," and also a shame that readers fail to object to such an untrue and unflattering portrayal. While she stops short of calling for an outright ban on this type of fiction, she does urge a boycott for the good of literature, society, and especially the ubiquitous Young Person.

ENGLISH NOVELS HAVE for a long time—from the days of Sir Walter Scott at least—held a very high reputation in the world, not so much perhaps for what critics would call the highest development of art, as for a certain sanity, wholesomeness, and cleanness unknown to other literature of the same class. This peculiarity has had its effect, no doubt, upon those very qualities of the national mind which produced it. It has increased that perfect liberty of reading which is the rule in most cultivated English houses; it has abolished the domestic Index Expurgatorius[1] as well as all public censorship; it has made us secure and unsuspicious in our reception of everything, or almost everything, that comes to us in the form of print. This noble confidence has been good for everybody concerned. It has put writers on their honour, and saved readers from that wounding consciousness of restraint or of danger which destroys all delicate appreciation. There are other kinds of literature in which the darker problems of the time can be fitly discussed, and, with a tolerably unanimous consent, English writers have agreed to leave those subjects in their fit place. The novel, which is the favourite reading of the young—which is one of the chief amuse-ments of all secluded and most suffering people—which is precious to women and unoccupied persons—has been kept by this understand-ing, or by a natural impulse better than any understanding, to a great degree pure from all noxious topics. That corruption which has so fatally injured the French school of fiction has, it has been our boast, scrupulously kept away from ours. It was something to boast of. We might not produce the same startling effects; we might not reach the same perfection in art, which a craftsman utterly freed of all restraints, and treating vice and virtue with equal impartiality, may aspire to; but we had this supreme advantage, that we were free to all classes and feared by none. Men did not snatch the guilty volume out of sight when any innocent creature drew nigh, or mature women lock up the book with which they condescended to amuse themselves, as they do in France. Our novels were family reading; and the result has been a sense of freedom, an absence of all suggestion of evil, in the superfi-cial studies of ordinary society, which it is impossible to overestimate.

---

[1]   List of objection; books that are restricted or banned.

"*Nous sommes tous d'un age mûr,*" said an irreproachable French matron to the English acquaintance whose eyes expressed a certain amazement at the frankness of some drawing-room narrative; "*j'espére que vous ne pensez pas que je parlerais comme ça devant des jeunes gens.*"[1] This idea, which is the very heart of French ideas on the subject, is quite foreign to our insular habits. We are accustomed both to read and to speak everything that comes in our way in the presence of *jeunes gens.* The habit has so grown upon us that to change it would involve a revolution in all our domestic arrangements. It would involve us in an amount of trouble which very few could face. We should require three or four packets from the library instead of one. We should have the nuisance of separating our children and dependents from our own amusements. We should no longer be able to discuss, as we do now continually, the books that we are reading and the thoughts we are thinking. This is a necessity from which we have been altogether free in the tranquil past; but it is an indulgence which only habit and the long use and wont of public security preserve to us now.

For there can be no doubt that a singular change has passed upon our light literature. It is not that its power has failed or its popularity diminished—much the reverse; it is because a new impulse has been given and a new current set in the flood of contemporary story-telling. We will not ask whence or from whom the influence is derived. It has been brought into being by society, and it naturally reacts upon society. The change perhaps began at the time when Jane Eyre made what advanced critics call her "protest" against the conventionalities in which the world clothes itself. We have had many "protests" since that time, but it is to be doubted how far they have been to our advantage. The point to which we have now arrived is certainly very far from satisfactory. The English mind is still so far *borné*[2] that we do not discuss the seventh commandment with all that effusion of detail which is common on the other side of the Channel, though even in that respect progress is daily being made; but there are points in which we alto-

---

[1] "We live in a mature age; I hope you do not think that I speak like this in front of young people."
[2] Restricted or self-restrained.

gether outdo our French neighbours. To a French girl fresh from her convent the novels of her own language are rigorously tabooed; whereas we are all aware that they are the favourite reading of her contemporary in this country, and are not unfrequently even the production, with all their unseemly references and exhibitions of forbidden knowledge, of young women, moved either by the wild foolhardiness of inexperience, or by ignorance of everything that is natural and becoming to their condition. It is painful to inquire where it is that all those stories of bigamy and seduction, those *soi-disant*[1] revelations of things that lie below the surface of life, come from. Such tales might flow here and there from one morbid imagination, and present themselves to us as moral phenomena, without casting any stigma upon society in general; but this is not how they appear. They have taken, as it would seem, permanent possession of all the lower strata of light literature. Above there still remains, it is true, a purer atmosphere, for which we may be thankful; but all our minor novelists, almost without exception, are of the school called sensational. Writers who have no genius and little talent, make up for it by displaying their acquaintance with the accessories and surroundings of vice, with the means of seduction, and with what they set forth as the secret tendencies of the heart—tendencies which, according to this interpretation, all point one way. When the curate's daughter in *Shirley* burst forth into passionate lamentation over her own position and the absence of any man whom she could marry,[2] it was a new sensation to the world in general. That men and women should marry we had all of us acknowledged as one of the laws of humanity; but up to the present generation most young women had been brought up in the belief that their own feelings on this subject should be religiously kept to themselves. No doubt this was a conventionalism; and if a girl in a secluded parsonage is very much in earnest about a husband, there is no effectual reason we know of why she should not lift up her "protest" against circumstances. But things have gone very much further since the days of *Shirley*. We have grown accustomed to the reproduction,

---

[1] So-called.
[2] Reference to Caroline Helstone, character in Charlotte Brontë's *Shirley* (1849).

not only of wails over female loneliness and the impossibility of finding anybody to marry, but to the narrative of many thrills of feeling
much more practical and conclusive. What is held up to us as the story
of the feminine soul as it really exists underneath its conventional
coverings, is a very fleshly and unlovely record. Women driven wild
with love for the man who leads them on to desperation before he
accords that word of encouragement which carries them into the
seventh heaven; women who marry their grooms in fits of sensual
passion; women who pray their lovers to carry them off from husbands
and homes they hate; women, at the very least of it, who give and
receive burning kisses and frantic embraces, and live in a voluptuous
dream, either waiting for or brooding over the inevitable lover,—such
are the heroines who have been imported into modern fiction. "All
for love and the world well lost," was once the motto of a simple but
perennial story, with which every human creature had a certain sympathy—the romance that ended pleasantly in a wholesome wedding, or
pathetically in a violet-covered grave. But the meaning has changed
nowadays. Now it is no knight of romance riding down the forest
glades, ready for the defence and succour of all the oppressed, for
whom the dreaming maiden waits. She waits now for flesh and
muscles, for strong arms that seize her, and warm breath that thrills
her through, and a host of other physical attractions, which she indicates to the world with a charming frankness. On the other side of the
picture it is, of course, the amber hair and undulating form, the warm
flesh and glowing colour, for which the youth sighs in his turn; but
were the sketch made from the man's point of view, its openness would
at least be less repulsive. The peculiarity of it in England is, that it is
oftenest made from the woman's side—that it is women who describe
those sensuous raptures—that this intense appreciation of flesh and
blood, this eagerness of physical sensation, is represented as the natural sentiment of English girls, and is offered to them not only as the
portrait of their own state of mind, but as their amusement and mental
food. Such a wonderful phenomenon might exist, and yet society
might be innocent of it. It might be the fault of one, or of a limited
school, and the mere fact that such ravings are found in print might
be no great argument against the purity of the age. But when it is

added that the class thus represented does not disown the picture—that, on the contrary, it hangs it up in boudoir and drawing-room—that the books which contain it circulate everywhere, and are read everywhere, and are not contradicted—then the case becomes much more serious. For our own part we do not believe, as some people do, that a stratum of secret vice underlies the outward seeming of society. Most of our neighbours, we know, are very good sort of people, and we believe unfeignedly that our neighbours' neighbours resemble our own. It is possible to believe that very fine people or very shabby people are profoundly wicked, but as for the world as represented on our own level we know that it is not so. The girls of our acquaintance in general are very nice girls; they do not, so far as we are aware—notwithstanding a natural proclivity towards the society, when it is to be had, of their natural companions in existence—pant for indiscriminate kisses, or go mad for unattainable men. And yet here stands the problem which otherwise is not to be solved. It is thus that Miss Braddon and Miss Thomas, and a host of other writers, explain their feelings. These ladies might not know, it is quite possible, any better. They might not be aware how young women of good blood and good training feel. The perplexing fact is, that the subjects of this slander make no objection to it. Protests are being raised everywhere in abundance, but against this misrepresentation there is no protest. It seems to be accepted by the great audience of the circulating libraries as something like the truth. Mr. Trollope's charming girls do not, now that we know them so well, call forth half so much notice from the press as do the Aurora Floyds of contemporary fiction. Is, then, the picture true? or by what extraordinary impulse is it that the feminine half of society thus stigmatises and stultifies its own existence?

The question is one at which we may wonder, but to which we can give no answer; and it is a very serious matter, let us look at it as we will. It may be possible to laugh at the notion that books so entirely worthless, so far as literary merit is concerned, should affect any reader injuriously, though even of this we are a little doubtful; but the fact that this new and disgusting picture of what professes to be the female heart, comes from the hands of women, and is tacitly accepted by them as real, is not in any way to be laughed at. Some change must have been wrought upon the social mind ere such things could be tolerated at all; and even now we are not awakened out of our calm to a full consciousness of the change. When we are so, then we will, of course, according to our natural English course of action, take tardy measure of precaution. We will attempt, in the face of all our traditions and habits, to establish the Index Expurgatorius; we will lock up the books which are not for the *jeunes gens;* we will glance, ourselves, with curiosity and a sense of guilt, "just to see what it is like," over the objectionable portion of our library parcel, and we will make up our minds to say nothing of it before the girls. Vain thought! If the girls are such as they are therein described, one book or another will do them little harm; and if the picture is false, why do they accept it? So far from showing any difficulty on this point, it is those very books, according to all appearances, which are most in demand. The *Times* deals them the crowning glory of its approval. The critical journals, if they do not approve, at least take the trouble to discuss; and "the authorities at the great circulating libraries," as somebody says—those sublime critics who sit at the fountainhead of literature, and enlarge or choke up at their pleasure the springs of our supply—find it impossible to resist the public craving for its favourite food. Mr. Mudie,[1] too, may utter a "protest," but it is futile in face of the protests of fiction. We confess to having felt a sense of injury in our national pride when our solemn contemporary, the *Revue des Deux Mondes*,[2] held up in one of its recent numbers the names of Miss Annie Thomas and Mr. Edmund Yates[3] to the admiration of the world as representative novelists of England. And yet, after all, though the acknowledgment naturally costs us a pang, the Frenchman was right. Such writers are purely, characteristically English. They are not brilliantly wicked like their French contemporaries. The consciousness of good and evil hangs about them, a kind of literary fig-leaf, a little better or worse than nothing. Though it is evident that the chatter of imaginary clubs or still more imaginary studios is their highest idea

---

[1]   Charles Edward Mudie (1818–90), proprietor of the largest and most influential circulating library.

[2]   French literary review, published 1831–1944.

[3]   Edmund Yates (1831–94), English journalist and novelist.

of social intercourse, still the guardsmen and the painters do not talk so freely nor half so cleverly as they would have done on the other side of the Channel. That sublime respect for sentimental morality and poetic justice which distinguishes the British public, stands forth in them beyond all question. The wicked people are punished and the good people are rewarded, as they always should be; and there are exquisite bits of pious reflection which make up to the reader for a doubtful situation or an equivocal character. This, however, is what we have come to in the eyes of our neighbours. It is not so serious as the moral question, but it is in its way very serious. A critic, indeed, may deceive himself when he looks across the mists and rains of the Channel; but if he is guided by what English papers say—by what advertisements say—by the evidence of circulating libraries and publishers' announcements—how can he judge otherwise? The glories of the moment are in the hands of Miss Thomas and her class. Whether it be in appreciation, or contempt, or amazement at the extraordinary character of such successes, the fact remains that our weekly critics never fail to say something about their productions; and is not *Maga* also now beguiled to the further extension of their fame? It is humbling, but it is true.

And the fact is all the more humbling when we consider the very small amount of literary skill employed in the construction of these books. In France, again, it is the other way. A wicked novel there may be very disgusting, but it is generally clever, and sometimes possesses a certain hideous sort of spiritual interest. When the vilest of topics happens to fall into the hands of such an anatomist as Balzac, or under the more human touch of Victor Hugo,[1] there is something of calm science in the investigation—a kind of inexorable and passionless dissection which renders even such studies impressive. But English sensational books of the day have no such attraction. We do not gulp down the evil in them for the sake of the admirable skill that depicts it, or the splendour of the scenery amid which it occurs. On the contrary, we swallow the poorest of literary drivel—sentiments that are adapted to the atmosphere of a Surrey theatre—descriptions of society which

---

[1] Honoré de Balzac (1799–1850) and Victor Hugo (1802–85), French novelists in the new realist style.

show the writer's ignorance of society—style the most mean or the most inflated—for the sake of the objectionable subjects they treat. The novels which crowd our libraries are, for a great part, not literature at all. Their construction show, in some cases, a certain rude skill, in some a certain clever faculty of theft; but in none any real inventive genius; and as for good taste, or elegance, or perception of character, these are things that do not tell upon the sensational novel. The events are the necessary things to consider, not the men; and thus the writer goes on from one *tour de force* to another, losing even what little natural gift might belong to him in its over-exercise, but never losing the most sweet voices which he has once conciliated.

Such at least is the evidence of the newspapers. *Rupert Godwin*, for example, the last work published by Miss Braddon, although published only a few days, is already, according to the advertisements, in the fourth edition.[1] Yet it would be difficult to point out one single claim it has to popular approval. We have met with many curious things in these lower regions of bookmaking, but it has never been our fate to meet with any piece of literary theft so bare-faced and impudent as this book. The story is copied in all its important particulars from Mr. Charles Reade's well-known and powerful novel of *Hard Cash*[2]—a work, we need not say, as far above the lower world into which *Rupert Godwin* has been born as it is possible to conceive. The story of *Hard Cash*, as everybody knows, is that of a sailor captain, who confides his hard-won money to the care of a banker, and, being cheated, goes mad, and is only rescued after many moving adventures by sea and land, his wife and children in the meanwhile being left destitute. In *Rupert Godwin* the conception is so far varied that the sea-captain is stabbed, and left for dead by the wicked banker; but all the other incidents may stand as above narrated. There are two pairs of lovers, son and daughter of the respective banker and victim, in both books; there is a madhouse in both books, and a clerk who betrays his master, and a marvellous recovery for the killed and mad hero. The only little difference is, that in one book this hero is a certain glori-

---

[1]   Originally serialized as *The Banker's Secret* in 1864, *Rupert Godwin* was published in 1867.
[2]   Published in 1863.

ous sailor, dear to our hearts, noble old knight of romance, simple old English seaman, David Dodd, altogether one of the finest conceptions in English fiction; and in the other a miserable ghost called Westfield, about whom nobody knows anything nor cares anything. How such an amount of self-confidence, or confidence in the folly of the public, could be attained as is displayed in this publication, it would be difficult either to explain or to understand. Mr. Reade is not yet a classic. He is one of the most powerful of contemporary writers; and though it may be possible to borrow with small acknowledgment a French story, it is temerity, indeed, to plagiarise so well-known a production. Yet this is what Miss Braddon has ventured to do. She has taken the bones of the tale, as a poor curate might take a skeleton sermon. Having no flesh to put upon them, it is true that, honester so far than the curate, she leaves the bones as she found them; and, notwithstanding a liberal mention of violet eyes and golden hair and dark Spanish beauty, presents her personages to us in a skeleton state. But this, it would appear, makes no difference to an admiring public. Here is the compiler's own account of the reception given to this piece of stolen goods:—

> *Rupert Godwin* was written for, and first appeared in, a cheap weekly journal. From this source the tale was translated into the French language, and ran as the leading story in the *Journal pour Tous.* It was there discovered by an American, who retranslated the matter back into English, and who obtained an outlet for the new translation in the columns of the *New York Mercury.* These and other versions have been made without the slightest advantage to the author, or indeed without the faintest approach to any direct communication to her on the subject. Influenced by the facts as here stated, the author has revised the original, and now offers the result for what it is—namely, a tale of incident, written to amuse the short intervals of leisure which the readers of popular periodicals can snatch from their daily avocations, and also as a work that has not been published in England, except in the crude and fragmentary shape already mentioned.

The public has rewarded this noble confidence in them by consuming already three editions of this much-produced tale. Three nations, accordingly, have united in doing honour to *Rupert Godwin*. England, France, and America have seized upon it with that eager appreciation which is the best reward of genius. Most probably before this present page has seen the light it will have been reviewed in more than one leading journal with praise proportioned to its popularity. Was there ever literary phenomenon more inconceivable? We stand aghast with open mouth of wonder, and are stricken dumb before it. Miss Braddon has, without doubt, certain literary claims. *Aurora Floyd*, notwithstanding its unpleasant subject (though we don't doubt that its unpleasant subject has been in reality the cause of its great success), is a very clever story. It is well knit together, thoroughly interesting, and full of life. The life is certainly not of a high description, but it is genuine in its way; and few people with any appreciation of fiction could refuse to be attracted by a tale so well defined. The *Doctor's Wife*[1] strikes even a higher note. It is true that it is to some extent plagiarised, as was pointed out at the time of its publication, from a French story; but the plagiarism was so far perfectly allowable that it clearly defined wherein the amount of license permitted by English taste differs from that which comes natural to the French. Other books of Miss Braddon's have not been unworthy, to some extent, of the applause bestowed upon them. There has been a good story now and then, a clever bit of construction, even an inkling of character. She is the inventor of the fair-haired demon of modern fiction. Wicked women used to be brunettes long ago, now they are the daintiest, softest, prettiest of blonde creatures; and this change has been wrought by Lady Audley, and her influence on contemporary novels. She has brought in the reign of bigamy as an interesting and fashionable crime, which no doubt shows a certain deference to the British relish for law and order. It goes against the seventh commandment, no doubt, but does it in a legitimate sort of way, and is an invention which could only have been possible to an Englishwoman knowing the attraction of impropriety,

---

[1]   *The Doctor's Wife* (1864) was adapted from French novelist Gustave Flaubert's (1821–80) *Madame Bovary* (1857).

and yet loving the shelter of law. These are real results which Miss Braddon has achieved, and we do not grudge her the glory of them; but yet we cannot conceive how the *éclat*[1] of such triumphs, great as it may be, should cover a piece of imposture. The boldness of the feat is the only thing that does in any way redeem it; and that is not an excuse either for literary larceny or that marvellous public credulity and folly, which is the really alarming feature in the transaction. The author of *Rupert Godwin* has compelled the world to accept not only a copy, but a very miserable copy, by the mere form of her name. She has palmed off upon three intelligent nations, according to her own account, a fairy changeling, bewitched out of natural beauty into decrepitude and ugliness, and France, England, and America have taken the imp at her word. This is a power which the greatest of writers might envy. It is one of the finest privileges of a great name. To have made such an impression upon your contemporaries that the whole civilised world thus acknowledges your sway, is a thing rarely achieved even by the greatest. But it has been achieved by Miss Braddon; and in sight of such a climax of fame and success, what can any one say?

We feel disposed, however, to emulate to some extent that pertinacious critic who once, as the story goes, took upon him to annotate the course of a sermon, by announcing the real authorship of its finest paragraphs. "Turn that man out," cried the aggrieved incumbent. "That's his own," said the critic. In like manner there is something in *Rupert Godwin* which is Miss Braddon's own. When the poor widow's virtuous and lovely daughter earns her scanty living on the stage, she is made the victim of one of those romantic abductions which used to be so frequent (in novels) forty or fifty years ago. As it happens, it does her no harm either in reputation or anything else, and, in short, is of little service anyhow except to fill up so many pages; but it is purely original and not copied. This it is only just to say. A foolish young marquess sets his heart upon the queen of beauty in the stage tableaux, and declares himself ready, as foolish young marquesses, our readers are aware, are so apt to do, "to lay his coronet at her feet, and make her Marchioness of Roxleydale"; a desire which the villain of the piece immediately seizes

---

[1]   Stir or excitement.

upon by way of carrying out his own vile projects. And accordingly Miss Braddon, with a stroke of her wand, brings back out of the ancient ages that post-chaise with the locked doors and the impassible man on the box with which we are all so perfectly acquainted. The lovely Violet is thus carried off to the old decayed house, with the old half-imbecile housekeeper, whom also we know. But we are bound to say that the young lady takes the accident with the composure becoming a young lady of the nineteenth century. Half-way on the road, when they stop to change horses, she satisfies herself that the pretext of her mother's illness, by which she has been inveigled into the carriage, is false, and sinks back relieved, with a profound sense of gratitude to heaven. She is rescued, as we have said, and the whole affair passes off in the calmest way, as such a natural accident might be supposed to pass. This abduction is Miss Braddon's own. And so is the episode of Esther Vanberg, a ballet-girl, who dies a most exemplary death at the Star and Garter, Richmond, after having been thrown by a wicked horse which she had ordered her lover, a young duke, to buy for her for a thousand pounds. The horse is bought, and runs away and breaks the reckless young woman's spine, and she then makes an edifying end which would become a saint, and leaves her duke touchingly inconsolable, though this also is utterly unconnected with the story. Esther's beauty had been of the demoniac order in her appearances on the stage. She inhabited a *bijou* mansion in Bolton Row; her drawing-room was approached by "a richly decorated staircase, where nymphs and satyrs in Florentine bronze smirked and capered in the recesses of the pale grey wall, relieved by mouldings and medallions in unburnished gold." Tropical flowers shaded the open windows, and the room was furnished with amber satin. Yet all this, and the hunter worth a thousand pounds, and circlets of diamonds, and flounces of the richest lace, all bought with her duke's money, seems to be considered by Miss Braddon quite consistent with relations of the purest character between the duke and the opera-dancer. And when she dies in this perfectly admirable way, the duke remains a kind of spiritual widower, to carry out all the last intentions, and build a monument over the grave of his love. In such an ethereal and lofty way are things supposed to be managed between young English dukes and ballet-girls. These episodes are both Miss

Braddon's very own. We recognise in them the original touch of the artist; and no doubt it is thus she has indemnified herself for giving up her natural faculty of construction, and using somebody else's story. Notwithstanding the undiminished success which has attended the essay, we cannot but think it is a pity. Honesty is the best policy. A writer whose gift lies in the portrayal of character, in delicate touches of observation, or sketches of real life, may possibly find it practicable to take the mere framework which has served another man; but for an author whose sole literary gift is that of construction, it is a pity. Miss Braddon has proved that she can invent a story. She can do it much better than she can discriminate, or describe, or even talk; and though it may save trouble, it is the sacrifice of her own powers she makes when she thus borrows from another. If we could hope that it was Mr. Reade who had done it, the matter would be very much less important; for Mr. Reade has many gifts, and can play upon his audience as on an instrument, and move us to tears or laughter as is permitted to very few. Miss Braddon cannot do this; but if she can fill up the circulating library, and be translated into French, and retranslated into American, she certainly does owe her *clientelle* the exercise of her one faculty. Such privileges have duties attached to them; and a prophet in whom the public thus believes should at least give of her own to that believing public. She never invented any circumstance so extraordinary as this public faith and loyal adherence which she seems to have won.

Miss Braddon is the leader of her school, and to her the first honours ought naturally to be given, but her disciples are many. One of the latest of these disciples is the authoress of *Cometh Up as a Flower*,[1] a novel which has recently won that amount of public approval which is conveyed by praise in the leading papers and a second edition. This book is not a stupid book. There is a certain amount of interest and some character in it. The young lover is, in his way, a real man—not very brilliant certainly, nor with any pretence of intellectuality, but as far removed as possible from the womanish individual so often presented to us ticketed as a man in ladies' novels; and so is the

---

[1] The actual author of this novel is Rhoda Broughton (1840–1920), but Oliphant is under the impression that it is by Annie Thomas.

middle-aged husband. The wonderful thing in it is the portrait of the modern young woman as presented from her own point of view. The last wave but one of female novelists was very feminine. Their stories were all family stories, their troubles domestic, their women womanly to the last degree, and their men not much less so. The present influx of young life has changed all that. It has reinstated the injured creature Man in something like his natural character, but unfortunately it has gone to extremes, and moulded its women on the model of men, just as the former school moulded its men on the model of women. The heroine of *Cometh Up as a Flower* is a good case in point. She is not by any means so disagreeable, so vulgar, or so mannish, as at the first beginning she makes herself out to be. Her flippancy, to start with, revolts the reader, and inclines him to pitch the volume to as great a distance from him as is practicable; but if he has patience a little, the girl is not so bad. She is a motherless girl, brought up in the very worst way, and formed on the most wretched model, but yet there is a touch of nature in the headstrong creature. And this of itself is a curious peculiarity in fiction generally. Ill-brought-up motherless girls, left to grow anyhow, out of all feminine guardianship, have become the ideal of the novelist. There is this advantage in them, that benevolent female readers have the resource of saying "Remember she had no mother," when the heroine falls into any unusual lapse from feminine traditions; but it is odd, to say the least of it, that this phase of youthful life should commend itself so universally to the female novelist.[1]

. . .

These are sentiments which everybody is aware a great many vulgar clever women think it clever and striking to enunciate. The misery of such unhappy ones as throw themselves out of the society of their own sex, their pitiful strivings after the recognition of any stray strong-minded woman who will look over their imperfections, should be

---

[1]   Oliphant here quotes passages introducing the heroine and her father, and relating the heroine's preference for friendships with men rather than with women.

sufficient answer to it in any serious point of view. But there is a great deal that is unlovely which is not immoral, and false to every human and natural sentiment without being positively wicked. This is one of the popular bits of falsehood by which lively-minded young women are often taken in and led to misrepresent themselves. And it is another curious feature in second-rate women's books. As a general rule, all the women in these productions, except the one charming heroine, are mean and envious creatures, pulling the exceptional beauty to pieces. Shall we say that the women who write ought to know? But the fact is, that a great many of the women who write live very contentedly in the society of other women, see little else, find their audience and highest appreciation among them, and are surrounded and backed up and applauded by their own sex in a way which men would be very slow to emulate. The pretence is one which only a vulgar mind could make. The man who scorns, or pretends to scorn, women's society, is generally a fool; what should the woman be? But it is one of those popular falsehoods which hosts of people repeat without in the least meaning it. It seems to imply a certain elevation above her neighbours of the speaker; although the very same woman, if brought to the test, would shrink and recoil and be confounded if her silly and false aspirations could be realised. Of course the patent meaning of it on the lips of a girl like the heroine of the book before us is, that the society she prefers is that of the man with whom she is falling in love, and who has fallen in love with her, and that for the moment the presence of other people is rather a bore than otherwise.

This story, as we have already said, is interesting, not because of its particular plot or incidents, but as a sample of the kind of expression given by modern fiction to modern sentiments from the woman's point of view. Nelly Lestrange has no particular objections to meet her soldier out of doors whenever he pleases to propose it. He takes her in his arms after he has seen her about three times, and she has still no objection. The girl is innocent enough according to all appearance, but she has certainly an odd way of expressing herself for a girl. She wonders if her lover and she, when they meet in heaven, will be "sexless passionless essences," and says, God forbid! She speaks, when a loveless marriage dawns upon her, of giving her shrinking body to the disagreeable bridegroom. There may be nothing wrong in all this, but it is curious language, as we have said, for a girl. And here let us pause to make a necessary discrimination. A *grande passion* is a thing which has to be recognised as possible wherever it is met with in this world. If two young people fall heartily and honestly in love with each other, and are separated by machinations such as abound in novels, but unfortunately are not unknown in life, and one of them is compelled to marry somebody else, it is not unnatural, it is not revolting, that the true love unextinguished should blaze wildly up, in defiance of all law, when the opportunity occurs. This is wrong, sinful, ruinous, but it is not disgusting; whereas those speeches about shrinking bodies and sexless essences are disgusting in the fullest sense of the word. Would that the new novelist, the young beginner in the realm of fiction, could but understand this! We will quote the last scene—the only scene in which there is much evidence of dramatic power in this novel. In it the poor little heroine, in her despair, flies in the face of all right and honour and virtue, yet is not revolting, nor yet nasty—which in her quite innocent impassioned moods, in her daring tone, and reckless little sayings, she frequently and unpardonably is. Everything that is worst to bear has happened to the unfortunate Nelly. Her lover's letters have been abstracted; she has been taught to think him false to her; she has married for that reason, and to save her father's life, the unattractive Sir Hugh, and her father has died the day after, losing to her all the comfort of her sacrifice; and then, in a moment when she is left alone, there comes suddenly her true lover, heartbroken with her perfidy, to look at her for the last time; and they speak to each other, and find out how it is that they have been separated. He is going to India, and it is their last meeting:—[1]

· · ·

Now, this is very objectionable, no doubt, and as wrong as it can be, but it is not disgusting. In the circumstances it is not unnatural. Great

---

[1] Oliphant quotes a long passage in which Nell begs to be taken along to India and her lover refuses, on the grounds that it would risk both their salvations.

love and despair, and the sense of an irredeemable useless sacrifice and a horrible mistake, might excuse if they did not warrant, such an outbreak. The difference is very clear and easily to be defined. At such a moment the reader forgives, and his mind is not revolted by a hopeless burst of passion, even though possible vice and the greatest of social sins is involved in it. And there is no sin involved in the light talk and nasty phrases which may mean nothing; yet to everybody of pure mind it is those latter which are most disgusting. Nor is this distinction an arbitrary one. When a human creature is under the influence of passion, it may be moved to the wildest thoughts, the most hopeless impulses, suggestions utterly foreign to its natural character; but its utterance in its cooler moments expresses the ordinary tenor of life. A woman, driven wild by the discovery of domestic fraud and great wrong, might propose any sin in her frenzy, and yet might be innocent; whereas a woman who makes uncleanly suggestions in the calm of her ordinary talk, is a creature altogether unredeemable and beyond the pale. This distinction is one which goes deeper than mere criticism. It is a point upon which social literature and society itself go much astray. When people who scarcely know each other, and do not care for each other, are obliged to meet, the lightest of talk naturally comes in to fill up the stray moments; and it is very handy for the novelist who has many stray corners to fill up; but now and then a point of some kind must be given to this light social froth. If not wit, which is not always at hand, why then a little licence, a touch of nastiness— something that will shock if not amuse. This is the abomination in the midst of us. Perhaps the indication it would seem to give of darker evil concealed below may be false—and we not only hope but believe that it is false—but of itself it is the height of unloveliness.

After our free-spoken heroine has come to the climax of her fate, she becomes consumptive and reflective after that loftily pious kind which generally associates itself with this species of immorality; for sensual literature and the carnal mind have a kind of piety quite to themselves, when disappointment and incapacity come upon them. The fire which burned so bright dies out into the most inconceivably grey of ashes; and the sweetest submission, the tenderest purity, take the place in a second of all those daring headstrong fancies, all that self-will and self-indulgence. The intense goodness follows the intense sensuousness as by a natural law;—the same natural law, we presume, which makes the wicked witch of romance—the woman who has broken everybody's heart, and spent everybody's money, and desolated everybody's home—sink at last into the most devoted of sisters of charity. The good women who follow the rule of St. Vincent de Paul would be little flattered by the suggestion.

We do not feel ourselves capable of noticing, although what we have just said recalls them to our mind, certain very fine and very nasty books, signed with the name of a certain Ouida, it is to be supposed a woman also.[1] They are so fine as to be unreadable, and consequently we should hope could do little harm, the diction being too gorgeous for merely human faculties. We note, in glancing here and there through the luscious pages, that there is either a mass of glorious hair lying across a man's breast, or a lady's white and jewelled fingers are twined in the gentleman's chestnut or raven curls—preferably chestnut; for "colour" is necessary to every such picture. Our readers will have remarked that, even in the crisis of her misery, the poor little heroine of *Cometh Up as a Flower* could not refrain from throwing her hair in "splendid ruddy billows" over her lover's shoulder; and the amount of use got out of the same powerful agent in *Strathmore* and *Idalia* seems something remarkable. Hair, indeed, in general, has become one of the leading properties in fiction. The facility with which it flows over the shoulders and bosoms in its owner's vicinity is quite extraordinary. In every emergency it is ready for use. Its quantity and colour, and the reflections in it, and even the "fuzz," which is its modern peculiarity, take the place of all those pretty qualities with which heroines used to be endowed. What need has a woman for a soul when she has upon her head a mass of wavy gold? When a poor creature has to be represented, her hair is said to be scanty, and of no particular colour. Power, strength, a rich nature, a noble mind, are all to be found embodied in this great attribute. Samson, being a Jew, had probably black locks, which would be against him; but otherwise

---

[1]   Pen name of Marie Louise de la Ramée (1839–1908), English novelist. Her best-known works include *Strathmore* (1865) and *Under Two Flags* and *Idalia* (both 1867).

Samson would have made a great figure in these days, if indeed Delilah had not outdone him with amber floods of equal potency. Amber is the tint patronised in the works of Ouida. It is the only idea that we have been able to evolve out of her gorgeous pages, if indeed it can be called an idea. With other and more orthodox writers the hue is gold or red. When the conception demands a milder shade of colouring, auburn, and even chestnut (with gold reflections), are permissible; but when a very high effect is intended, red is the hue *par excellence*. Red and gold, in all its shades, are compatible with virtue; amber means rich luxurious vice; whereas the pale and scanty locks are the embodiment of meanness and poverty of character. As for black and brown, which were once favourites in fiction before it took to violent colouring, they are "nowhere." They may be permitted now and then in a strictly subordinate position, but they have nothing to do with the symbolism of modern art.

Red is the colour chosen by Mr. Edmund Yates[1] to characterise the heroine of one of his many productions, the Margaret of *Land at Last*. She has, as a matter of course, "large, deep, violet eyes," and "long, thick, luxuriant hair, of a deep-red, gold colour; not the poetic 'auburn'— not the vulgar 'carrots'—a rich metallic red, unmistakable, admitting of no compromise, no darkening by grease or confining by fixature—a great mass of deep-red hair, strange, weird, and oddly beautiful." She is picked up in the street by the artist-hero, who is equally, as a matter of course, subjugated at once by this gorgeous combination of colour. Margaret makes great play with her hair, like all the other ladies. If she does not take to sweeping it over her lover's breast all at once, she lets it over her own shoulders "in a rich red cloud," which comes to the same thing; and notwithstanding that she tells him with beautiful frankness the story of her life, into which "the usual character—without which the drama of woman's life is incomplete—a man!" had come at an early age, poor Ludlow marries her, despite all the remonstrances of his friends. Then ensues a long and sufficiently clever description of the failure of this red-haired heroine to adapt herself to the dulness of a respectable life. It is very hard work

---

[1]   *Land at Last, The Forlorn Hope.* [Author's note.] Published in 1866 and 1867, respectively.

for her, as may be supposed. When she goes to visit her dull mother-in-law at Brompton, she sees in the Row, as she passes, faces that remind her of her former history; people pass her in mail-phaetons and on high-stepping horses, while she walks, who would place both at her disposal at a word. She will not say the word, but naturally, as she pursues her walk, she loathes her own bondage more than ever; and in the evening, when she plays to her good, stupid, adoring husband, dreams come upon her of the balls of other days—of "Henri so grand in the 'Cavalier seul,'" of the "*parterre* illuminated with a thousand lamps glittering like fireflies, ... and then the cosy little supper, the sparkling iced drink." Such sublime recollections carry her far away from the solemn quiet of Elm Lodge. And she has a baby and hates it; and her husband loves her so much, and is so unspeakably good to her, that she grows mad with disgust and misery. And, in short, an awful crisis is visibly coming, and comes by the reappearance of the man, her first love, who, it turns out was not her seducer, but her husband. So that the wretched creature has made a victim in cold blood of the unhappy artist—marrying him, as the villain used to marry an unsuspecting woman in the old novels, because he was a quite hopeless subject for any other treatment, and because she wanted comfort and a home! The scene in which she calmly informs Ludlow of these facts—of her utter indifference to himself and her child, her devotion to another man, and, finally, of her previous marriage—has considerable dramatic power, if it were not that the vile audacity of one party, and the feebleness of the other, take from it the interest which should belong to a death-and-life struggle. The idea is so far original that Margaret is at no period of her career a repentant Magdalene; and neither is she tempted by passion into her base and treacherous crime. She marries Ludlow in cold blood for a home, without any delusion on the subject, knowing that he is a good and innocent man, and that she is bringing him disgrace and ruin. The best touch in the book is the woman's stupid ignorance and insensibility, which leads her to imagine that she can return, as she says, to her husband, after having been the wife of another man—a delusion out of which she is speedily driven when the wretched reprobate to whom she goes back turns her away with a cruelty and insensibility equal to her own. So far this is true enough, and no attempt is made to clothe vice in an attractive form; but yet it is undeniable that the author throughout gives to his red-haired woman a lofty superiority over all the good people in his book. She—with the rich red cloud over her shoulders, her silence, her abstraction, the secret contrasts she is making in her own mind between the respectable suburban life and that of the illuminated *parterres* and ice drinks of her former state of being, and the profound disgust which fills her—is evidently, in Mr. Yates's eyes, a creature much above the level of those dull women whose talk is of babies. She sails about among them in sullen state, and he feels that she is a banished angel—a creature of a higher sphere. Her disgraceful and abominable secret, though of course he duly punishes it, still elevates her above the dull mother and gushing sister of her artist-husband. And when her real husband has disdainfully spurned her, she becomes a heroine. When she is found, she makes a little speech of self-defence, "I acknowledge my sin, and, so far as Geoffrey Ludlow is concerned, I deeply, earnestly, repent my conduct"; she says, "Have those who condemned me—and I know naturally enough I am condemned by all his friends—have those who condemned me ever known the pangs of starvation, the grim tortures of houselessness in the streets? Have they ever known what it is to have the iron of want and penury eating into their souls, and then to be offered a comfortable home and an honest man's love? If they have, I doubt very much whether they would have refused it." And she makes an edifying end, watched and counselled and cared for by the model of womanly virtue, who all this time has been saving up for poor Ludlow. Such is the story. It is a little departure from the established type of the golden-haired sorceress, and the author does not try to soften her guilt by any touches of sentiment; but still it is clear that he feels her to be a superior woman. He may praise his other personages in words, who are contented people, making the best of their lives; but Margaret, who makes the worst of it, and to whom respectability is intolerable, and who dreams of cosy suppers and iced drinks, is evidently, though be says he disapproves of her, fashioned after a much higher ideal. Mr. Yates goes into her ways and thoughts in detail, while he contents himself with weak plaudits of "Geoff, dear old Geoff," from all the painter's surroundings. To his taste it is evident that the wicked-ness of the woman, her heartlessness and self-indulgence, and utter blindness to everybody's feelings but her own, render her profoundly interesting; and his good women are very dull shadows by her side. We do not forget that years ago this used to be the reproach addressed to Mr. Thackeray, and that the cleverness of Becky and the silliness of Amelia[1] were very favourite objects of reprobation to virtuous critics. But Thackeray did not dwell upon Becky solely because she was wicked. She was infinitely clever, amusing, and full of variety. The fun in her surmounted the depravity. But at the present day this is no longer the case. There is no sort of fun, no attraction of any sort, about such heroines as the Margaret in *Land at Last*. Their interest is entirely fictitious, and founded solely upon their wickedness. The creature is a loathsome cheat and impostor, and therefore she is worthy of being drawn at full length, and presented to us in all the convolutions of her stupid and selfish nature. Such seems to be the view of fiction adopted even by such a writer (greatly above the ordinary sensational average) as Mr. Yates, whom, by the way, artists in general are little indebted for the flippancy and coarseness of the picture he gives of them. Beer and pipes are not refined accessories certainly, but yet their presence on the scene scarcely necessitates the production of Charley Potts as the representative painter. It is not complimentary to English art.

Another book by the same author—whose productive powers fill us with awe and wonder—is the *Forlorn Hope*, in which the story turns upon the forlorn and hopeless passion of a doctor, already married, for a fair young patient, who returns his love. The doctor's wife, in a fit of tragic but only too clear-sighted jealousy, poisons herself, and leaves him free; but the poor, pretty, consumptive Madeline, who is the object of his love, marries somebody else just at the moment when her physician is beginning to permit himself to think of approaching her, and henceforward can only purchase a little intercourse with her hopeless lover by falling very ill and dying in his hands. Now it goes utterly against all social morality to introduce lovemaking between a doctor and his patient. There are even hard-hearted critics who have

---

[1] Characters in Thackeray's *Vanity Fair* (1847–48).

objected to the idyll of melancholy passion as set forth in the pure and pensive pages of *Doctor Antonio*,[1] notwithstanding that the scene is Italy, and the story as spotless as imagination could conceive. Doctors and patients have no right to fall in love with each other; it goes in the face of all the proprieties and expediencies of life. A young physician may, it is true, be permitted to appreciate the beauty and excellence of the sweet nurse in a sickroom, who ministers along with him to the sick mother or father or brother; but when she herself becomes his patient, a wall of brass rises between them. Yet Mr. Yates's sympathies evidently go with the physician, and it appears only natural to him that the golden-haired patient (pale gold in this case, which is angelic—not red gold, which is of the demons) should quite obliterate in Dr. Wilmot's mind the reserved and dark-complexioned wife who waits for him at home. This poor woman does not right herself even by suicide. The facts of the case give her husband, when he finds them out, a great shock; but not so great a shock as does the marriage of the delicate Madeline, who, angel of purity as she is, evidently feels it quite legitimate on her part to recall her medical lover, and enact little scenes of despairing love on her deathbed, and die happy in his arms, with a sweet indifference to the fact of her husband's existence. It is no doubt very melancholy that people should obstinately persist in marrying the wrong person, as indeed is visible in real life as well as in novels; but how far it is expedient to call in the right man, whom you have not married, as your medical attendant, may, we think, be questioned. The suggestion is not a pleasant one.

As Miss Thomas has been mentioned in the beginning of this paper, we may say, in justice to her, that she has freed herself to some extent from the traditions of her school. Her two last books[2] are neither immoral (to speak of), nor *horsey*, which is akin to immoral. They are very frothy, and deal with a world which is not the ordinary world around us—a world where there is either very gorgeous upholstery or very shabby meanness, and no medium between them; but still the books are not nasty. *Played Out*, in fact, is not a bad story. The

---

[1] Novel (1856) by Giovanni Ruffini (1807–81).
[2] *Played Out; Called to Account.* [Author's note.] Both published in 1867.

little heroine Kate is very tiresome in her changeableness, but still she is a well-known character, whom we have met so often that we feel a certain interest in her, and indignation at the amazingly senseless way in which her prospects are thrown away. The device by which this is accomplished is one which is becoming about as general as the golden hair. It is used in both Miss Thomas's books—in *Cometh Up as a Flower*—in a lively and clever novel called *Archie Lovell*,[1] which is a little earlier in date—and no doubt in a host of others if we could but remember. It is a device not very creditable either to the invention or the good taste which suggested it. In all these books the heroines are made to spend a night accidentally in the society of a man with whom they have been known to flirt. It is done in the purest innocence, and in that curious fortuitous way with which things happen only in novels. Chance alone on both sides brings it about, but yet it becomes known, and the consequences are generally disastrous. Kate Lethbridge, for instance, in *Played Out*, is persuaded to step into a railway carriage in which her friend is going off to London, and which is supposed to wait ten minutes at a little country station, to enable him to spend these ten minutes pleasantly. And the moment she has entered it the train sweeps away, and the young lady's reputation is ruined for life. This expedient, it must be allowed, is a very poor one; and it is a curious sign of the absence of all real inventive power in this kind of literature, that it should be so often employed. In *Called to Account*, Miss Thomas enters upon the less safe ground of married life, and displays to us, among a number of "grandly-simple" beauties, with the usual sublime attribute of golden locks, a scanty-haired pale-coloured woman, who makes mischief and destroys domestic peace, yet turns out very good at the end, and goes into the Sister of Mercy business with much applause on all hands. Here, too, all unhappy pair are condemned to rouse everybody's suspicion, and to risk their character by being shut up together in a cave for some twenty-four hours or so, though happily, as they are all but killed by the experience, scandal is silenced. Certain curious symptoms of the kind of culture prevalent in the region to which this class of literature belongs, are,

---

[1] Published in 1866.

however, to be gleaned out of these books—a real contribution to our knowledge of our species. The first of these gives us a sketch of the favourite literature of the hero who is, like so many heroes, a man of letters publishing novels in magazines, and otherwise contributing to the instruction of the public. He is, besides, a clerk in a government office, a university man, and has suddenly and unexpectedly become heir to a fine estate. We are told to glance round his sitting-room in his absence, with the view of throwing light upon his tastes and pursuits—and this is what we find:—

> The recesses on either side of the fireplace were occupied with broad shelves, and these were filled with books—original editions most of them, of the standard modern novelists. An independent oak book-stand, placed within reach of the one armchair in the room, might be supposed to contain the more special favourites of that room's occupant, and there Fielding and Smollett, Wycherly and Ben Jonson, Spenser and Sidney, Bon Gaultier, Bacon, Addison, Ingoldsby, and a host of other wits, poets, essayists, dramatists, humorists, and scholars, stood in amicable array.

Our readers will admire the admirable conjunction of names herein assembled, and the charming way in which they relieve and heighten each the effect of the other. Bacon and Addison leashed together, and marching between Bon Gaultier and Ingoldsby, is a true stroke of genius;[1] and there can be no doubt that a very peculiar light is thrown upon the "tastes and pursuits, if not on the character of my hero," by the fact that his shelves are filled with the standard modern novelists in the "original editions." It is intelligible that people who read nothing but standard modern novelists should produce such books as are now under review. The second passage we shall quote is also a description

---

[1] Francis Bacon (1561–1626), English courtier, philosopher, and natural historian; Joseph Addison (1672–1719), classicist and essayist; Théophile Gautier (1811–72), or "Le Bon Théo," French man of letters. *The Ingoldsby Legends* were a collection of poems and narratives published in 1840, supposedly by "Thomas Ingoldsby" but actually by clergyman R.H. Barham (1788–1845).

of a room—a room which the hero—again a literary man—of *Called to Account* thinks so perfect, that he never tires of raving about the exquisite taste which has arranged it. It must have been done by "a woman of genius essentially human," he says. We do not go into the paraphernalia of silver lamps, "shallow silver urns, classical in design and execution," and reflected in "immense sheets of plate-glass," but go on to its more purely artistic features:—

> On either side of these glasses were niches (oval-shaped at the top in the wall, which was coloured a faint warm cream-colour) containing marble statuettes about two feet high. Venus and Hercules, Apollo and Diana, were chosen as the respective types of beauty and strength.... In one recess by the side of the fireplace, a small semi-oblique piano stood, with a pile of loosely arranged music on it. In the corresponding recess there was a ruby velvet shrine, composed of a pedestal and curtains for the glorious goddess, who is grander and more perfect in her mutilated beauty than anything else the world has seen in marble, a nearly life-size copy of "Our Lady of Milo." ... And pictured suggestions of the past and the future were not wanting; for Raphael and Fornarina, Dante and his Beatrice, and a Madonna with the warm soft beauty of a moonbeam, all looked upon one from the walls.

This amazing combination strikes the poet-hero as half divine. Very likely Miss Thomas imagines that the relation of the Fornarina to Raphael, and that of Beatrice to Dante, were identical; and that it is very fine and classical to talk of the Venus as Our Lady of Milo.[1] Such wonderful exhibitions of the uneducated intelligence which has

---

[1] Oliphant criticizes Thomas for conflating profane and divine love and art. Fornarina was the supposed mistress of Italian artist Raphael (1483–1520) and the model for his *Portrait of a Nude Woman* (c. 1518); Beatrice Portinary (1266–90) was the inspiration for Italian poet Dante Alighieri's (1265–1321) *Vita Nuova* (1292) and *Divine Comedy* (1314–15). Dante's love for Beatrice was mystical and spiritual, not physical. The *Venus de Milo* is a classical Greek statue in the Louvre in Paris; the statue is being inappropriately compared to images of the Madonna.

caught up a name here and there, and is bold enough to think it knows what they mean, are very astonishing. Truly, a little learning is a dangerous thing.

We have gone as far as human patience can go in our survey, and leave off with the certainty that we have left a great deal that is more objectionable still untouched. In one novel, which we do not attempt to notice here, but which lately passed through our hands,[1] we remember that the chief interest turns on the heroine's discussion with herself as to whether or not she will become the mistress of a very fascinating man she happens to be brought in contact with. Her decision eventually is on the side of virtue, but she takes the whole question into consideration with the most frank impartiality. In another[2] the central point is a certain secret passage leading from the chamber of the profligate master of a house into a room occupied by an old general and his charming young wife—a passage which the villain uses once too often, finding himself at last in presence of the insulted husband. But it is needless to multiply instances. It would be a task beyond our powers to enter into all the varieties of immorality which the novelists of the day have ingeniously woven into their stories. In these matters the man who writes is at once more and less bold than the woman; he may venture on positive criminality to give piquancy to his details, but it is the female novelist who speaks the most plainly, and whose best characters revel in a kind of innocent indecency, as does the heroine of *Cometh Up as a Flower*. Not that the indecency is always innocent; but there are cases in which it would seem the mere utterance of a certain foolish daring—an ignorance which longs to look knowing—a kind of immodest and indelicate innocence which likes to play with impurity. This is the most dismal feature among all these disagreeable phenomena. Nasty thoughts, ugly suggestions, an imagination which prefers the unclean, is almost more appalling than the facts of actual depravity, because it has no excuse of sudden passion or temptation, and no visible boundary. It is a shame to

---

[1] *Which Shall It Be?* [Author's note.] Published in 1866 by novelist Mrs. Alexander (1825–1902).

[2] *Guy Deverell.* [Author's note.] Published in 1865 by Irish novelist Joseph Sheridan Le Fanu (1814–73).

women so to write; and it is a shame to the women who read and accept as a true representation of themselves and their ways the equivocal talk and fleshly inclinations herein attributed to them. Their patronage of such books is in reality an adoption and acceptance of them. It may be done in carelessness, it may be done in that mere desire for something startling which the monotony of ordinary life is apt to produce; but it is debasing to everybody concerned. Women's rights and women's duties have had enough discussion, perhaps even from the ridiculous point of view. We have most of us made merry over Mr. Mill's crotchet on the subject, and over the Dr. Marys and Dr. Elizabeths;[1] but yet a woman has one duty of invaluable importance to her country and her race which cannot be over-estimated— and that is the duty of being pure. There is perhaps nothing of such vital consequence to a nation. Our female critics are fond of making demonstrations of indignation over the different punishment given by the world to the sin of man and that of woman in this respect. But all philosophy notwithstanding, and leaving the religious question untouched, there can be no possible doubt that the wickedness of man is less ruinous, less disastrous to the world in general, than the wickedness of woman. That is the climax of all misfortunes to the race. One of our cleverest journals took occasion the other day to point out the resemblance of certain superficial fashions among ourselves to the fashions prevalent among Roman women at the time of Rome's downfall. The comparison, no doubt, has been made again and again, and yet society has not become utterly depraved. But yet it has come to have many very unlovely, very unpromising, features in it. We are no preacher to call English ladies to account, and we have no tragical message to deliver even had we the necessary pulpit to do it in; but it certainly would be well if they would put a stop to nasty novels. It would be well for literature, well for the tone of society, and well for the young people who are growing up used to this kind of reading. Considering how low the tone of literary excellence is, and

---

[1] Reference to J.S. Mill's efforts on behalf of women's suffrage and to Elizabeth Blackwell (1821–1910) and Elizabeth Garrett Anderson (1836–1917), the first women in Britain to be certified as doctors.

how little power of exciting interest exists after all in these equivocal productions, the sacrifice would not seem a great one.[1]

SOURCE

Blackwood's Edinburgh Magazine 102 (September 1867).

SELECTED SECONDARY READING

Jay, Elisabeth. *Mrs. Oliphant: A Fiction to Herself.* Oxford: Clarendon Press, 1995.

Williams, Merryn. *Margaret Oliphant: A Critical Biography.* New York: St. Martin's Press, 1986.

Trela, D.J., ed. *Margaret Oliphant: Critical Essays on a Gentle Subversive.* Selinsgrove, PA: Susquehanna University Press, 1995.

---

[1] In a separate column, Oliphant goes on to review favorably Anthony Trollope's *The Claverings* and *The Last Chronicle of Barset* (both 1867), as well as Anne Thackeray Ritchie's (1837–1919) *The Village on the Cliff* (1866).

A REMONSTRANCE
(NOVEMBER 1867)

Mary Elizabeth Braddon

MARY ELIZABETH BRADDON (1835–1915) was born in London of Irish parents, both of whom wrote sporadically for periodicals, especially the *Sporting News*. After her parents separated, Braddon briefly went on the provincial stage as "Mary Seyton" to support herself and her mother. However, she soon turned to writing, and by 1860 she was back in London, contributing to publisher John Maxwell's penny magazines and soon after moving in with him. (They married in 1874, after his estranged and institutionalized wife died.) The next couple of years were busy ones, as she wrote for and helped edit Maxwell's publications and also launched her novel-writing career, initially under a number of pseudonyms and then under her own name. With the unprecedented successes of *Lady Audley's Secret* (1862) and *Aurora Floyd* (1863), early and excellent examples of the sensational novel subgenre, Braddon's career was assured. She continued to write more than 70 novels in a wide range of styles, as well as shorter fiction and a few plays and poems.

In 1866, Maxwell and Braddon launched *Belgravia*, a monthly literary magazine. Initially, at least, Braddon sought to use her position as "conductress" of *Belgravia* to elevate her literary reputation above that of mere popular novelist. However, when she found herself under attack in other periodicals, notably in *Blackwood's* and the *Pall Mall Gazette*, she decided to use her own magazine to fight back and to denounce what she referred to in a letter to her literary mentor, novelist Edward Bulwer-Lytton, as the "little carping criticisms which *teach* me nothing, & indeed seem intended only to wound & annoy" (10 October [1867]).

In "A Remonstrance," Braddon assumes the voice of Captain Shandon, a character in William Makepeace Thackeray's novel *Pendennis* (1848–50) who founds the *Pall Mall Gazette* as a journal written "by gentlemen for gentlemen." In 1865, publisher George Smith and editor Frederick Greenwood had founded an evening paper by that name, and in 1867 the real *Pall Mall Gazette* accused Braddon of plagiarism. While the accusation related to *Circe*, a novel by Braddon that was running in *Belgravia* under the pseudonym Babington White (and which was admittedly based on a similar story in French), the attack was motivated more by an ongoing feud between Maxwell and Greenwood than by any desire to preserve literary purity. Braddon's forceful, satirical response to Greenwood ranges knowledgeably across historical and national boundaries to muster examples of ill-judged literary criticism, and it demonstrates Braddon's spirited command of a range of rhetorical tools to defend her own literary honour.

"All life whatsoever is but a chaos of infirmities; and whoso will reprehend must either be a god amongst men without fault, or a byword to men for his foul tongue."

Captain Shandon to the Editor of the "Pall-Mall Gazette"

Sir,—When untimely death takes a man from the friends he loves and the places that have been familiar and dear to him, his spirit still hovers over the walks he trod in the flesh, and, from the darksome shore where he stalks joyless and unquiet amongst kindred ghosts, he looks back to that busy world where he once had a place, and notes with interest the great conflict from which he has been withdrawn. And as the fond father, from his lonesome wanderings in the undiscovered country, turns with looks of yearning to the children he has left behind him, so the man of letters watches the literary bantling from which grim death reft him, eager to see how the frail nursling fares in stranger hands. From this land of shadows, I, Charles Shandon, survey with looks of wonder the dealings of a class of men whom I was once proud to call my brothers. Alas, they have changed sadly since that day; and there are some among them now whose hands no honest man would care to take in friendship.

The old times and the old troubles come back to me, and I fancy myself sitting in the little room in the Fleet prison—sure 'twas pleasant times we had there in those days; and it grieves me to see the place is gone, and shabby hoardings and tawdry flaunting bills disfigure the old walls, behind which I once found no unpleasant home. I fancy myself sitting there, I say, with a desk on my knee, writing for dear life; while my wife looks up from her work every now and then—poor patient soul!—and little Mary plays with Pendennis's watch-chain; and noble Warrington scowls at me from under his dark thoughtful brows; and Bungay the publisher waits impatient to hear my prospectus of the *Pall-Mall Gazette*.

I'll own, sir, I was a little proud of that prospectus; and I think of it still with as much satisfaction as a ghost can feel in the petty triumphs of the life that is over. It had the genuine ring; and there are not many among your literary hacks nowadays who could write such a sentence as that which Pendennis pronounced the crowning beauty of the composition. "We address ourselves to the higher circles of society; we care not to disown it. The *Pall-Mall Gazette* is written by gentlemen for gentlemen; its conductors speak to the classes in which they live and were born. The field-preacher has his journal; the radical free-thinker has his journal—why should the gentlemen of England be unrepresented in the Press?"

Now, sir, there was of course some little of the tradesman's trick and bombast in this splendid paragraph; but I protest, on my honour, that when I wrote it I meant to keep this promise; and I believe that the *Pall-Mall Gazette*, while under my direction, rarely outstepped the limits which a gentleman prescribes for himself even when he is most acrimonious. The names of such contributors as Warrington and Pendennis were, indeed, a sufficient guarantee for the carrying out of intentions somewhat boldly put forth in my prospectus. Those two young men were gentlemen by birth and education. We had not yet come to the flippancy and self-conceit of the semi-educated journalist. We were often bitter. We had our pet antipathies and our trade interests; but we were always gentlemen; and when it pleased us to hate anybody, we gave utterance to our hatred in a decent and gentleman-like manner.

These, sir, were the tactics of the *Pall-Mall Gazette* while conducted by your humble servant.

What, sir, shall I say of it now?—Can I call it a journal written by gentlemen for gentlemen? Not content, Mr. Editor, with having purloined that noble sentence of which I was so justly proud, you are doing all you have the power to do to change it into a byword and a reproach. A journal written by gentlemen for gentlemen, quotha! A bundle of cuttings from other papers, garnished with flippant and frivolous comment; and little carping, spiteful paragraphs; and prurient harpings upon subjects that decency best reprobates by decent avoidance; and sham letters from sham correspondents, all breathing the same malignant feeling against some one or something respected by other people; and, to give spice to the whole, an occasional forgery.

This, sir, is the journal written by gentlemen for gentlemen, which you conduct, and which I peruse with unutterable regret.

Now, sir, I am not going to plead the cause of a certain Mr. Babington White, whose book you have chosen to condemn. The right of the critic to his opinion is indisputable; whether it be the *Edinburgh Review*, which is pleased to laugh at Mr. Wordsworth; or the *Quarterly*, which must have its joke about young Mr. Tennyson; or the united critics of France, who band themselves together to laugh down and extinguish M. Hugo and the romantic school which he has inaugurated; or the "Highflyers at Buttons," who prefer Mr. Tickell's *Iliad* to Mr. Pope's popular version of the same epic;[1]—the critic for the moment is omnipotent, the Imperator of literature, supreme in the exercises of self-assumed and irresponsible power. But when you outstep the limits of criticism to carry on a crusade, not against the writer of the work you dislike, but against the Lady who conducts the Magazine in which the work appeared, I declare that you are guilty of a paltry and cowardly proceeding, eminently calculated to bring lasting discredit on the journal you edit, the proprietors of which are, I fear, unaware of the harm your foolish zeal is likely to inflict upon their property.

We will begin at the beginning, sir, if you please, and review this tilting match against a literary windmill. In the first place you criticise Mr. White's book, and stigmatise, as a dishonest translation, a novel, founded on a French drama, from which source the English writer has taken only the broad idea of his characters, and the general bearing and moral of his story. But then he has translated about half a page of the French writer's dialogue, that half-page being the keynote of his theme, and he has thus enabled you to quote a parallel passage, and by a little clever manipulation to make it appear to your readers (who, you speculate, are not acquainted with the French drama) that the whole work is a mere translation, or, in your less guarded assertion, "a novel stolen from the French." This, sir, is a specimen of the sham-sample system, in which the malevolent critic plagiarises the artifice of the dishonest chapman. Mr. Babington White may boldly proclaim his right to take his inspiration from a foreign source, as the greatest writers have done before him; and whether his book be good or bad, there is no man of letters who will deny the justice of his plea. You have demanded that this writer should "come forward," or be "produced," for your satisfaction. Where, sir, is your pillory? Where your tribunal?

---

[1] Famous examples of discredited criticism in the eighteenth and nineteenth centuries. Lord Francis Jeffrey (1773–1850), editor of the *Edinburgh Review*, reviled Wordsworth and other early Romantic poets; J.W. Croker (1780–1857) savaged Tennyson's early poetry in the *Quarterly Review*; Victor Hugo's (1802–85) 1830 play *Hernani* sparked a controversy between defenders in France of the neoclassical style and of the new Romantic style that even resulted in a duel; English poets Thomas Tickell (1685–1740) and Alexander Pope (1688–1744) both published translations of the *Iliad* in 1715, setting off a literary feud between Pope and Tickell's sponsor, critic Joseph Addison (1672–1719).

By what right, sir, do you ask to know more of any author than the book which it is your pleasure to review, and the name on the title-page of that book? Mr. White may elect to claim the privilege exercised by Junius;[1] for in the republic of letters there is no license accorded to the greatest which does not belong to the least. If he is to be heard of in the future, his quality will be best proved by the work which shall bear his name: if he is to return to the obscurity from which your clamorous censures have lifted him, it can be no more necessary for you to know what manner of man he is than it is necessary for him to discover the name of that accomplished critic who, in truculence of temper and choice of diction, resembles rather the Jeffreys of the Bloody Assize[2] than the caustic chief of the *Edinburgh Review.*

But now, sir, we come to a very different kind of journalism; and I blush to find that the history of the newspaper press, like other histories, repeats itself, and that the days of the *Age* and the *Satirist* seem to be coming back to us.[3] You receive, or in some manner become possessed of, a letter purporting to be written by Miss Braddon—a letter so obviously absurd, that an editor who could allow it to appear without some previous inquiry as to its authenticity must be, indeed, alike anxious to inflict injury and reckless of the reputation of the journal. The letter appears, however; and the next day appears another letter, with an anonymous signature, hinting that the book you had condemned was not written by Mr. Babington White, but by a popular lady novelist. And in your next impression appears a third letter, in which a clerk's error is twisted into an attempt at falsification, and in which a bookbinder's blunder is taken advantage of for the misspelling of Mr. Babington White's name; and from this time forward it is to be observed that your subtle sense of humour exhibits itself in the uniform misspelling of this writer's name, the writing of which with two *b*'s instead of one appears to you in the light of a very

---

[1] Reference to a collection of letters signed "Junius," published in 1772; Junius's identity has never been settled, so the pseudonym has had to stand as the author of the letters.

[2] As Lord Chief Justice, Lord George Jeffreys (1648–89) presided over a notorious series of trials and executions following the defeat of the Duke of Monmouth, illegitimate son of Charles II and a pretender to the British throne.

[3] Satiric periodicals published earlier in the nineteenth century.

exquisite joke, and, indeed, a complete extinction of Mr. White and his literary pretensions; just as I have no doubt the adherents of Richard Plantagenet thought they gave the finishing stroke to all claims of Henry VII when they described him as "one Henry Tidder."[1] It appears, sir, that Miss Braddon is only informed of what is going on after the publication of the third foolish letter. She writes immediately to inform you that the letter purporting to bear her signature is a forgery.

Now, sir, what would be the first impulse of a "gentleman" upon discovering that by any carelessness of his he had inflicted on a lady the serious wrong involved in the publication of a very foolish letter? and moreover, a letter which, had the public been in any way dissatisfied with the Magazine she conducts—and it would appear happily they are not—might have inflicted real trouble and annoyance upon her in her capacity of Editor. Would not the gentleman writing for gentlemen hasten to apologise for his unwitting furtherance of a malicious plot, and would he not take immediate steps to discover the spiteful blockhead who had put this cheat upon him? Such, sir, was not your conduct. You positively abstain from any expression of regret that your paper should have been made the vehicle of private malice; and with unparalleled audacity you tell Miss Braddon that it would better have become her to write the letter which she did not write, or, in other words, that the malicious blockhead who forged her signature possessed a finer sense of honour than the lady herself! And then, sir, Miss Braddon, with natural indignation, writes to offer a reward of one hundred guineas for the discovery of the forger, and she calls upon you to reciprocate her offer. This letter you suppress, and this offer you ridicule. Mr. Babington White, whose only real offence, if offence it be (?), is that he has founded an English novelette on a French drama, is, you say, a far more reprehensible person than the spiteful blockhead who forged a lady's signature to a ridiculous letter, in the hope of placing her in a false position with the subscribers to *Belgravia* and the public generally.

---

[1] In other words, Henry Tudor, who defeated Richard III in 1485 and became the first Tudor king.

And then, sir, when the voice of the Press shouts in your ear that your conduct is discreditable to journalism, you are goaded into a feeble expression of being "very sorry," and you precede this tardy piece of repentance by asserting that you have no machinery applicable to trace out the dastardly forgery. You forget, sir, that your employer is a publisher and the owner of a rival magazine to the *Belgravia*. If his signature was forged, is there no machinery by which he would essay to discover the forger? Would he be content to do nothing? It appears, sir, that your machinery is at the ready service of the scoundrel who forged Miss Braddon's signature, and that you can print and reprint the felonious document just as your caprice dictates; and thus your machinery can repeat the annoyance, to this it is quite equal; but you have no machinery that will throw any light upon, or assist in any way to drag to justice, the miscreant who deals in forgery, and who is so conveniently on the alert for an opportunity. Whenever, sir, your own signature—that of Frederick Greenwood, editor of the *Cornhill Magazine*—shall be forged, as Miss Braddon's has been, with the same malicious intent to injure the Magazine you conduct, then, no doubt, you will find some machinery to trace out the wrong-doer, and make him amenable to the criminal law.

Your next editorial disregard of duty, sir, is worthy of all that has gone before. The same spiteful blockhead who palmed upon you the forged letter now imposes upon your simplicity a preposterous advertisement, published in a Utrecht paper on Thursday September 26th;[1] and this absurdity, without any authentication or guarantee, you quote and comment upon in your journal of Saturday the 28th. Sharp work, this Mr. Editor, and suggestive too! It is not difficult for the conspirator who inserted the advertisement to contrive to give notice of its appearance in anticipation of the ordinary postal delivery; and it is a fact not generally known, that a newspaper published in Utrecht on Thursday does not reach the General Post-office in

---

[1] The Editor of the paper refuses, in his issue for October 15, to state from whom he received this mendacious advertisement, and he declines to give any aid to trace the anonymous concoction. It is hoped, however, that either the Burgomaster of Utrecht, or the solicitor to her Majesty's Consul at Amsterdam, will eventually unravel this unprincipled sequence to the forgery of Miss Braddon's name. [Author's note.]

London until Saturday. But what can I say of the editor who unconsciously lends himself to so pitiful an affair! And the cause of all this plotting and counter-plotting, the forgery, the anonymous letters, the spurious advertisement from a Dutch newspaper, the wilful suppression of Miss Braddon's letters, is to show—what? Only that Mr. Babington White derived the characters in his story from a French drama, and did not consider himself bound to blazon the fact upon his title-page any more than William Makepeace Thackeray considered himself bound to tell the world that he derived the broad idea of his wonderful Becky Sharp, with her tricks and lies and fascinations, and elderly adorer, and sheepdog companion, from the Madame de Marneffe of Honoré de Balzac;[1] or any more than that great writer's accomplished daughter is bound to proclaim that the pre-Raphaelite word-painting for which she has been so highly commended is a trick of style exactly identical with, if not directly derived from, the style of Gustave Flaubert.[2]

Why, sir, if you better knew the literature you profess to represent, you would better understand the silliness of this childish outcry; you would know that Le Sage borrowed the plan of his *Diable Boiteux* from the Spanish of Guevara, and that he derived the materials of *Gil Blas* from the Spanish drama;[3] you would know that, without acknowledgment or sense of compunction, Sterne took whole pages *verbatim* from Rabelais, and helped himself with a very free hand to the gems of erudition and quaint conceits which he found in Burton's *Anatomy of Melancholy*;[4] you would know that Molière, in a notorious sentence, confessed to taking his material wherever he found it.[5] I daresay the

---

[1] Character in French novelist Honoré de Balzac's (1799–1850) *Cousin Bette.*

[2] Reference to novelist and essayist Anne Thackeray Ritchie (1837–1919), whom Braddon compares to French realist novelist Gustave Flaubert (1821–80).

[3] French dramatist and novelist Alain-René Le Sage (1668–1747) based his novel *Le Diable Boiteux* on a story by Spanish writer Luis Vélez de Guevara (1579–1644), but *Gil Blas* is now generally accepted to be a completely original work.

[4] English novelist Laurence Sterne (1713–68), whose best-known work is an early stream-of-consciousness style novel, *Tristram Shandy* (1760–67); among Sterne's acknowledged influences are the comic works of the French writer François Rabelais (1490–1553), and English writer Robert Burton's (1577–1640) sprawling philosophical treatise *The Anatomy of Melancholy* (1621).

[5] Molière, pen name of Jean Baptiste Poquelin (1622–73), French playwright.

little carping critics of Grub-street had their fling at the Yorkshire parson who wrote *Tristram Shandy*—the chief characters of which, by the way, Lord Lytton reproduced, regenerated, and ennobled in his immortal *Caxtons*.[1] Yet who protests? who dare to shout "literary thief" here? No doubt Vadius and Trissotin[2] found plenty to say about the dishonesty of Jean-Baptiste Poquelin, alias Molière. And yet, sir, I would rather have an ounce of Molière's genius, or a pennyweight of Laurence Sterne's wit, than a pound of your honesty, marketable as the commodity may be; or of that keen sense of honour which permitted you to record the experiences of a spy who did not disdain to misrepresent himself as a "man on strike," and who did not scruple to hob and nob with the deceived journeymen tailors, in order to give the world at large, and the master tailors in particular, the benefit of knowledge obtained by that petty treason.[3]

I doubt, sir, if you know how much you promised when you so boldly appropriated the best sentence in my prospectus. A journal written by gentlemen for gentlemen! Have you any idea what that implies? and can you for a moment imagine that gentlemen write, or that gentlemen care to read, such stuff as you have written, or caused to be written, upon this Babington-White question? Is it the part of a gentleman to deal in imputations that he cannot maintain, to give ear to the backstairs gossip of a printing-office, or take his crude information from some underhand source, and then, after making his charge by means of hints and innuendoes, to suppress the letter that calls upon him to substantiate his accusation? Is it the part of a gentleman to war against a woman, or to give ridiculous prominence to an insignificant matter in order to injure a trade rival? No, sir: if ever you are so happy as to fall into the society of gentlemen, you will discover that urbanity is the distinguishing mark of a gentleman's conduct; and that a courteous reverence for womankind—whether it be my Lady Mary in her chariot going to St. James's Palace in all her glory of diamonds and court-plumes, or only

---

[1] Novel by Braddon's literary mentor, Edward Bulwer-Lytton (1803–73), later first Baron Lytton.
[2] Characters in Molière's play *The Learned Ladies*; both characters are writers.
[3] Reference to activities leading up the 1866 establishment of a national journeyman tailors' union.

poor Molly the housemaid scrubbing her master's door-step—is a senti-ment at once innate and inextinguishable in a gentleman's mind.

Go to school, Mr. Editor, and learn what it is to be a gentleman. Learn of Addison and Steele, whose papers are models of all that is gentle and gentlemanly in literature.[1] Observe with how light a rod those elegant writers chastise the follies of their age. Remark how wide their sympathies, how inexhaustible their good humour, how dignified their sarcasm, how polished their wit. And understand from these qualities how it happened that those papers, designed for the amusement of an idle hour in the day that gave them to the town, have become the standard of taste in journalism, and the delight of intellectual mankind. Learn of Jeffrey and of Brougham,[2] those masters of critical sword-play, who had no need to fall to fisticuffs, like dirty little boys in the gutter, in order to belabour the object of their antipathy. Those gentlemen, sir, were the high-priests of literature: they offered up their victim with something of the solemnity attend-ing a pious sacrifice; and, as the leper-priest of the mediaeval legend felt his leprosy leave him at the moment when he offered the supreme sacrifice, so these masters of the art of criticism banished from their minds all party spirit and all personal feeling while engaged in the performance of their self-assumed function. Above all, sir, study the writings of William Makepeace Thackeray, from whose great mind you derived the title which your mistaken policy has so degraded.

As for the Lady whom you have attacked, I do not think she need fear any ill results from your malevolence. Adverse criticism loses its power to sting from the moment in which it ceases to be disinterested. Do you think the friends and readers of Alexander Pope valued his genius any the less after reading the libels of Lord Hervey?[3] No, sir; they only

---

1. The *Tatler* (1709–11) and the *Spectator* (1711–12), written by Addison and Irish drama-tist Richard Steele (1672–1729), served as models of tasteful periodical literature for their own and subsequent generations.

2. Lord Henry Brougham (1778–1868), journalist and politician. Brougham was one of the founders of the prestigious *Edinburgh Review*.

3. Lord John Hervey (1696–1743), poet and vice chamberlain under Queen Caroline, along with poet Lady Mary Wortley Montagu (1689–1767), engaged in a long-running literary feud with Pope. Hervey's *Letters from a Nobleman at Hampton Court* (1733) attacks Pope's humble origins and physical deformities.

thought that my lord hated the poet very furiously, and expressed his antipathy in very poor and feeble language. The town may possibly have derived some small entertainment from the *Epistle to a Doctor of Divinity from a Nobleman at Hampton Court*, but the lordling's silly rhymes can have robbed the poet of no single admirer. Miss Braddon, I imagine, has no higher aspiration than to please that novel-reading public which has hitherto applauded and encouraged her efforts to amuse its leisure hours; and I am sure her readers will not withdraw their support from her because she has been made the subject of a most unmanly attack in a journal which professes to be written by gentlemen for gentlemen. The English mind, sir, is quick to resent anything that savours of persecution; and if you have the interests of your paper at heart, you will do well in future to refrain from these noisy onslaughts upon popular female novelists; which are more characteristic of the disappointed author of two or three unappreciated novels than of the gentleman editor who writes for gentlemen readers.

I have the honour to be, sir,

Your predecessor and humble servant,

Charles Shandon.

Hades, October 1867.

SOURCE

Belgravia 4 (November 1867).

SELECTED SECONDARY READING

Carnell, Jennifer. *The Literary Lives of Mary Elizabeth Braddon: A Study of Her Life and Work.* Hastings: Sensation Press, 2000.

Robinson, Solveig C. "Editing *Belgravia*: M.E. Braddon's Defense of 'Light Literature.'" *Victorian Periodicals Review* 28.2 (1995): 109–22.

Wolff, Robert Lee. "Devoted Disciple: The Letters of Mary Elizabeth Braddon to Sir Edward Bulwer-Lytton, 1862–1873." *Harvard Library Bulletin* 22.1 (1974): 1–35; 22.2 (1974): 129–61.

Wolff, Robert Lee. *Sensational Victorian: The Life and Fiction of Mary Elizabeth Braddon.* New York: Garland, 1979.

ON FICTION AS AN EDUCATOR
(OCTOBER 1870)

Anne Mozley

ANNE MOZLEY (1809–91) was born in Gainsborough and grew up in Derby, one of 12 children in a family that made notable contributions to publishing and journalism. Her father was a bookseller and publisher, and two brothers carried on the family business. Her mother supervised the children's rigorous educations: the boys were educated at various grammar schools and at Charterhouse, while the girls were educated at home by governesses and masters. Anne later lauded the benefits of being continually exposed to serious adult conversation during her childhood.

Three of the Mozley sons went to Oxford, and Thomas and James formed especially close associations with the leaders of the Oxford Movement, John Henry Newman and Edward Pusey. Thomas and an elder brother John married Newman's sisters Harriet (a minor novelist) and Jemima. These close collegial and family ties proved important to Anne's literary career. Not only did her brother James's ten-year editorship of the *Christian Remembrancer* provide her an entrée for reviews and articles, but Newman chose her to edit his *Letters and Correspondence*, which were published in 1891, the year of her death.

Mozley built a solid reputation as a reviewer and editor, contributing to *Bentley's Quarterly Review*, as well as the prestigious *Saturday Review* and *Blackwood's Edinburgh Magazine*. Selections of her essays from the latter two periodicals were reissued anonymously as *Essays on Social Subjects* (1868) and *Essays from Blackwood* (1892). In addition to editing Newman's and her brother James's letters, she also edited a number of religious poetry anthologies in the 1830s and 1840s. From 1842 on, she edited the children's periodical *Magazine for the Young*, where one of her contributors was Charlotte Yonge, who would herself go on to edit the long-running children's magazine *Monthly Packet.* Mozley's literary work tapered off in the 1880s as she, like her brother Thomas, gradually lost her eyesight.

"On Fiction as an Educator" originally appeared in *Blackwood's*, and it addresses the perennial question of the value of didactic versus aesthetic literature. Citing examples from the lives of great writers, Mozley builds a compelling case that it is imaginative literature that ignites the sparks of genius in children. "Early childhood," she claims, "is the time when wonder, curiosity, expectation, susceptibility, and pleasure itself, are separate from personal consciousness." Didactic literature, especially that written specifically for children, can "work no wonders of this kind" because it does not challenge children to expand beyond their own experiences and knowledge.

While Mozley initially concerns herself only with the education and experiences of boys, towards the end of the essay she explicitly considers the education of girls as well. Since few girls could gain access to the kinds of systematic education touted for boys—and even fewer "women of acknowledged genius" had the benefit of such education—Mozley notes that fiction, including drama, must play an even more important role for women in providing "the awakening touch" of self-awareness and love of learning.

WE BELIEVE THAT EVERY ONE who reads at all, every one to whom books were anything in childhood—and it may be taken for granted that all readers in manhood were readers in childhood—every man who ever took up a book for his diversion, can look back to some particular book as an event in his inner history; can trace to it a start in thought, an impulse directing the mind in channels unknown before, but since familiar and part of his very being. He perhaps wonders how the book, being such as it is, should have wrought such marvels, but of the fact he cannot doubt: he was different after reading it from what he was before; his mind was opened by it, his interests widened, his views extended, his sense of life quickened. And he will surely find that the book thus influential came to him by a sort of chance, through no act of authority or intention. He seemed to find it for himself: it was a discovery. His teachers had surrounded him with books, whether of instruction or amusement, suited to his dawning faculties; but to these, however well adapted to their purpose, he can trace no conscious signal obligation. No doubt he owes much to them, but the methods and processes are lost. As far as his mind is stored and cultivated they have an important share in the work: but his memory is treacherous as to individual services. They are associated with the routine of duty, when the fancy is hard to enlist. Because they were suited there was nothing to startle.

Books are founders of families as well as men—not meaning the great books, the folios that overshadow the world of thought and teach ages and generations to write and think with a family likeness— the Aristotles, Augustines, Bacons,[1] and so forth; but books of infinitely less weight, composed under certain conditions of fervour and vivacity. For we take it that no book gives the start we mean, let who will be the author, which was not composed in heat of spirit to satisfy a necessity for expression, and with vigour of execution.

It may be granted that of all reading novel-reading, as usually performed, is the slightest of intellectual exercises—one that may be discontinued with least perceptive loss to the understanding. As we view the enormous amount of novels issuing from the press, it can be said of few that any of the readers for whom they are expressly written are materially the better for them. A chat with a neighbour, or a nap, or a game at bezique[2] would fulfil every purpose they effect on the jaded, hack-

---

[1] Aristotle (384–322 BC), Greek philosopher; Augustine (AD 354–430), saint and philosopher of the early Christian church; Francis Bacon (1561–1626), English philosopher.
[2] French card game.

neyed attention. Any one of the three modes of passing an hour would leave as lasting an impression as the average serial manufactured for the monthly demand by even fairly skilful hands—that is, on the mind familiar with such productions. Yet to judge by the autobiography of genius, the novel plays a part second to none—we might almost say, the foremost part—in the awakening of its powers. It is a point on which memory and present observation are not only not agreed, but strangely and absolutely at odds. There is no comparison between the novel of recollection and the novel of to-day. We do not mean in literary merit, but in the sway and telling power on the reader. Who can forget his first novel? the tale that entranced his childhood, introducing him to those supreme ideas of hero and heroine; opening a new world to him—not the nursery, school-room, play-ground world, but a veritable field of cloth of gold, of beauty, achievement, adventure, great deeds, success! He reads the story now, and wonders where its power lay—that is, unless his lucky star threw some masterpiece in his way, such as *Ivanhoe*, entrancing to childhood, and still delightful at every age. But this is a chance. The exquisite vision of life may have come in the shape of a classical story—the action is stilted to his mature taste, the language turgid. Or in a tale of chivalry, he can only laugh now at impossible feats of heroism. It may have been an historical romance, such as *Thaddeus of Warsaw*,[1] which Thackeray harps upon: the whole thing strikes him as at once false and dull. It may have been a tale of passion, flimsy to his mature judgment, though the author's heart was in it. His mind can scarcely, by an effort, revive even a faint echo of the old absorbing excitement; but not the less is he sensible of a lasting influence—a permanent impression, following upon the first enchantment.

Who that has felt it but will class such hours among the marked ones of his life? what a passionate necessity to unravel the plot, to pursue the hero in his course; what a craving for the next volume, stronger than any bodily appetite; what exultation in success; what suspense when the crisis nears; what pity and tears in the tragic moments; what shame in these tears—the shame that attends all strong emotions—as they are detected by unsympathising, quizzing

---

[1] Novel (1803) by English novelist Jane Porter (1776–1850).

observers; shame leading to indignant protesting, pertinacious denials, haunting the conscience still, and deceiving no one! What a blank when the last leaf is turned, and all is over!

Who cannot contrast the weariness with which he now tosses the last novel aside, with the eager devices of his childhood to elude pursuit and discovery, to get out of earshot, or to turn a deaf ear, when the delightful book is in his grasp which is to usher him into another world? What ingenuity in hiding, behind hedges, in out-houses and garrets—nay, amongst the beams and rafters of the roof, to which neither nurse nor governess, nor mamma herself, has ever penetrated. Even the appearance of the book devoured under these circumstances lives a vivid memory—torn page, thumb-marks, and all. But it is the way of such things to disappear when their mission is accomplished—to elude all search; though for some we would willingly give as much as ever book-hunter did for a rare pamphlet.

If it were possible, as has been more than once attempted, by a system of rigorous and vigilant exclusion, to confine an intelligent child's education within certain exactly defined limits—to impart what is called an admirable grounding in all exact knowledge, and at the same time to shut out every form of fiction from its mind—to allow it to receive no impressions through the fancy—to compel its powers of thought and perception into one prescribed direction—to suffer it to read and hear nothing but fact, to imbibe nothing but what is called useful knowledge, to receive its history purified of all legend, its grammar without illustration, its arithmetic without supposed cases, its religion through direct precept only,—and to compare it with another child of equal age and powers, which had learnt nothing laboriously, nothing but through unrestricted observation and the free use of its senses—knowing nothing that lessons teach, reading, if it could read, only for amusement,—but familiar from infancy with legendary lore, fairy tales, and the floating romances of social life,—some interesting conclusions might be drawn. As the first case is an impossible one, we can only surmise which mind would be most developed, which would be possessed of the truest, because most clearly and largely apprehended knowledge. Either system is mischievous followed out to its full length: these victims of experiment or neglect would each be wanting, perhaps permanently, in supremely important elements of intellectual power; but there is no doubt what would be the voice of experience as the extent of loss where the higher faculties are in question. All the men of genius who tell us anything of themselves give it—whether intentionally or not—in favour of feeding and exciting the imagination from the first dawn of thought, as a condition of quickening that faculty in time, and sustaining the human race at a due elevation.[1] There are indeed dry men, who are satisfied with the restrictive system which made them what they are, by stopping some of the mind's outlets for good and all; while Fancy's child, on the contrary, is often painfully conscious of something missing, some strength needed to carry out the brain's conceptions: but satisfaction with an intellectual status is no warrant for its justice. The poet has both types in his thought when he pictures the model child, the growth of the system of his day, as

> A miracle of scientific lore.
> Ships he can guide across the pathless sea,
> And tell you all their cunning: he can read
> The inside of the earth, and spell the stars;
> He knows the policies of foreign lands;
> Can string you names of districts, cities, towns,
> The whole world over, tight as beads of dew
> Upon a gossamer thread; he sifts, he weighs;
> All things are put to question; he must live
> Knowing that he grows wiser every day
> Or else not live at all, and seeing too
> Each drop of wisdom as it falls
> Into the dimpling cistern of his heart;[2]

---

[1] Bearing upon our subject is a well-considered lecture recently delivered and since published by Lord Neaves on *Fiction as a Means of Popular Teaching*. The line of thought leads him chiefly to dwell on the value of parable and fable as moral teachers for all time and every age. His numerous examples in prose and spirited verse are not only apt and varied, but show a familiar acquaintance with the literature, both European and Oriental, of the subject. [Author's note.] Lord Neaves (1800–76) was a classicist who became rector of the University of St. Andrews in Scotland; the lecture Mozley cites was delivered and published in 1869.
[2] These and the other long poetry excerpts are from Wordsworth's *Prelude*.

and contrasts the little prig with the child expatiating, all unconscious of self, in the free range of fiction and fairy-land. It is thus Wordsworth congratulates Coleridge on their mutual escape:—

Oh! where had been the man? the poet where?—
Where had we been, we two, beloved friend,
If in the season of unperilous choice,
In lieu of wandering, as we did, through vales
Rich with indigenous produce, open ground
Of fancy, happy pastures ranged at will,
We had been followed, hourly watched, and noosed,
Each in his several melancholy walk;
Stringed, like a poor man's heifer, at its feed,
Led through the lanes in forlorn servitude;
Or rather like a stallèd ox, debarred
From touch of growing grass, that may not taste
A flower till it have yielded up its sweets
A prelibation to the mower's scythe?

It is common, however, for men of genius to complain in their own case of a defective intermittent education in a tone which gives it for elaborate training; it is their grievance against their special belongings or against society generally. They assume their imagination a giant no chains could have bound; while exacter, more varied, and deeper knowledge would have added strength and power to their crowning faculty. We discover this querulous humility in men who have acquired distinction; to whom, therefore, the world allows the privilege of talking at themselves. They are aware of inequalities, and perhaps feel themselves pulled back by deficiencies which would not have disturbed them had their education been more regular and systematic at some early period than they were left to themselves, and allowed to follow their own devices. Under the desired circumstances their powers would have been more on a level. This is probable, but the level might be attained through the checked exuberance of their highest and most distinguishing faculty; a sacrifice they would be little prepared for, though the average of capability might be raised.

Mr. Galton,[1] in his work on hereditary genius, asserts genius to be irrepressible. To us it seems, like all other kindling matter, to need a spark; and whatever is not inherent, but imparted, may be wanting. It may be wanting either through abject circumstances, or effectual repression in childhood, the period when the divine touch is given—given in some moment of careless leisure, through the medium of delight, using fancy for its ministrant. There is a critical moment in childhood when it is open to impressions with a keener apprehension than at any other period of existence. Scenes and images strike on the dawning mind, and elicit a flash of recognition, which later on in life, and taken in through gradual processes, would effect no such marvel. It is perhaps when the first glimpse of the possibilities of life falls on a just-awakening intelligence that the light is caught most readily, and tells most lastingly on the intellect. The idea must not only interest, it must be new—something hitherto undreamt of. A child's first apprehension of poetic fiction is a revelation,—fiction, that is, that either tells something absolutely new, like the heroic aspect of life—great deeds and wonderful adventures— or which gives an insight into the passions, the stir, and excitement of manhood. Nothing written for children can produce this commotion in the whole nature; it must be something absolutely out of the sphere of experience, representing life in a new and wonderful aspect, of which before there was no conception, and which yet is recognised at once for truth. And, as we have said, it must be come upon by accident and at unawares. There is fiction, noble fiction, in all classical training; but men don't look back upon their lessons for the moment of illumination we speak of. Probably it has come before to them; for early childhood is the time when wonder, curiosity, expectation, susceptibility, and pleasure itself, are separate from personal consciousness. It is when a child is lost in a book or heroic tale, to the utter forgetfulness of self, that the germ springs into life. The poet is *made* as well as born. It is here that the making begins. Walter Scott had received his bent at three years old, long before he could read, when he shouted the ballad of Hardyknute to the annoyance of his aunt Janet's old bachelor visitors.[2]

---

[1]   Francis Galton (1822–1911), English scientist; his *Hereditary Genius* appeared in 1869.
[2]   According to his biographer John Lockhart, Scott claimed the ballad of "Hardyknute" was the first poem he ever learned.

Children's tales of the moral sort, however well told, and however valuable for safe reading and innocent amusement, work no wonders of this kind. A child's story deliberately treats of matters with which the child is familiar; all the grown-up characters are drawn from his point of view. Miss Edgeworth wrote thing better than "Simple Susan,"[1] but it touches on no new ground. No one looks back upon it as a starting-point of thought. Still less influential in this direction are those that draw society; that bring boys and girls together, and make them talk and act upon one another as it is supposed that boys and girls do act. At best, a child learns appropriate lessons for its own conduct from them. Miss Sewell's valuable tales on the one hand, and Tom Brown on the other,[2] open out no vision of life; they are not of the fiction that sows the seeds we mean, though they induce swarms of imitators amongst their older readers and admirers: no doubt, for one reason, that a child's criticism, its questioning satirical temper, is at once roused—the posture of mind least akin to inspiration. In the domestic tale there is a constant appeal to the probable. Here the child cannot but feel as a judge. It has quick sight to detect bombast and want of nature, which might have passed current in unfamiliar scenes, and enacted by men and women. And because verse is more out of the range of a child's critical judgment than prose, and a tale sung is lifted into a higher region than a tale said, we find romance in harmonious numbers take the first place as instigator and stimulant to the latent spark of genius. How much of our poetry, for instance, owes its start to Spenser! when the *Fairy Queen*[3] was a household book, and lay on the parlour window-seat! Before the drawing-room table had a literary existence, the window-seat fulfilled its function as the home for the light literature of the day. The parlour window was the form of popularity Montaigne[4] affected to despise and dread for his essays, as placing him within everybody's reach—not of critics only. Clearly the window-seat was better adapted for the explorations of childhood than its modern substitute, as being easily climbed into, more snug and retired,

[1] Children's story (1800) by English novelist Maria Edgeworth (1767–1849).
[2] Anna Sewell (1820–78), English writer of moral tales for children; *Tom Brown's Schooldays* (1857) by Thomas Hughes (1822–96)
[3] Edmund Spenser (1552–99), English poet whose best-known work is *The Faerie Queene* (1590–96).
[4] Michel de Montaigne (1533–92), French philosopher.

a miniature study, in fact, presenting a hiding-place from curious observers behind the curtain; and the window itself, a ready resource for wandering eyes, when the labour of reading, of attention, even of excitement, demanded a pause. "In the window of his mother's apartment lay Spenser's *Fairy Queen*," writes Johnson of Cowley,[1] "in which he very early took delight to read, till, by feeling the charms of verse, he became, as he relates, irrecoverably a poet. Such are the accidents," he goes on to say, "which, sometimes remembered, and perhaps sometimes forgotten, produce that particular designation of mind and propensity for some certain science or employment which is commonly called genius." With his self-chosen studies Cowley acquired that disinclination for the asperities of a formal education which mature genius so often laments, "and he became such an enemy to all constraint, that his master never could prevail on him to learn the rules of grammar." Pope[2] says, "I read *the Fairy Queen* with infinite delight at twelve." Dryden[3] calls Milton the poetical son of Spenser; and all recent biography gives to Spenser the same preeminence as a prompter of the nation's genius. And this not only because the flow of his verse and his charm of narrative naturally attract children, but that the brilliancy and the strangeness and the utter difference between life as he draws it, and life as the child knows it, especially qualifies it for the work. The *Fairy Queen* does not so much suggest imitation as other poems do of equal power, but it awakes a faculty. The poets adduced never followed their first teacher; they caught nothing from him but the impulse—the flash. Another remarkable and eventful impulse of the same nature, and for the same reason, was the publication of the *Arabian Nights*,[4] awaking power without give its direction. To this Wordsworth testifies:—

> Dumb yearnings, hidden appetites are ours,
> And *they must* have their food ....

---

[1]   Abraham Cowley (1618–67), English poet, dramatist, and essayist; he was included in Samuel Johnson's (1709–84) *Lives of the English Poets* (1779).

[2]   Alexander Pope (1688–1744), English poet.

[3]   John Dryden (1631–1700), English poet.

[4]   *The Arabian Nights* (1850) were translated into English by explorer Richard Francis Burton (1821–90).

In that dubious hour,
That twilight when we first begin to see
This dawning earth, to recognise, expect,
And in the long probation that ensues
The time of trial, ere we learn to live
In reconcilement with our stinted powers.
... Oh! then we feel, we feel,
We know where we have friends. Ye dreamers then,
Forgers of daring tales! We bless you then,
Imposters, drivellers, dotards, as the ape
Philosophy will call you; *then* we feel
With what, and how great might ye are in league,
Who make our wish, our power, our thought a deed,
An empire, a possession,—ye whom time
And seasons serve; all faculties to whom
Earth crouches, the elements are potter's clay,
Space like a heaven filled up with northern lights
Here, nowhere, there, and everywhere at once:

and Dr. Newman,[1] in his recollections of early childhood, writes: "I used to wish the Arabian Tales were true; my imagination ran on unknown influences, on magical powers and talismans .... I thought life might be a dream, or I an angel, and all this world a deception, my fellow-angels by a playful device concealing themselves from me, and deceiving me with the semblance of a material world."

Dryden gives it as his opinion that "it is the genius of our country-men to improve upon an invention rather than to invent themselves"; and though he is speaking of the obligations of our earlier English poets to Italian sources, rather than of the mission of Oriental fancy to help Western imagination to the use of its wings, yet his argument takes that direction, and shows the necessity of a first impulse from without in opposition to the irrepressible theory lately put forth. No doubt a work of far less decided force of invention falling on a kindred fancy

---

[1]   John Henry Newman (1801–90), English writer on religion and education; later a cardi-
nal in the Roman Catholic Church.

effects the same purpose. We have always regarded the *Autobiography of David Copperfield* as in some points imaging Charles Dickens's own early experiences. When his hero amuses Steerforth at school with repetitions of his early novel-readings, we doubt not they were the tales that had impressed the author's own childhood, and given the bent to his genius. When little Copperfield pays his first visit to Mr. Micawber in the Marshalsea, and recalls on his way Roderick Random's[1] consignment to that dreary prison, and there encountering a debtor whose only covering was a blanket, it was probably the recollection of a similar vivid startling impression on his own feelings which made the humours of prison-life at all times a congenial subject for his pen.

Curiously illustrating this view is Cobbett's[2] history of what he calls his intellect. Cobbett's was certainly an irrepressible character; but the intellect which gave such weight and impetus to it needed an awakening which, except for an accident, might not have happened in childhood—the age essential for its full development. And unless Swift[3] had chosen to express himself through the medium of fiction (so to call it), his mind, however congenial with Cobbett's, would never have come in contact with it at the impressible period, and probably never at all. It is one of the main gifts of influence to know the right means to an end, and Swift knew invention to be his means, saying, "In my disposure of employments of the brain, I have thought fit to make invention the master, and to give method and reason the office of its lackeys."[4]

· · ·

Who can tell how much Cobbett's admirable style, so remarkable in a self-educated man, turned upon an early acquaintance with such a model? The choice and collocation of words owe much to early preference, and the rhythm which first charms the ear.

---

[1] Character in novel by Irish novelist Tobias Smollett (1721–71).
[2] William Cobbett (1763–1835), English journalist and political activist.
[3] Jonathan Swift (1667–1745), Irish writer.
[4] Mozley here quotes a long passage from Cobbett's autobiography, in which he describes finding and buying a copy of Swift's *Tale of a Tub* (1704).

The child's first visit to the theatre plays a telling part in the memory of genius. Our readers will recall Charles Lamb's vivid recollections of his first play, *Artaxerxes*,[1] seen at six years old, when the green curtain veiled heaven to his imagination—when, incapable of the anticipation, he reposed his shut eyes in the maternal lap—when at length all feeling was absorbed in vision. "I knew nothing, understand [sic] nothing, discriminated nothing. I felt all, loved all, wondered all, was nourished I could not tell how." And Walter Scott, at four, shouting his protest, "But ain't they brothers?" as Orlando and Oliver[2] fought upon the Bath stage. Goethe's[3] childhood-recollections are all of the theatre and living actors and puppets, his earliest and lasting inspiration. But the excitement of the scene commonly makes a child too conscious of the present, and of his own part in it, for the magic of new impressions to work undisturbed. A clever child is stimulated to immediate imitation of what it sees. The sight of the actors, the gaudy accessories, the artificial tones, lower the level. The noblest language, the most impressive scenes, don't work on the mind as they do pictured by the busy absorbed fancy. No child reading *Macbeth* or the *Midsummer Night's Dream* could conceive the idea of composing a play; but, taken to the theatre, play-writing proposes itself as an obvious amusement. "It is the easiest thing in the world," said Southey,[4] at eight years old an *habitué*, "to write a play." "Is it, my dear?" said the lady he addressed. "Yes," he answered; "for you know you have only to think what you would say if you were in the place of the characters, and to make them say it": a notion very current with children, who expect the words to come with the situation, but unpromising for future success. We find always a period of gestation between the first prompting and great achievement.

The most striking conjunction of favourable circumstances for intellectual education is seen where severe study imparts the strength essential

---

1   Charles Lamb (1775–1834), English essayist; Lamb probably remembers the operatic version of *Artaxerxes* by Thomas Augustine Arne (1710–78).

2   Characters in Shakespeare's *As You Like It.*

3   Johann Wolfgang von Goethe (1749–1832), German Romantic poet.

4   Robert Southey (1774–1843), English Romantic poet; one of the group known as the Lake Poets.

to the forcible development of ideas, and gives vigour to the mind's conceptions, yet leaves leisure and opportunity in the season of "unperilous choice" for the due working and entertainment of happy accidents; infusing new images through the medium of pleasure, the more delightful from an experience of task-work and labour imposed. The intellect labours still, but it rejoices even in a strain to full tension, exacted neither by duty nor teacher's will, but by curiosity catching a glimpse of what life may be, and what the world offers, to its choicer spirits. Where to these is added the excitement of stirring times, and the clash and conflict of great interests, we recognise the circumstances under which Milton's genius developed itself, and later on the school of our Lake poets. Sometimes great political events are sufficient of themselves to give the stimulus to childhood, providing they are viewed from a sufficient distance, and are absolutely removed from personal participation. In times of great wars, great tragedies, great discoveries, vast social changes, indelible impressions are made on the minds of children, who hear of them as they hear a fairy tale or the things that happened once upon a time. We see such an influence telling on the little Brontë children, in their remote seclusion, who lived in a permanent excitement about the Duke of Wellington, and used to invent stories, of which the Marquess of Douro[1] was the hero. But infancy rarely gets the proper ring of those public stimulants. In wealthy well-regulated households the children are in the nursery when telegrams bring their startling news, and the paper at the breakfast-table tells of the hero falling in battle, of great cities besieged, of new lands discovered, the earth's treasures brought to light, kings dethroned, emperors taken captive, and a nation's joy suddenly turned to mourning. Therefore, still to prefigure the terms and shocks of fate—the deeper emotions of manhood—and to prepare heart and soul for their keen reception and eloquent portrayal, must infancy be fed on fictitious wonders, joys, and sorrows, and so learn the difference between life as the mass use and treat it, and life in its nobleness, fascinations, its capabilities; thus providing it with a pictured experience and standard of comparison.

---

[1] Fictionalized versions of Arthur Wellesley, Duke of Wellington (1769–1852), and of his son, the Marquis of Douro, featured in Charlotte Brontë's juvenilia.

As the world goes, however, it is not only that the child is out of sight of excitements, but that the excitements of common life are small and piecemeal; intolerable to eager expectation, if this be really all. Life is rarely seen in picturesque circumstances; where it is, doubtless it makes a deep impression. Any disinterested emotion from public events leaves an indelible mark on the memory of childhood. To find mamma crying "because they have cut the Queen of France's head off," was an intellectual stimulus of the noblest sort for little girls fourscore years ago, but one which does not often come in the way of little girls. We old folks cannot regret the humdrum exterior of our insular existence (if in the painful—we trust it may also be passing—excitement of fierce war between neighbour nations[1] we may use the expression), knowing that emotion means discomfort and worse. We are content that the infant should establish it as an axiom that grown-up people do not cry, nor allow themselves in any turbid irregularities. It is well that joys and griefs should hide their disorder from young eyes troublesomely inquisitive in such matters, and treasuring up in memory every abnormal display of passion as something rare and startling—if seen, that is, under dignified or elevating circumstances, for the excesses of ill-temper are not what we mean. Not the less is it part of a really liberal education to know of such things with realising power; one, we assert, which fiction can alone adequately perform. History tells of great sorrows and great successes, but it is only poetry and fancy that can make them felt. It was the old woman's stories, listened to by Burns[2]—she who had the largest, wildest collection in the whole country, of tales and songs about witches, apparitions, giants, enchanted towers, and dragons—that enlarged his imagination for the reception of heroic fact, and made reading the lives of Hannibal and William Wallace[3] such an epoch. History of itself, eagerly apprehended in childhood, ministers to personal ambition; and premature ambition does not, we think, lead to the fulfilment of its hopes. The boy who devours Plutarch's lives[4] of great men hopes to rival them.

---

[1] The Franco-Prussian War (1870–71).

[2] Robert Burns (1759–96), Scottish poet.

[3] Hannibal (247–183 BC), Carthaginian general; William Wallace (c. 1270–1305), Scottish patriot.

[4] Plutarch (c. 46–119), Greek historian, whose *Parallel Lives* paired stories of famous Greeks and Romans.

Fiction proper induces dreams, it may be, of personal aggrandisement, but it more naturally sets the child upon weaving tales of his own, in which self is forgotten.

But if works of fancy perform such wonders on the masculine mind—if to it men of genius trace their first consciousness of thought, the beginning of their present selves—much more is this the case with women. If women, learning fact in a slipshod, inaccurate, unattractive way, are at the same time cut off from fiction, as by some strict, scrupulous teachers they are, where is the wonder if their interests and intellect alike stand at a low level? Miss Thackeray's sleeping beauty,[1] before the awakener comes, personates with little exaggeration the mental famine in which some girls grow up to meagre womanhood, learning dull lessons, practising stock-pieces, hearing only drowsy family talk of "hurdles and pump-handles," and adding their quota to the barren discourse, like Cecilia in the story, with "Mamma, we saw ever so many slugs in the laurel walk—didn't we, Maria? I think there are a great many slugs in our place."

There are many women desultory, restless, incorrigible interrupters, incapable of amusing themselves, or of being amused by the same thing for five minutes together, who would have been pleasanter and so far better members of society if once in their girlhood they had read a good novel with rapt attention—one of Walter Scott's or Miss Austen's, or, not invidiously to select among modern great names, if the Fates had thrown it in their way, *Sir Charles Grandison*[2]—entering into the characters, realising the descriptions, following the dialogue, appreciating the humour, and enchained by the plot. If they had once been interested in a book, their attention once concentrated out of themselves, the relaxed unsteady faculties must have been nerved and tightened by the tonic, not for the time only, but with lasting results.

Very few girls have the chance of thorough good training; nor do we find that women of acknowledged genius have been exceptionally fortunate in this respect. But we find more distinctly in them

---

[1] Anne Thackeray Ritchie (1837–1919), English novelist; her *Five Old Friends and a Young Prince* (1868) retold a number of classic fairy tales in a contemporary manner.

[2] Novel (1754) by Samuel Richardson (1689–1761), which features a model gentleman as hero.

even than in men the recognition of fiction as the awakening touch, and this often allied with acting, and through the drama. Mrs. Thrale was a pet of Quin's, and taught by him to declaim. At six years old she followed his acting of *Cato* with absorbed attention.[1] It was one of Garrick's offices to stimulate female genius. He helped to make Hannah More.[2] It is curious in this relation to observe, towards the end of the last century, the success, intellectually speaking, of a girls' school at Reading, conducted by a French emigrant and his wife.[3] Dr. Valpy, indeed, was their friend, and his influence in direct teaching might tell for much, but acting was part of its system. We are not commending this excitement for girls, but merely noting for our argument's sake that three distinguished women, whose names are still household words among us, were pupils at this school—Miss Mitford, Mrs. Sherwood,[4] and Jane Austen. Any reader acquainted with Miss Mitford's works will recall a very bright account, in her most glowing effusive vein, of a school-play, and of the girls who acted it. On Mrs. Sherwood, her much-enjoyed residence at this school, and share in its excitements, made as deep an impression; though she dwells on her school-days avowedly to lament the want of religious training—a deficiency, under the circumstances, not to be wondered at. As for Jane Austen, she went to this same school at Reading, when too young to profit much by the instruction imparted there, because she would not be parted from her elder sister Cassandra; but deep impressions may be given and thought awakened before lessons of much consequence are learnt. Here the taste for private theatricals was probably acquired which suggested such admirable scenes in *Mansfield Park*.

---

[1] Hester Thrale Piozzi (1740–1821), friend and biographer of Samuel Johnson; James Quin (1693–1766), leading actor; Joseph Addison's (1672–1719) popular tragedy *Cato*.

[2] David Garrick (1717–79), English actor, playwright, and impresario. Hannah More (1745–1833) was a member of the Blue Stocking women's group; best known for her didactic tracts, one of her tragedies was produced by Garrick.

[3] The Abbey School in Reading was run by a Mme. St. Quintin; Richard Valpy was headmaster of the Reading grammar school from 1781–1830, where he adapted plays for the boys to perform.

[4] Mary Russell Mitford (1787–1855), English essayist and dramatist; Mary Butt Sherwood (1775–1851), English children's author.

But at this date, when education proper was not thought of for girls, the drama had everywhere an education part to play. Madame de Genlis,[1] as a child of five, enacted Love with such grace, and looked so charming in fitting costume—pink silk, blue wings, quiver, bow, and all—that her mother had several suits of it made for week-day and Sunday, only taking off the wings when she went to mass. At about the same age she read *Clélie*, Mlle. de Scudery's wonderful romance of ten volumes,[2] with its maps of the kingdom of tenderness; caught the infection before she could write, and dictated novels in her turn. These novels of Mlle. de Scudery, prolix to the utmost point of unreadableness, were supreme influences in their own day. The offspring of a genuine enthusiasm in their author, the fact that they took time and protracted the *dénouement* beyond the capacity of modern patience, did not prevent the youth of her day devouring them with an enthusiasm as ardent, and they were fit instruments for the purpose we indicate. Both for knowledge of character, in however quaint disguise, and power of description, they bear favourable comparison with many a popular novel of our day, while in elevation of sentiment they stand on a higher level altogether than our own sensational literature. We find the same combination of acting and novel-reading in the childhood of Madame de Staël,[3] though she came into the world when education had been started as the favourite theme of the philosophers, and women took it up as the panacea with more than manly faith. Fancy was then in disgrace. Madame Necker objected to novels—her daughter must receive a severe classical train-ing; and Madame de Genlis, who felt teaching her specialty, and in her capacity of educationist would have quenched the Fairy Tale once for all, longed to take the clever girl in hand "to make a really accom-plished woman of her." But the drama and the novel were not the less a necessity and passion for the child of genius who cut out paper kings and queens, and gave them each their heroic or passionate part, and

---

[1] Stéphanie Felicité, Madame de Genlis (1746–1830), French educational writer and governess to one of the French princesses.

[2] Madeleine de Scudéry (1607–1701), French novelist and literary hostess; *Clélie* (1654–60) was one of her many long *romans à clef*.

[3] Germaine Necker de Staël (1766–1817), French-Swiss essayist and novelist.

undutifully smuggled *Clarissa*[1] under her lesson-books, declaring years after that Clarissa's elopement was one of the great events of her youth. But novels read in childhood, whether by Scudery or Richardson, imparted little of their own tone; this was all caught from society and the family, from the living voice of the practical view of things taken by the world around. Their influence might thus seem to be rather intellectual than moral, though we would not presume on this notion so far as to suffer a child knowingly to read what offends propriety or right feeling.

The child, awaking to its powers, begins to be the same self it will be to the end, occupied in the same speculations, open to the same interests. With relation to society it knows itself a child; but in its inmost consciousness, from early boyhood to old age, it knows no change. To this innermost consciousness the class of children's books proper, with their juvenile feats and trials and lessons, ministers nothing. They are too easy to understand—they keep the mind where it is, instead of stretching it out of itself. They have indeed a most valuable purpose; where they are to be had they are practically essential for the average run of children. Yet genius did, in fact, very well without them. As Walter Scott says, in recalling his first acquaintance with Hotspur, Falstaff, and others of Shakespeare's characters,—"Children derive impulses of a powerful and important kind from hearing things which they cannot entirely comprehend. It is a mistake to write down to children's understanding. Set them on the scent, and let them puzzle it out."

It is a very natural prejudice, if only a prejudice, to assume that the nature of the fiction that influenced the first thought of ourselves and our ancestors is better suited to the work than what characterises our own age; but we believe there is reason in the view. The more invention is pure and direct, the less it is mixed with analysis and elaborate psychological speculation, the less it inquires into causes, or stops a plain tale at every turn to tell the reason why, the more congenial it is to a fresh and hungry curiosity. The structure of all the poetry and fiction recorded to have wrought marvels upon infantile brains is

---

[1] Novel (1747–48) by Richardson.

simple, and may be fully apprehended; while the high and deep thought beneath bides its time, and grows with the growth. Spenser, Shakespeare, Bunyan, Goldsmith,[1] Walter Scott, Coleridge, Southey, and much of Wordsworth, are all adapted to every stage of thinking humanity. The boast of our own age is the reverse of simplicity. Men not only do things, but the reader has to get to the bottom of why they do them. All the science of instinct is investigated to account for each action. The reverencers of that "wonderful poem" and nine times told tale, *The Ring and the Book*,[2] think it small reproach that no child could read it—that he would probably feel repulsion towards it rather than attraction; but the poetry that repels childhood wants one main stay of fame and continuance. The sensational novel is as little adapted to a child's taste, with its stock corps of knaves, dupes, villains, and favourites of fortune. He may run through it for the incident, but it can make no footing in the memory. The superior claims on sympathy of vice over virtue is an acquired idea. As an educator it is nowhere, for it damages the intellect as much as the moral nature to be early entangled in the quandaries of crime and a polluted conscience; to view them with the feelings rather of a participator and condoner than a judge. As for the drama, no plays now answer so well as the detestable burlesque—a wallowing in the mire—which no child could relish, after it understood the end and aim, without permanent moral and intellectual degradation.

The motives now for exercising invention are of a more plodding commonplace order than they were of old, when praise rather than solid pudding was the inducement to the pains of composition. The knack of writing novels with ease, and putting together creditably imaginary talk, incident, and description, is an acquirement of our time. It is astonishing how many people can do it well who would not have dreamed of putting pen to paper a hundred years ago. Then it was considered necessary to have a story to tell as a preliminary—the novelist's capital, so to say. It is clear that this is quite a secondary

---

[1] John Bunyan (1628–88), English author and preacher; Oliver Goldsmith (1730–74), Irish author.
[2] Epic verse-novel (1868–69) by Robert Browning (1812–89).

condition in much modern novel-writing. Start your characters, and the story is expected to evolve itself. There must be plot and story, in the true sense of the words, to engage and hold a child's attention. But Nature is not lavish of this crowning effort of invention, so that the quantity of our so-called fiction tells nothing for the extent of its influence; while the direction it takes, either as being didactic, and obtruding a moral or philosophic purpose, or as ministering to a base rather than an aspiring curiosity, or as surveying things with a nicety and minuteness of investigation alien to the spirit of childhood, seems still to throw us back upon the old models—the few typical achievements of genius—as the natural chosen nurses and cultivators of the higher faculties,—models which probably owe their form and excellence to some remote originator; for as there is nothing so rare as invention in its strictest sense and highest walk, it follows that of inventors proper, whether in verse or prose, there must be fewer than of any other class the world owns.

SOURCE

Blackwood's Edinburgh Magazine 108 (October 1870).

SELECTED SECONDARY READING

Jordan, Ellen. "Sister as Journalist: The Almost Anonymous Career of Anne Mozley." Paper presented at RSVP Conference, New York City, September 2001.

Wingerd, Kathy L. *New Voices in Victorian Criticism: Five Unrecognized Contributors to Victorian Periodicals*. Diss. Kent State University, 1987. Ann Arbor: UMI, 1988.

BROWNING'S POEMS
(DECEMBER 1870)

Elizabeth Julia Hasell

Born in Cumbria near Penrith, ELIZABETH JULIA
HASELL (1830–87) was the daughter of the lord and lady
of the manors of Dacre and Soulby. She was educated at
home and excelled at languages, teaching herself Latin,
Greek, Spanish, and Portuguese. According to "Pages from
the Story of My Childhood," an autobiographical sketch
published in 1876 in *Blackwood's Edinburgh Magazine (Maga)*,
she began writing at an early age. Inspired by reading Walter
Scott's *Ivanhoe* when she was nine, she wrote a three-act play
entitled "The Siege of D'Arcy Castle" (set at the nearby Dacre
Castle). According to her account, she first "rather shirked
any love-making," only to find "the fighting more unman-
ageable than the love-making." She continued to write
throughout her youth, penning a long narrative poem about
a knight buried in the nearby Dacre Church and, at age 13,
a "grand historical tragedy" on the battle of Hastings, which
was inspired by reading Racine on Aristotle's dramatic unities.
While the adult Hasell laughed at her juvenilia, she also credited the effort of trying to write verses in her youth with
underpinning "the many hours of happiness" she had since
experienced when reading the classics.

Hasell began working as a literary critic in about 1858,
when she began contributing essays to *Maga* and to the
Quarterly Review, for whom she reviewed Lord Derby's translation of the *Iliad*. She made her reputation as a critic of clas-

sical and southern European literature, and she was invited to contribute the volumes on Calderon and Tasso (both 1877) to Blackwood's *Foreign Classics for English Readers* series. She also reviewed the major works of Tennyson for *Maga* and of Robert Browning for *St. Paul's Magazine,* and she published essays on the elegy, the sonnet, and the ode. In addition to her critical and translating work, she was evidently a tireless educator in the Lake District, walking great distances to lead classes and deliver lectures until her death in 1887.

The following essay is the first of a two-part series on Browning's major works, published in *St. Paul's Magazine* in 1870 and 1871. It is among the first wave of critical reappraisals of Browning after the publication of his epic *The Ring and the Book* (1868–69). While Hasell acknowledges the validity of some earlier criticisms of Browning's poetry—notably the awkwardness and ugliness of some of his imagery, his use of colloquialisms, the morbidity of some of his characters, and his occasional obscurity—she points to the genius underlying his work. The difficulty, she claims, lies in Browning's desire to go beyond the traditional bounds of drama and poetry, "to paint the light in its fountain instead of on land and sea ... the life inside the brain and heart, instead of that same life revealed in the human form divine." When the experiment succeeds, as it does in "Childe Roland," the result is poetry "as unsurpassed in [its] ever-gathering swell of rich, full sound, as in the excitement of [its] visual imagery."

BROWNING HAS BEEN PARTIALLY known already to one generation of the British public. A second has risen up since the appearance of his first poem, before whom he modestly takes his stand in his latest book, as still a candidate for the favour which their fathers refused him. There is every sign that it will be accorded to him. Everything seems to show that the many are at length about to concur in the passionate admiration of the few, and to make up (as they are wont) for unreasonable neglect in the past by undiscriminating eulogy in the present. This, though the better extreme of the two, is neither satisfactory to the author so treated, when he is such a man as Browning's poems reveal himself to be, nor altogether good for those who indulge in it; while its effect on the young, who have a taste to form and a model to select for imitation, is sure to be bad, leading them to mistake a master's defects for merits, and to copy them, while possibly overlooking his perfections altogether. The present seems, therefore, a good time for an attempt to consider the most noticeable matters in Browning's works—the great qualities they reveal, the deficiencies they betray; what things his varied powers have achieved already, and what we may be justified in yet expecting from them.

Those powers are varied indeed, far beyond a poet's ordinary equipment; and at times, from their very number and size, an encumbrance instead of a help to their possessor. His proficiency in logic, his skill in metaphysics, his keen wit, and his delight in verbal subtleties, are frequently too much for him, and impel him to display them out of season. The bard wrestles in him with the philosopher, and gets a fall; the humorist trips up the poet.

Much as Browning has written,—doubtless, for one reason, because he has written so *much*,—he has not done full justice yet to some of his poetical endowments; and it is now to be feared that they will never receive it at his hands. Instead of cherishing and making them yield their utmost for our benefit, he has often preferred to elaborate other talents, great in their way, but not the poet's peculiar heritage. Take, for an instance, satire, which is the application to mean and base objects of that genius which "detects identity in dissimilar" as well as the "difference in similar things"; which thus uses a heaven-sent torch to light up the recesses of a tavern; which is as useful a gift to an orator as to a poet, to a Demosthenes as to a Juvenal, to Dryden the polished and witty prose-writer as to Dryden the satirist in verse.[1] This power is a favourite with Browning, who certainly possesses it abundant in measure and trenchant in quality. He has employed it with singular success;

---

[1] Demosthenes (384–322 BC), renowned Greek orator and stylist; Juvenal (c. AD 55–127), Roman satirical poet; John Dryden (1631–1700), English poet, dramatist, and critic.

but then to its employment he has not unfrequently sacrificed poetry. We look all in vain for poetry in his clever pictures of the half-conscious, refined, ecclesiastical, and the quite conscious, vulgar cheat—"Bishop Blougram" and "Mr. Sludge."[1] We read those two monologues for the knowledge of human nature displayed in them, for the portrait each man paints in them unintentionally of himself, while he is using his skill against his neighbours or in his own defence; but we only call them *poems* because they are written in a sort of blank verse.[2] How if Browning had made less of this lower gift in order to make the very most of its higher companion, his poetic genius, the insight to which the ideal is revealed and the skill which exhibits it by means of realities? How if there had been added to his vigorous imagination, to his great dramatic faculty and to his fine ear for music, an artistic conscience; and if he had firmly resolved to maintain it in its rightful dominion over his other powers? Then we should have lost some interesting metaphysical discussions which now overbalance and spoil the harmonious proportions of his poems; some admirable traits of character now revealed to us at the expense of dramatic propriety; some racy expressions and exquisitely funny rhymes, which now impart a flavour of grotesqueness to poems which should be purely sublime or beautiful. In a word, we should have lost the Browning whom we know; and we who know him can scarcely refrain from tears at the thought. But what a poet we should have gained! A diver who, having gone down deeper than his compeers, fetched us up nothing but pearls of price; never disappointing us by bringing up vile things instead—precious in his eyes because he had found them at a depth of so many fathoms.

This last thought leads us to the greatest hindrance to Browning's attainment of universal popularity; that popularity which rewards the poet whose genius has breadth as well as depth; the love of simple-minded women and children as well as of men, of uneducated persons as well as of the learned. The hindrance to winning such

---

[1] Poems from *Men and Women* (1855) and *Dramatis Personae* (1864).
[2] Sometimes of this kind:—
   The caddy gives way to the dram-bottle.
       —"Mr. Sludge the Medium" [Author's note.]

acceptance as this lies in Browning's deficient sense of beauty in his choice of subjects. Doubtless as much skill may be shown in painting an ugly as a beautiful face, a dirty farmyard as a glorious lake; but who, even of observers with a special knowledge of painting, looks at the two sorts of pictures with equal pleasure? While to the child, or to the unlearned, the subject is almost everything, the execution nothing. Even so Browning's knowledge of human nature, his very skill in tracking its devious windings and detecting its sins in their closest lurking-places, have injured his power of exciting universal interest, by tempting him to choose subjects which would best display this knowledge, without regard to their intrinsic beauty. Some of his best-known poems make the reader shudder, even while he most admires their cleverness, by the physical or moral horrors which they set before him. And when the child or intelligent rustic, who has laughed loud over the delicious "Piper of Hamelin," and cried for joy as the good horse Roland's hoofs smite the Aix pavement,[1] tries to read more of the book which delighted him so much, he finds there little that he can understand, except poisonings, stabbings, and stranglings, varied by public executions of different degrees of cruelty, which culminate in the burning alive of a man before a slow fire.

This want of feeling for the paramount claims of the beautiful may be the reason why a writer, who knows every hole and corner of the classics, has only drawn one poem from (pre-Christian) Greek sources; why the repose so familiar to him in the masterpieces of the ancients is the quality in which his own works are most deficient; why, though delighting in his adopted country's art, though well knowing (as his poems bear witness) how the sculptor feels as he watches some godlike form grow beneath his hand, the painter as he looks up to his own Madonna smiling down upon him from her golden light; the musician as the wave of sound swells round him responding to his conception; yet when he comes to deal with his own art, it is too often discords of music, the snake-enfolded struggler of sculpture, the plague-stricken form of painting that Browning has chosen for his own portion as a poet.

---

[1] References to "The Pied Piper of Hamelin" from *Dramatic Lyrics* (1842) and "How They Brought the Good News from Ghent to Aix" from *Dramatic Romances and Lyrics* (1845).

His love of abnormal types of character, of morbid conditions of mind, of exceptional crimes as subjects for his verse, will hinder Browning's popularity (in the widest sense of the term) even more than that other barrier about which so much has been said—his peculiarity of style.

Nevertheless this barrier exists also. Browning is the Carlyle of verse; a lover, like that great writer, of odd nicknames,[1] and a coiner of new and forcible expressions; like him, inclined rather to run risks in the attempt to "snatch a grace beyond the reach of art"[2] than to incur the reproach of tameness by following her beaten track; like him, through native originality unconstrained where another man would be odiously affected, applauded where that other would be deservedly hissed; but also, like him, in the cloud which sometimes obscures his meaning; and, therefore, even as he, neither to be imitated with tolerable effect nor to be understood without preliminary initiation. It was chiefly from unwillingness to undergo the trouble of that initiation in an unknown author's favour that the last generation received Browning's first poems as they did. When the new aspirant for poetic honours invited chance listeners to hear him

Talk as brothers talk
In half-words, call thing, by half-names,

and proposed confidentially to

Leave the mere rude
Explicit details: 'tis but brother's speech
We need, speech where an accent's change gives each
The other's soul,[3]

---

1   Witness "Bluphocks" and "Gigadibs." [Author's note.] Characters from *Pippa Passes* (1841) and "Bishop Blougram's Apology."
2   Line from Alexander Pope's (1688–1744) poem *An Essay on Criticism* (1711).
3   *Sordello.* [Author's note.] Play (1840) that tells the story of a troubadour caught up in the conflicts of thirteenth-century Italy; Sordello also figures in Dante Alighieri's (1265–1321) *Purgatory.*

can we wonder if men, whose typical poet was Byron, who complained of Wordsworth's difficulties, stood aghast at *Paracelsus*[1] and *Sordello*, and turned from them exclaiming, "Non lectore tuis opus est, sed Apolline libris?"[2] Is it marvellous if they thought the "Now die, dear Aureole" of Festus, at the close of his friend's long-winded death-bed harangue, the most sensible thing in *Paracelsus?* or if they complained that while Sordello's first poet,[3] always profound, is only sometimes obscure, his second, only sometimes profound, chose to be obscure always? Or can we be surprised if even the wiser section, who had learned from Coleridge that there is a kind of obscurity in an author which is a compliment to the reader, felt the compliment here too much for their modesty, and longed for less respect and more information?

But this sort of talk is now a thing of the past. Browning has modified his style, though he still throws us a hard lyric nut, a "Respectability," a "Popularity," to crack every now and then.[4]

The British public grumbled for awhile, and then patiently learned Browningesque as it before learned Carlylese. So that for the present the advantages of a picturesque way of putting things remain for the reader's sensible enjoyment; its attendant disadvantages have retired from his immediate observation. Nevertheless, they should not be left out of sight in an attempt to estimate their employer's genius; for they must hinder his naturalisation among those men of other lands and other ages whom every great poet addresses next to those of his own day and country, and they mark that mind of which they are the natural outgrowth as (whatever its greatness) still below the measure of the stature of those who sit serene on the Parnassian summit.

We do not, of course, mean that the unquestionable (though much exaggerated) difficulty of Browning's first poems is due to style alone. It is caused fully as much by their subject. For in them a step is endeavoured to be taken beyond epos, beyond drama, for which no firm

---

1   Poem (1835) based on the story of a sixteenth-century physician and alchemist; Festus is one of Paracelsus' companions.

2   Epigram from Martial: "Your books don't need a reader, but an Apollo." In other words, "no one except the god of obscure oracles could understand your text."

3   Dante. [Author's note.]

4   Two poems from *Men and Women*.

footing can be secured. They are an attempt to paint the light in its fountain instead of on land and sea, glittering in its beams; the life inside the brain and heart, instead of that same life revealed in the human form divine. They could not, therefore, but prove (artistically speaking) failures, though failures worth more than some successes; gallant, if unauthorised and unavailing, efforts to annex alien dominions to the realms of poesy, and efforts from which many a victory might be confidently predicted for the champion when marching steadily beneath her banners.

To resume, however, our considerations of Browning's style, it is obviously a hindrance to dramatic success by being too marked and peculiar for dialogue. The illusion, which it is the aim of the drama to produce, is the result of a well-understood compromise between the real and the ideal; and it is an infringement of the terms of this compromise to require the spectator, who has already conceded that the foreign personages before him may talk English verse, to grant further that they may all use the same style of abrupt transition and startling metaphor. Imagine a Platonic dialogue by Carlyle. Would the speaker, now on this side, now on that, seem any other than the same man addressing us from various positions? Even so it requires all Browning's great dramatic talent to neutralise the effect of his style upon his plays.

Those plays are eight in number, besides two short dramatic sketches, each admirable in its way: *A Soul's Tragedy*, for the sly fun of the legate's address; "In a Balcony," for the tragic force compressed into its brief space.[1] Of the longer dramas, *Colombe's Birthday*[2] is a true and graceful picture of a young heart passing in one short day from girl to woman, from the vanities of the world's outward show to the knowledge and choice of deeper and better things. The speech of Valence, the youthful Duchess's humble but heroic defender, glorying in his apparently unrequited love for her, is a very noble one.

Pippa Passes, the most unique, is deservedly the best known and best loved of Browning's plays. What fancy could be more charming than this of the sweet child who spends her holiday in playfully imagining

---

[1] *A Soul's Tragedy* was published in 1846; *In a Balcony* appeared in *Men and Women*.
[2] Published in 1844.

herself by turns the four people she supposes the happiest in her town while she sings those pretty songs which now enhance, now alleviate, their real misery; who lies down at night, unconscious alike of the good she has effected and the evil she has escaped, commending herself to Him who, while she knew it not, had perfected His praise out of her mouth? Here, too, both the author's lyric and dramatic talent find expression, and mutually support one another. The scene between Ottima and Sebald is powerfully tragic; and the contrast between the hoarse accents of their guilt and the fresh pure voice outside is as over-powering to the spectator as to themselves. Still, are not the dark shades, both here and in a subsequent scene, laid on with a somewhat coarse hand? Are not painful features obtruded on us in this play more than was absolutely needful?

Of the plays which are regular tragedies, *A Blot in the Scutcheon* is incomparably the best. *King Victor and King Charles* follows it after a certain interval.[1] The four personages of this last play are well drawn and well contrasted; the wily father with the open-hearted son, the artful minister with the noble-minded wife. We have always admired the catastrophe; when the hoary schemer, baffled by his son's plain honesty, has recourse to truth at last, and, by its aid, attains the privi-lege of dying with the crown, the object of his life's desires, on his head. But the *Blot* is at once more thoroughly tragic in subject, and worked out with more completeness. It is a play in which not a stroke is wasted, in which every speech and every circumstance contributes to the final result. Though English in its colouring, though it depends for its catastrophe on the modern code of honour, yet this tragedy is Greek in the unexpectedness of the discovery on which it turns, and in the sense of an inevitable impending woe which pervades it. The contrast between the prosperous splendour of the doomed house and its hidden disgrace, between Mildred's seemingly innocent beauty and her real guilt, is most impressive. Nor can any two characters be more touching in their sadness than those of Mildred and her lover; the girl looking up, loving but hopeless, to the hand which she feels must strive in vain to lift her from the abyss into which it plunged her

---

[1] Published in 1843 and 1842, respectively.

first; the youth's frank nature subdued to unaccustomed deceit, and his brave arm unnerved by his consciousness of guilt. In all the domain of tragedy there are few more pathetic speeches than Lord Mertoun's, as he lies mortally wounded, to the man whom hoped to call his brother.[1]

. . .

The dramatic power exhibited in this tragedy and in *Pippa* is of a very high order. And in all Browning's plays we feel that we are watching real men and women, not mere impersonated virtues and vices; while his best characters are strong and individual conceptions, unfolded to us naturally by their own words and deeds. Where there is a failure, it is caused by the dramatist placing too many of his personages on his own level in point of intellect, so that their reasonings display a suspiciously uniform correctness, their wit a too equal brilliancy. For it cannot be denied that Browning sometimes pushes his speakers unceremoniously aside to take their place himself. King Victor's reflection on the loathsomeness of a crafty old age should have been made by some bystander. Colombe's courtiers reveal their selfishness with uncourtly frankness. Poor Young Mertoun speaks of his own youth more like an older man talking of a boy than a boy talking about himself. Ignorant Phene[2] turns a critic's eye on the students' self-conceit. And even dear little Pippa herself is rather high-flown and strained in her first salutation to the daylight, and her "Best people are not angels quite" is over-mature and unchildlike.

This disposition to lend the author's brain as well as his tongue to his characters appears oftener still in Browning's monologues; and oftenest of all in that series which form his latest work. In the "Experiences of Karshish,"[3] this fine description of the risen Lazarus's state—

---

[1] Hasell here quotes Mertoun's speech from act 3, scene 1 of *The Blot in the Scutcheon.*
[2] Character in *Pippa Passes.*
[3] "An Epistle Containing the Strange Medical Experience of Karshish, the Arab Physician" from *Men and Women.*

> The spiritual life around the earthly life,
> The law of that is known to him as this—
> His heart and brain move there, his feet stay here,

is not within the competence of the supposed writer. The young David *reasoning* out the hope of the future in "Saul," the aged St. John *arguing* against the unbelief of later times (and this, too, in a style so remote from that of his published sayings as to give full proof of their verbal inspiration), are anachronisms of thought which at once direct our gaze from the supposed to the real speaker.[1]

The three monologues most entirely free from such faults are two which belong to the Italy of the renaissance, and one which depicts the darker side of monastic life. Each of these portrays a different kind of wickedness at its height. Each is a legitimate, because a poetic, exercise of the tremendous power of satire possessed by its writer. And each gives proof of how disinterested he is in its employment; since he forbears all appeal to the ill-nature of his readers by directing its lightnings against evil-doers remote from them, instead (like the older satirists) of aiming them at the sinners at their doors. The "Soliloquy of the Spanish Cloister"[2] is alike too well known and too horrible for quotation. It is a picture (ghastly in its evident truth) of superstition which has survived religion; of a heart which has abandoned the love of kindred and friends, only to lose itself in a wilderness of petty spite, terminating in an abyss of diabolical hatred. The ordinary providential helps to goodness have been rejected; the ill-provided adventurer has sought to scale the high snow-peaks of saintliness,—he has missed his footing,—and the black chasm which yawns beneath has engulfed him.

Yet more terrible than the outspoken Spaniard is the smooth Italian prince in "My Last Duchess," with his polished reserve, his agreeable dilettanteism and his cold-blooded cruelty. The way in which that accomplished art-patron (while displaying her portrait to

---

[1] "Saul" is from *Men and Women*; St. John is the speaker in "A Death in the Desert" from *Dramatis Personae*.

[2] This poem and "My Last Duchess" are from *Dramatic Lyrics*.

his intended new father-in-law's envoys) calmly divulges the fact that he could criticise his first wife's deportment. as well as her picture, and that, liking the former worse than the latter, he gave commands for her death, chills the blood with horror.

Worse still, in one respect, than this model husband, is the model bishop whom we overhear ordering "his tomb in St. Praxed's Church."[1] We shudder as we listen to that mitred worldling invoking the saints, yet dying, as he lived, without God; viewing his disgraceful past without remorse, his terrific future without concern; nay, unable to discern that future at all, blocked out, as it is, to his contracted vision by the rose marble and lapis lazuli, the sculptured frieze and choice Latin inscription for which he wrestles with his sons' avarice, the ornaments of that magnificent tomb which is to enable him to triumph even in death over a hated rival. It has been remarked that we must go to Juvenal alike for an adequate parallel to this poem, or to the withering sarcasm of the first part of "Holy-Cross Day,"[2] in which a Jew (forced to listen to a sermon from even such a bishop) pours forth the indignation which, as he says

Overflows, when to even the odd,
Men I helped to their sins, help me to their God.

And if the great Roman's severity of satire is here equalled or outdone, who, after all, need feel surprised? For what heathen satirist had ever folly like this to scourge? The old world's decayed civilisation showed him man faithless only to his own moral sense and to the ideal that philosophy had set before him. A Christian's lapse into paganism involves the disregard of a greater Guide, and the rejection of a diviner prize. In the awful procession formed by all who have heard the gospel, if "those who are being saved" have joys unknown to the best heathen, in like manner must those who are perishing far surpass the worst of the elder day in their folly, their guilt, and their misery.

---

[1] "The Bishop Orders His Tomb at St. Praxed's Church" from *Dramatic Romances and Lyrics.*
[2] From *Men and Women.*

No wonder, then, that these monologues (masterpieces of their kind) appal us while we admire. Gentle readers (if sensation novels have left any) will wonder how their author bore the preliminary study: just as the beholder of certain pictured horrors marvels how the artist could ever endure to paint them. We have asked ourselves the same question before now, especially when reading (in the *Dramatis Personae*) the ghastly tale of the dying girl and her hoard of gold.[1] And we came to the conclusion that, just as critics mark with surprise in lofty and pure-minded Dante a strange attraction to the physically nauseous and repulsive, like that which dragged the old Greek (protesting the while aloud) to satiate his eyes on the loathsome corpse by the wayside; even such a power do similar spectacles in the moral world exercise over Browning. But we must not lead any one to suppose that his satire gleams phosphorescent over such dark spots alone. Let us thankfully remember how it plays over the Italian nobleman's love for his town with its drum and fife, and all its little stirs; how it casts a new though not a favourable light on the hero of Schiller's "Glove"; how it illuminates the silliness of the mediaevalist in "The Flight of the Duchess";[2] and how it once condescends to enact the part of the good-natured lightning of the electric machine, and sport, all fun and no danger, for the children's amusement in "The Piper of Hamelin."

Nor should we omit to notice the deep-rooted convictions, alike moral and religious, from which Browning's severer satire springs; or fail to acknowledge that if he sometimes disallows the claims of the beautiful, he is never unmindful of those of the truth. He approaches the subject of religion oftener than is the wont of modern poets, and he handles it more satisfactorily. Shakspeare, Spenser,[3] and Milton knew in Whom they believed, defective as is the last-named's creed. But Pope only proclaims the worship of an unknown God. And the

---

[1]   Reference to "Gold Hair: A Legend of Pornic."

[2]   Reference to "Up at a Villa—Down in the City" from *Men and Women*. Both Browning's and German Romantic poet Friedrich Schiller's (1759–1805) poems "The Glove" are based on an old French tale in which a lady tests her suitor by dropping a glove into a lion pit; "The Glove" and "The Flight of the Duchess" are from *Dramatic Romances and Lyrics*.

[3]   Edmund Spenser (1552–99), English poet whose best-known work is *The Faerie Queene* (1590–96).

bulk of modern poetry gives the reader too much this sort of impression of its writer's mind: "We are not sure that the Christian faith is true, nay, we shrewdly suspect it to be false; but those who held it in the olden time, and the unlettered who believe it now, form charming themes for verse. See that knight taking his sword from the altar, that pale votaress kneeling before the shrine; listen to those peasants' evening hymn, or to the preacher before whose accents the listening crowd sways like corn before the wind; we need not inquire whether their faith be true or false, but let us diligently improve, for artistic purposes, the beauty of its manifestations."

Not so, says the poet before us. This faith is true, and in its truth lies its beauty. Strong in this conviction, he does not fear to contemplate those who hold it in weakness, in ugliness, even in vulgarity; because to his eye there gleams through the earthen pitcher the Fire from heaven, behind the rough shell the Pearl of Price, beneath the field's thistles and nettles the hidden Treasure.

To him the most interesting of all historic periods is that when on wrecked humanity, after the long and stormy night, the Sun of Righteousness first arose. By force of contrast, the other epoch which seems most to have engaged his attention is that of the revival of Greek learning and art in Europe, with all the loss and gain which have resulted from it to the Christian Church. Most graphic is his picture of the faith and love of primitive times in the unargumentative portion of "A Death in the Desert." Yet more remarkable is the "Epistle of Karshish," the most fascinating to thoughtful minds of all Browning's poems. An Arab physician of the first century describes, in a letter to a learned friend, his interview with the risen Lazarus. He is inclined to consider the man's story a case of mistaken trance; he is anxious to display no other than a medical interest in the matter, and for that purpose intersperses his account with descriptions of natural curiosities. But when he comes to mention the patient's perfect health and unearthly peace, he betrays a stronger disposition to believe his tale than he likes to acknowledge to himself. He fights against the conviction; after saying that this Lazarus believes his awakener to be God and yet Man, he apologises for the very mention of so monstrous an assertion. Yet the affected indifference with which he turns aside to describe a curious plant which he has seen, cannot hide his emotion at the bare possibility of that assertion's truth. This tone of forced calmness is maintained to the very close of the letter, and then the writer, ceasing to struggle against the truth which is shaking his spirit to its centre, exclaims:

> The very God! think, Abib, dost thou think?
> So the All-Great were the All-Loving too—
> So through the thunder comes a human voice
> Saying, "O heart I made, a heart beats here!
> Face, my hands fashioned, see it in Myself,
> Thou hast no power, nor may'st conceive of Mine,
> But love I gave thee with Myself to love,
> And thou must love Me who have died for thee!"
> The madman saith He said so: it is strange.

This is a very fine poem. It is not merely that it gives us a sense of pleasurable surprise, by presenting to us from so strange and unexpected point of view the great, well-known history; nor only that it is true to human nature in its picture of man's ignorance taking great for small and small for great things: it derives its especial excellence as a work of art from the way in which it shows us the awful truth which it enshrines, first glimmering from afar, next lighting up one face fully amid the darkness, and then at last flooding the beholder with a sudden blaze of glory.

Two of Browning's noblest lyrics also are on religious subjects. His "Saul," though, as we have mentioned, an anachronism, is still a grand expression of faith in God; and the uprising of all nature at the close of the poem, to sympathise with the truth new-born in David's soul, is a beautiful conception. The latter part of "Holy-Cross Day " (strange end to its sarcastic beginning) is the appeal of men faithful to their portion of revealed truth, the persecuted Jews, against their Christian oppressors, who hold their larger heritage in unrighteousness. It is expressed with a force of pathetic indignation which is wonderfully striking. At the opposite pole to these poems we have that profoundly instructive caricature of the exalters of sovereignty at the expense of love among the divine attributes—Caliban gazing with mingled fear and hatred on his own image, magnified in his Setebos and projected into the clouds for him to worship.[1]

These five poems are among the best known, as they are among the finest of their author. On the other hand, his "Christmas Eve" and "Easter Day" have hardly yet received the attention they deserve.[2] The first-named is a strange mixture of the lightest sport with the gravest earnest. Its humour, now broad as in the account of the congregation of Zion Chapel, now subtle as in the German professor's lecture, is enhanced by the same far-fetched trisyllabic rhymes as those which, in the "Hamelin Piper" and "Flight of the Duchess," compete with the fun of *Ingoldsby Legends*.[3] But this humour, perilous from its close juxtaposition with sacred things, is still far from being irreverence; for there stands behind it so strong a conviction of the importance of religious truth, that the possessor of that conviction can affect to jest with the absurdities of that truth's adherents. From a beginning quaint and laughable to excess, the poem rises to a vast height of moral as well as poetic sublimity. It was written at Florence, and by the strong grasp it takes with one hand of the homeliest and commonest earthly matters, with the other of high and heavenly things, might please the great spirit who hovers over Arno, and who did the self-same thing (but on a vaster scale and with unapproachable dignity) in his own mighty poem.

The main idea of "Christmas Eve" is that a Christian cannot despise his meanest or most erring brethren; if he allows himself so to do, he ceases to be a Christian any longer. A subsidiary thought is that it is one thing, and that most dangerous, to

> Sit apart, holding no forms of creeds,
>   But contemplating all,

---

[1] "Caliban upon Setebos" from *Dramatis Personae*, based on the character from Shakespeare's *Tempest*.

[2] Published together in 1850.

[3] *The Ingoldsby Legends* were a collection of poems and narratives published in 1840, supposedly by "Thomas Ingoldsby" but actually by clergyman R.H. Barham (1788–1845).

and quite another (being indeed our bounden duty) to prove all things, and hold fast that which is good. Its supposed speaker seeks shelter one Christmas Eve from a storm among the congregation of an ugly meeting-house in the squalid outskirts of a town. There, after hearing the preacher deduce the doctrine of the most holy Trinity from the dream of Pharaoh's baker, he (to the pious horror of his neighbours) falls asleep, and dreams. In that vivid dream he believes himself to have rushed out, disgusted by the preacher's perversion of Scripture and by his hearers' spiritual pride, and to be walking alone on the hillside. There, reflecting on the scene which he has left, he considers how he first attained the knowledge of God in lonely meditation, and thinks he may leave others to seek Him in their narrow shrines, standing aloof from them himself to commune with Him in the great temple of His works. He is reproved by a vision. The storm has ceased: the moon breaks through the cloud-masses which walled her in, and a resplendent lunar rainbow spans the vault of heaven, the fit herald of the greater glory which approaches—the presence of Him who at this season first came down to visit His Church, revealed on the same errand to the astonished gazer. Then he remembers that promise to the assembled two or three which he had been disregarding,[1] and fears to have forfeited his own share in it by his contempt for his lowly brethren. He confesses his fault, and grasps the healing hem of the glorious vesture. Wrapped in its folds, he is borne over land and sea to Rome. Standing there at the door of St. Peter's, he thinks why it is that he is left outside while the Divine Presence goes within among the assembled worshippers. He sees how Infinite Mercy can bless the erring by means of the truth they still hold, without bidding its more enlightened children to receive the error because they love the truth. Just as his heart is rising to embrace these brethren whom his intellect cannot but disapprove, he is borne away once more. He now finds himself at a lecture-hall in Göttingen,[2] which he enters unbidden, hoping to gain for his mental powers what Rome denied them. The lecturer gravely propounds,

---

[1] See Matthew 18:20.
[2] Home of famous university; center of secular thought, as Rome is a center of religious thought.

> Whether 'twere best opine Christ was,
> Or never was at all, or whether
> He was, and was not, both together,

and the believer cannot listen to him long. Yet is he struck by the homage rendered to that Name even by those who have lost their hold of all that can explain and justify it. He tries to hope that these men's lips deny a truth that their hearts receive unknowingly, and is tempted, amid these charitable thoughts, to grow careless of creeds, to

> a mild indifferentism,
> Teaching that all our faiths (though duller
> His shine through a dull spirit's prism)
> Originally had one colour.

But as he so muses he finds to his terror that he has lost hold of the saving garment altogether. Nor does he recover it till he has acknowledged, repentant,

> Needs must there be one way, one chief,
> Best way of worship: let me strive
> To find it, and when found, contrive
> My fellows also take their share.

He feels that man, the conscript in life's battle, must "buy the truth and sell it not," alike for the sake of the dying around him and for his own. Thereupon he grasps the vesture once more—and awakes, on the seat as before beneath the preacher, who is just conducting his discourse; whence, consenting on reflection to drink even from the poorest chalice the water of life which refreshes the sick and around him, he (with a prayer for the like blessing on both Pope and professor) rises to join in the humble congregation's evening hymn.

So ends one of the boldest combinations of incongruous materials ever successfully essayed—a poem which makes the reader smile at first, and then thrills him with awe—the awe not taking away his power to smile, the surface absurdities not diminishing the awe. The two descriptions, of the rainbow at night and of St. Peter's with its myriads of breathless worshippers, would be pointed out as beauties in any poem; while there is a power in the divine apparition (suggested, not described) which unspeakably comforts and elevates the soul.

In the companion of "Christmas Eve," "Easter Day," a man tells of an awful vision which he saw on that blessed morning—the product, as he tries to think, of his disordered fancy stimulated by an aurora of intense brightness, but which he sometimes inclines to believe a dread reality; so that, while seeming a living man among the living, he may be, in truth, one already tried, sentenced, and undergoing his doom. He had been examining his own heart, he says, when he looked up, and, lo! the heavens were on fire, the great day had come, and he must stand before his Judge—his own conscience pronouncing his condemnation, because he had chosen the world for his portion instead of Him who made it. The light dies away; all is over, and he hears his sentence proclaimed. Different crimes find different penalties. His sin has been the preference of earthly to heavenly joys. His punishment is to live for ever among the seeming-real shows of the now vanished world, an exile from heaven and from God. At first he thinks this doom a light one; for is there not enough beauty on the earth to give the mind endless satisfaction? "Nay," replies the Judge, "not a mind that knows this fairness in its imperfection, for the guarantee of that perfect-beauty which it must now never hope to see." If nature thus fails the soul, can it then find no delight in art? "No, for earthly art only charmed as a prophecy of that ideal which shall never now be realised." Can the spirit find no satisfaction then in knowledge? "The goal of knowledge has been reached." Ah, then! cries the disappointed man, let me at least love. Love gave my soul its purest joys in the life that has now vanished. Let it cheat itself into still loving its shadowy companions, and believing they can love again. "Try it, if thou wilt," is the final answer; "but must it not remind thee of that Love which might have been thine own?—the love which created, redeemed, and would have filled thy soul for ever, but which thou couldst not credit (so great was it), and didst cast away?" Then the soul discerns its hopeless misery, and prays, in its despair, at least for power to forget its state:—

Let that old life seem mine—no more—
With limitation as before,
With darkness, hunger, toil, distress:
Be all the earth a wilderness!
Only let me go on, go on,
Still hoping ever and anon
To reach one eve the better land.

XXXII.
Then did the Form expand, expand—
I knew Him through the dread disguise,
As the whole God within his eyes
Embraced me.

XXXIII.
When I lived again,
The day was breaking,—the grey plain
I rose from, silvered thick with dew.
Was this a vision? False or true?

The speaker knows not which; his fears tell him it was true, and that his own is now a hopeless case; his hopes oftener persuade him that all was but a warning, and that to him too the promise of Easter morn may yet find fulfilment.

The leading thought of "Easter Day" is, therefore, that so familiar to an Augustine, to a Herbert,[1] that there is no object adequate to fill the boundless capacity of a human soul, save He who made it for Himself. And this thought is enforced with an argumentative skill, and adorned by a poetic beauty, which will repay close examination; while the great theme is here treated with more uniform seriousness than in "Christmas Eve."

Both poems claim the Christian's gratitude by their unwavering and fearless faith; both command the critic's admiration by the mastery they

---

[1] St. Augustine (354–430), early Christian theologian; George Herbert (1593–1633), English metaphysical poet.

exhibit over the most unyielding materials, by their wonderful flights of fancy, and by the lofty beauty which they attain in their best passages.

The versification of "Christmas Eve" and "Easter Day" exhibits on a larger scale the qualities of strength and ease, conspicuous in their writer's lyrics, both in those which present us with familiar measures, and in those where (the musician of the prophecy in *Pippa* turning poet instead of painter) new combinations of sound are essayed and startling variations effected. Here, as we have said already, the peculiarities of the author's genius sometimes interfere with the reader's pleasure; for some of his short poems are effectually precluded by their subject from *pleasing*, in whatsoever else they may succeed. Others, not professedly comic, burlesque their theme by out-of-the-way rhymes and odd expressions, instead of setting it off for our admiration. Others, again, though fine in conception, exhibit failures in execution—such as the offence against good taste of the disagreeable similes, the grass which grows "scant as hair in leprosy," and the earth which breaks into "boils" and "blotches" in "Childe Roland."[1] With such faults must be classed quite needless descents from a high poetic eminence to a level of plain, perhaps ludicrous, prose—descents proper and natural in drama, which is a miniature representation of human life as a whole, but improper and very disturbing in lyric poetry, which aims at depicting single exalted moments of life taken by themselves. An instance of our meaning, and at the same time an exemplification of the saying that in some cases "the half is more than the whole," is afforded by "The Grammarian's Funeral," a poem which we may assume to be well known to those for whom we write. In it low words like "dab" and "queasy," and the prosaic and minute catalogue of the various complaints, and somewhat trivial studies, of the deceased mar the grave solemnity of the burial chant. They ill accord with the peculiar and very fine musical effect of the bearers' song, as they carry their beloved teacher's corpse to his lofty burying-place, their measured tread keeping time to the accents of their manly grief, swelling upwards in the long iambic line, to fall back regularly in the short succeeding adonic.[2] But after allowing for all

---

[1] From *Men and Women*; "The Grammarian's Funeral" is also from this volume.
[2] Metrical combination of a dactyl followed by a spondee.

drawbacks, we still find much delightful both to mind and ear in Browning's lyrics, and see in them one of his surest passports to immortality. Already his *Paracelsus* is opened oftener for the sake of those it contains than for any other reason. Some of them give fuller expression to their writer's love of nature, and close observation of her various aspects, than the longer poems, where such gifts are of necessity subordinated to "the proper study of mankind." Two of the lyrics[1] give a livelier idea of the scenery of north and south Italy than many volumes of travels. Others set before us the Venice of the past with graphic power. Of these, "In a Gondola"[2] is one of the smoothest and sweetest of its author's compositions—the ever-varying music of the poem conveying to the mind an ineffaceable impression of that passionate love of Italian hearts which laughs at death and fate, as the verse flows on, now languishing like the floating barque, now steady as the rhythmic beat of the oars, which bear the doomed pair onward; now broken by the bursts of song which rise from them ever and anon in fitful snatches as they sweep to their destruction. The same sense of how love is able to compress an eternity into an hour is the inspiring thought of "The Last Ride Together,"[3] where the full strong tide of feeling rolls, in wave after wave alike, each curling over and breaking in anapaestic form. But to English hearts the short poem entitled "The Lost Mistress" will be always dearer than these, alike for its simplicity and its self-restraint.[4]

• • •

There are three very noble lyrics in the later volume entitled *Dramatis Personae*, though in two of them—"Rabbi Ben Ezra" and "Abt Vogler"—the loftiness of the thoughts sometimes outsoars adequate clearness of expression. The first-named is a fine hymn of the aged, with its solemn expansion of the metaphor of man the clay, and time the wheel on which the great Potter shapes him. The swift movement

---

[1] "By the Fireside" and "The Englishman in Italy." [Author's note.] From *Men and Women* and *Dramatic Romances*, respectively.

[2] From *Dramatic Lyrics*.

[3] From *Men and Women*.

[4] Hasell here quotes the poem, from *Dramatic Romances and Lyrics*, in full.

of "Abt Vogler" echoes well (until its prosaic termination) the extemporiser's thoughts, who surveys with pride "the palace of music" he rears, and, mourning its disappearance, turns for relief to the Sole-Changeless, in Whom all fair things for ever abide. This is the last stanza but two:—

> All we have willed or hoped or dreamed of good shall exist;
>> Not its semblance, but itself; no beauty, nor good, nor power
> Whose voice has gone forth, but each survives for the melodist
>> When eternity confirms the conception of an hour.
> The high that proved too high, the heroic for earth too hard,
>> The passion that left the ground to lose itself in the sky,
> Are music sent up to God by the lover and the bard;
>> Enough that He heard it once: we shall hear it by-and-by.

"Prospice," the best known of the three, is a stirring and soul-uplifting strain, neither hard to understand, nor anywhere deviating into prose. Its peculiar staccato effect is similar to that of "Saul," though not produced in the same manner. For readers (if any there be) to whom Browning's remarkable and successful use of such metres is not known, we extract a briefer specimen, one of the most striking of his minor poems; in which the short line composed of two anapests (following and rhyming to the three of the longer line) represents by its abruptness the misery of the successful duellist, which, becoming too great for words, breaks off shorter yet in the last line of all.[1]

· · ·

The music of this poem is not of the old familiar sort, like that of "The Lost Leader" or "The Cavalier Tunes" on the one hand, or that of "Johannes Agricola," or "Any Wife to Any Husband" on the other;[2] but it suits the subject well, and, when once learned, clings closely to

---

[1] Hasell here quotes the second half of "Before and After" from *Men and Women*.
[2] The first two poems are from *Dramatic Romances and Lyrics*; the latter two are from *Dramatic Lyrics* and *Men and Women*.

the memory. There is another peculiar metre which is a favourite with Browning; it is that of this commentary on the saying, "Heaven is for those who have failed on earth," which we here present to our readers; premising that, beautiful as it is, they will see in it three instances (though very mild ones) of the faults we have already mentioned. The slightly-confused metaphor of the second stanza's first line, the imperfect rhyme of the same stanza's last word, and the very unpoetical expression at the end of the first stanza's second line, are unsought examples, on a small scale, of their author's occasional defects of taste. But they are here eclipsed by the splendour of one of the most effective contrasts ever drawn, the same figure noble in the sunshine, but standing out far nobler in the storm; and they are overpowered by the grandeur of the sufferer's final appeal from man to God.[1]

• • •

The last of Browning's short poems about which we can say a word at present is the romance which derives its name from Edgar's song in *King Lear:* a weird story invented to match a Shakspearean title, rather than, like Tennyson's beautiful Marianas,[2] an expansion of a Shakspearean idea. We would not fear to take any one who had read "Childe Roland to the Dark Tower Came" through carefully, for judge of many of our preceding observations. For the less favourable would be justified on a cursory inspection of its thirty-four stanzas, by a sufficiency of prosaic and careless expressions, and by more than a sufficiency of grotesque and painful metaphors; while the very real poetry, which these blemish without destroying, would prove of itself justice of our praise. The poem at first sight appears the recollection of a nightmare: the river, "so petty, yet so spiteful," its suicidal willows and its hidden horrors, the traces of deadly combat on its bank and the grim wheel of torture on the road, furnishing all the scenery of a fevered dream. But from amidst these wild forms there emerges a striking image of life, of its many disappointments, its strange successes;

---

[1]   Hasell here quotes the full text of "The Patriot" from *Men and Women.*
[2]   Reference to Tennyson's poems "Mariana" and "Mariana in the South."

and the mysterious story becomes a parable, sad yet inspiriting, of youth's desire attained when youth's illusions are no more, too late for joy, but not too late for duty; of the highest of all the kinds of courage, that of the man who, bereft of his early comrades, finds the stroke which he was to have struck with them brought unexpectedly within the reach of his single arm; who knows that whether he conquers or falls it must now be alone, yet nerves himself to do a man's part and to strike the blow, alike without sympathy and without applause. The teller of the tale has vainly sought the Dark Tower for years; there to perform some great, but unexplained adventure. After all his hopes have died away, left last of the goodly band who first vowed the enterprise along with him, he learns amazed and half incredulous, from a "hoary cripple with malicious eye," the right track to the Tower. He follows it in the evening light, over a long and dreary plain, amid the discouragement of fearful or loathsome sights, and yet sadder and bitterer memories. As he pursues his way, his object seems to draw no nearer; nor can he recognise the goal of his life-long wandering at first, as it rises up before him in the failing daylight. Then follow the last four stanzas of the poem, as unsurpassed in their ever-gathering swell of rich, full sound, as in the excitement of their vivid imagery:—

XXXI.

What in the midst lay but the Tower itself?
　　The round squat turret, blind as the fool's heart,
　　Built of brown stone, without a counterpart
In the whole world. The tempest's mocking elf
Points to the shipman thus the unseen shelf
　　He strikes on, only when the timbers start.

XXXII.

Not see? because of night perhaps? Why, day
　　Came back again for that! before it left
　　The dying sunset kindled through a cleft:
The hills, like giants at a hunting, lay,
Chin upon hand, to see the game at bay,—
　　"Now stab and end the creature—to the heft!"

XXXIII.

Not hear? when noise was everywhere! it tolled
  Increasing like a bell. Names in my ears,
  Of all the lost adventurers my peers,—
How such a one was strong, and such was bold,
And such was fortunate, yet each of old
  Lost, lost! one moment knelled the woe of years.

XXXIV.

There they stood, ranged along the hillsides, met
  To view the last of me, a living frame
  For one more picture! in a sheet of flame
I saw them and I knew them all. And yet
Dauntless the slug-horn to my lips I set,
  And blew. "*Childe Roland to the Dark Tower came.*"[1]

SOURCE

St. Paul's Magazine 7 (December 1870).

SELECTED SECONDARY READING

Wingerd, Kathy L. *New Voices in Victorian Criticism: Five Unrecognized Contributors to Victorian Periodicals.* Diss. Kent State University, 1987. Ann Arbor: UMI, 1988.

---

[1] Hasell concludes with a promise to discuss Browning's epic *The Ring and the Book* (1868–69) in a subsequent article.

JANE AUSTEN
(AUGUST 1871)

Anne Thackeray Ritchie

The eldest daughter of novelist William Makepeace Thackeray, ANNE THACKERAY (1837–1919) was born in London. When she was about three, her mother had to be institutionalized for mental illness, and Anne and her sister lived for a number of years with their paternal grandmother in Paris. Educated at home in a lively literary milieu, Anne began to write early under her father's guidance, and she also served as his amanuensis. Although she published her first essay in 1860 in the *Cornhill Magazine*, which her father edited, her work was actually first accepted by the publisher as an anonymous submission. She continued to write both nonfiction and fiction regularly for the *Cornhill* throughout her career.

Her first novel, *The Story of Elizabeth*, was published in 1863, and she continued to write fiction over the next two decades. Her best known novels include *The Village on the Green* (1867), *Old Kensington* (1873), *Miss Angel* (1875), and *Mrs. Dymond* (1885). After her marriage to her cousin Richmond Thackeray Ritchie in 1877, Ritchie turned increasingly to nonfiction prose. She published a number of respected literary biographies, including studies of Madame de Sévigné (1881), memoirs of Tennyson, Ruskin, and the Brownings (1892), and also a collection of studies of English women writers, *A Book of Sibyls* (1883). In 1907, when her husband was knighted for his work in the India Office, she became Lady Ritchie, and she became a fellow of the Royal Society of Literature in 1911.

The following essay was prompted by the publication in 1871 of the first biography of Jane Austen, by Austen's nephew James Edward Austen Leigh. In the essay, which begins with long quoted passages from Austen's juvenilia, also available to the public for the first time (and omitted here), Ritchie reflects on the pleasure of reading Austen and on the differences in the style of prose and heroines between Austen's generation and her own, a theme she had sounded in 1865 in an article for *Cornhill*, "Heroines and Their Grandmothers." Evincing the interest in the connections between an author's life and work that she would develop in later literary biographies, Ritchie emphasizes those aspects of Austen's character that seem to be reflected in her most compelling heroines. Austen's undoubted achievement in the public sphere was "to write six books that were masterpieces in their way—to make a thousand people the happier for her industry," Ritchie concludes, but that achievement was fully matched by her achievement in the private sphere: "She lived long enough to be loved by all those of her home."

"I did not know that you were a studier of character," says Bingley to Elizabeth. "It must be an amusing study."

"Yes, but intricate characters are the most amusing. They have at least that advantage."

"The country," said Darcy, "can in general supply but few subjects for such a study. In a country neighbourhood you move in a very confined and unvarying society."

"But people themselves alter so much," Elizabeth answers, "that there is something new to be observed in them for ever."

"Yes, indeed," cried Mrs. Bennet, offended by Darcy's manner of mentioning a country neighbourhood, "I assure you that we have quite as much of *that* going on in the country as in town."

Everybody was surprised, and Darcy, after looking at her for a moment, turned silently away. Mrs. Bennet, who fancied she had gained a complete victory over him, continued her triumph.[1]

THESE PEOPLE BELONG TO A WHOLE world of familiar acquaintances, who are, notwithstanding their old-fashioned dresses and quaint expressions, more alive to us than a great many of the people among whom we live. We know so much more about them to begin with. Notwithstanding a certain reticence and self-control which seems to belong to their age, and with all their quaint dresses, and ceremonies, and manners, the ladies and gentlemen in *Pride and Prejudice* and its companion novels seem like living people out of our own acquaintance transported bodily into a bygone age, represented in the half-dozen books that contain Jane Austen's works. Dear books! bright, sparkling with wit and animation, in which the homely heroines charm, the dull hours fly, and the very bores are enchanting.

Could we but study our own bores as Miss Austen must have studied hers in her country village, what a delightful world this might be!—a world of Norris's economical great walkers, with dining-room tables to dispose of; of Lady Bertrams on sofas, with their placid "Do not act anything improper, my dears; Sir Thomas would not like it"; of Bennets, Goddards, Bates's; of Mr. Collins's; of Rushbrooks, with two-and-forty speeches apiece—a world of Mrs. Eltons....[2] Inimitable woman! she must be alive at this very moment, if we but knew where to find her, her basket on her arm, her nods and all-importance, with Maple Grove and the Sucklings in the background. She would be much excited were she aware how highly she is said to be esteemed by the present Chancellor of the Exchequer,[3] who is well acquainted with Maple Grove and Selina too. It might console her for Mr. Knightly's shabby marriage.

All these people nearly start out of the pages, so natural and unaffected are they, and yet they never lived except in the imagination of one lady with bright eyes, who sat down some seventy years ago to an

---

[1] Passage from chapter 9 of *Pride and Prejudice*.
[2] Characters from *Mansfield Park*, *Pride and Prejudice*, and *Emma*.
[3] Robert Lowe, later Viscount Sherbrooke (1811–92).

old mahogany desk in a quiet country parlour, and evoked them for us. Of her ways and belongings we read for the first time in this little memoir written half a century after her death. For the first time we seem to hear the echo of the voice, and to see the picture of the unknown friend who has charmed us so long—charmed away dull hours, created neighbours and companions for us in lonely places, and made harmless mirth. Some one said just now that many people seem to be so proud of seeing a joke at all, that they impress it upon you until you are perfectly wearied by it. Jane Austen was not of these; her humour flows gentle and spontaneous, it is no elaborate mechanism nor artificial fountain, but a bright natural little stream, rippling and trickling and sparkling every here and there in the sunshine. We should be surprised now-a-days to hear a young lady announce herself as a studier of character. From her quiet home in the country lane this one read to us a real page from the absorbing pathetic humorous book of human nature—a book that we can most of us understand when it is translated into plain English; but of which the quaint and illegible characters are often difficult to decipher for ourselves. It is a study which, with all respect for Darcy's opinion, must require something of country-like calm and concentration, and freedom of mind. It is difficult, for instance, for a too impulsive student not to attribute something of his own moods to his specimens instead of dispassionately contemplating them from a critical distance.

So we gladly welcome one more glimpse of an old friend come back with a last greeting. All those who love her name and her work, will prize this addition, small as it is, to their acquaintance with her. *Lady Susan* is a short story complete in itself. It is very unlike her later works in many respects, and scarcely equal to them, but the *Watsons* is a delightful fragment, which might belong to any of her other histories. It is bright with talk, and character, and animation. It is a story which is not *Emma*, and which is not *Pride and Prejudice*, but something, between the two, and which was written—so the Preface tells us—some years before either of them was published.[1]

---

[1] Here Ritchie summarizes the plot of *The Watsons*, with long extracts.

• • •

Emma Watson, and Tom Musgrave, and the whole town of D——
in Surrey belong, without a doubt, to the whole generation of Miss
Austen's heroes and heroines. One would scarcely recognize Lady
Susan's parentage if it were not so well authenticated. It must have
been written early in life, when the author was still experimentalizing
(as young authors, and alas! some old authors are apt to do) with
other people's characters and creations, making them talk, walk, and
rehearse the play, until the real actors come on the stage; and yet even
this unpublished novelette possesses one special merit which gives so
great a charm to Miss Austen's art. She has a gift of telling a story in
a way that has never been surpassed. She rules her places, times, characters, and marshals them with unerring precision. Her machinery is
simple but complete; events group themselves so vividly and naturally
in her mind that, in describing imaginary scenes, we seem not only
to read them, but to live them, to see the people coming and going:
the gentlemen courteous and in top-boots, the ladies demure and
piquant; we can almost hear them talking to one another. No retro-
spects; no abrupt flights, as in real life: days and events follow one
another. Last Tuesday does not suddenly start into existence all out
of place; nor does 1790 appear upon the scene when we are well on
in '21. Countries and continents do not fly from hero to hero, nor do
long and divergent adventures happen to unimportant members of
the company. With Miss Austen days, hours, minutes succeed each
other like clock-work, one central figure is always present on the
scene, that figure is always prepared for company. Miss Edwards' curl-
papers are almost the only approach to dishabille in her stories.
There are postchaises in readiness to convey the characters from Bath
or Lyme to Uppercross, to Fullerton, from Gracechurch Street to
Meryton, as their business takes them. Mr. Knightly rides from
Brunswick Square to Hartfield, by a road that Miss Austen herself
must have travelled in the curricle with her brother, driving to
London on a summer's day. It was a wet ride for Mr. Knightly, followed
by that never-to-be-forgotten afternoon in the shrubbery, when the
wind had changed into a softer quarter, the clouds were carried off,

and Emma, walking in the sunshine, with spirits freshened and thoughts a little relieved, and thinking of Mr. Knightly as sixteen miles off, meets him at the garden door; and everybody, I think, must be the happier, for the happiness that one half-hour gave to Emma and her "indifferent" lover.

There is a little extract from one of Miss Austen's letters to a niece, which shows that this was not chance, but careful workmanship.

"Your aunt C.," she says, "does not like desultory novels, and is rather fearful that yours will be too much so. That there will be too frequent a change from one set of people to another, and that circumstances will be sometimes introduced of apparent consequence, which will lead to nothing. It will not be so great an objection to me. I allow much more latitude than she does, and think nature and spirit cover many sins of a wandering story...."

But, though the sins of a wandering story may be covered, the virtues of a well-told one make themselves felt unconsciously, and without an effort. Some books and people are delightful, we can scarce tell why; they are not so clever as others that weary and fatigue us. It is a certain effort to read a story, however touching, that is disconnected and badly related. It is like an ill-drawn picture, of which the colouring is good. Jane Austen possessed both gifts of colour and of drawing. She could see human nature as it was; with near-sighted eyes, it is true; but having seen, she could combine her picture by her art, and colour it from life.

In this special gift for organization she seems almost unequalled. Her picnics are models for all future and past picnics; her combinations of feelings, of gentlemen and ladies, are so natural and life-like that reading to criticize is impossible to some of us—the scene carries us away, and we forget to look for the art by which it is recorded. How delightful the people who play at cards, and pay their addresses to one another, and sup, and discuss each other's affairs! Take Sir Walter Elliot compassionating the navy and Admiral Baldwin—"nine grey hairs of a side, nothing but a dab of powder at top—a wretched example of what a seafaring life can do, for men who are exposed to every climate and weather until they are not fit to be seen. It is a pity they are not knocked on the head at once, before they reach Admiral Baldwin's age...."

The charm of friends of pen-and-ink is their unchangeablencss. We go to them when we want them. We know where to seek them; we know what to expect from them. They are never preoccupied; they are always "at home"; they never turn their backs nor walk away as people do in real life, nor let their houses and leave the neighbourhood, and disappear for weeks together; they are never taken up with strange people, nor suddenly absorbed into some more genteel society, or by some nearer fancy. Even the most volatile among them is to be counted upon. We may have neglected them, and yet when we meet again there are the familiar old friends, and we seem to find our own old selves again in their company. For us time has, perhaps, passed away; feelings have swept by, leaving interests and recollections in their place, but at all ages there must be days that belong to our youth, hours that will recur so long as men forbear and women remember, and life itself exists. Perhaps the most fashionable marriage on the *tapis* no longer excites us very much, but the sentiment of an Emma or an Anne Elliot comes home to some of us as vividly as ever. It is something to have such old friends who are so young. An Emma, blooming, without a wrinkle or a grey hair, after twenty years' acquaintance (she was, in truth, sixty years old when we first knew her); an Elizabeth Bennet, sprightly and charming, at over eighty years of age....

In the *Roundabout Papers*[1] there is a passage about the pen and ink friends my father loved:—

> They used to call the good Sir Walter the "Wizard of the North." What if some writer should appear who can write so *enchantingly* that he shall be able to call into actual life the people whom he invents? What if Mignon, and Margaret, and Goetz von Berlichingen are alive now (though I don't say they are visible), and Dugald Dalgetty and Ivanhoe were to step in at that open window by the little garden yonder? Suppose Uncas and our noble old Leather Stocking were to glide in silent? Suppose Athos, Porthos, and Aramis should enter, with a noiseless swagger, curling

---

[1]   Essays (1860–63) by William Thackeray.

their moustaches? And dearest Amelia Booth, on Uncle Toby's arm; and Tittlebat Titmouse with his hair dyed green; and all the Crummles company of comedians, with the Gil Blas troop; and Sir Roger de Coverley; and the greatest of all crazy gentlemen, the Knight of La Mancha, with his blessed squire?[1] I say to you, I look rather wistfully towards the window, musing upon these people. Were any of them to enter, I think I should not be very much frightened. Dear old friends, what pleasant hours I have had with them! We do not see each other very often, but when we do we are ever happy to meet ....

Are not such friends as these, and others unnamed here, but who will come unannounced, to join the goodly company, creations that, like some people, do actually make part of our existence, and make us the better for theirs? To express some vague feelings is to stamp them. Have we any one of us a friend in a Knight of La Mancha, a Colonel Newcome,[2] a Sir Roger de Coverley? They live for us even though they may have never lived. They are, and do actually make part of our lives, one of the best and noblest parts. To love them is like a direct communication with the great and generous minds that conceived them.

It is difficult, reading the novels of succeeding generations, to determine how much each book reflects of the time in which it was written; how much of its character depends upon the mind and the mood of the writer. The greatest minds, the most original, have the least stamp of the age, the most of that dominant natural reality which belongs to all great minds. We know how a landscape changes as the day goes on, and how the scene brightens and gains in beauty as the shadows begin to lengthen. The clearest eyes must see by the light of their own hour. Jane Austen's hour must have been a midday hour: bright, unsuggestive, with objects standing clear, without relief or shadow. She did not write of herself, but of the manners of her age. This age is essentially

---

[1] Characters from fiction by Scott; James Fenimore Cooper (1789–1850); Alexandre Dumas (1802–70); Laurence Sterne (1713–68); Samuel Warren (1807–77); Dickens; Richard Steele (1672–1729) and Joseph Addison (1672–1719); and Miguel de Cervantes (1547–1616).
[2] Character in William Thackeray's *The Newcomes* (1853–55).

an age of men and women of strained emotion, little remains of starch, or powder, or courtly reserve. What we have lost in calm, in happiness, in tranquillity, we have gained in intensity. Our danger is now, not of expressing and feeling too little, but of expressing more than we feel.

There is certainly a wide difference between Miss Austen's ladies and, let us say, a Maggie Tulliver.[1] One would be curious to know whether, between the human beings who read Jane Austen's books to-day and those who read them fifty years ago, there is as great a contrast. Have events happened within the last fifty years, feelings changed so rapidly as to turn many of the butterflies back into cocoons again, wrapping them round and round with self-involved, self-inflicted experiences, from which, perhaps, some higher form of moth might start in time, if such a metempsychosis were possible in natural history.

The living writers of to-day lead us into distant realms and worlds undreamt of in the placid and easily contented gigot age.[2] People are gifted with wider experiences, with aspirations and emotions that were never more sincerely spoken than they are now; but, for actual study of character, there seems but little taste. A phase, a mood of mind, a sympathy, is what we look for, and what we chiefly find among the present novelists. There are leaders of the school to whom this criticism does not apply; and yet it would be no disrespect to George Eliot to say that we know more of her own generous sympathies and of the inner minds of her creations than of their outward expression, or to Mrs. Oliphant to remember more vividly what Zaidee[3] and her sisters have felt than what they said. One reason may be, perhaps, that characters in novels are certainly more intimate with us and on less ceremonious terms than in Miss Austen's days. Her heroines have a stamp of their own. They have a certain gentle self-respect and humour and hardness of heart in which modern heroines are a little wanting. Whatever happens they can for the most part speak of gaily and without bitterness. Love with them does not mean a passion so much as an interest—deep, silent; not quite incompatible with a

---

[1] Heroine in George Eliot's *The Mill on the Floss* (1860).

[2] Reference to gigot or "leg-of-mutton" sleeves, popular in the early part of the nineteenth century.

[3] Character in novel by Margaret Oliphant (1828–97).

secondary flirtation. Marianne Dashwood's tears are evidently meant to be dried. Jane Bennet smiles, sighs, and makes excuses for Bingley's neglect. Emma passes one disagreeable morning making up her mind to the unnatural alliance between Mr. Knightly and Harriet Smith. It was the spirit of the age, and, perhaps, one not to be unenvied. It was not that Jane Austen herself was incapable of understanding a deeper feeling. In the last written page of her last written book, there is an expression of the deepest and truest experience. Anne Elliot's talk with Captain Benfield is the touching utterance of a good woman's feelings. They are speaking of men and of women's affections.[1] "You are always labouring and toiling," she says, "exposed to every risk and hardship. Your home, country, friends, all quitted; neither time nor life to be called your own. It would be too hard, indeed, (with a faltering voice,) if a woman's feelings were to be added to all this."

Farther on she says, eagerly:

> "I hope I do justice to all that is felt by you, and by those who resemble you. God forbid that I should undervalue the warm and faithful feelings of any of my fellow-creatures. I should deserve utter contempt if I dared to suppose that true attachment and constancy were known only by woman. No! I believe you capable of everything good and great in your married lives. I believe you equal to every important exertion, and to every domestic forbearance so long as—if I may be allowed the expression—so long as you have an object; I mean while the woman you love lives and lives for you. *All the privilege I claim for my own sex (it is not a very enviable one, you need not covet it) is that of loving longest when existence or when hope is gone.*"
>
> She could not immediately have uttered another sentence— her heart was too full, her breath too much oppressed.

Dear Anne Elliot!—sweet, impulsive, womanly, tender-hearted— one can almost hear her voice, pleading the cause of all true women.

---

[1] The following passages actually occur in chapter 23 of *Persuasion*, in which Anne Elliott and Captain Harville are talking about Captain Benwick. The italics are Ritchie's.

In those days when, perhaps, people's nerves were stronger than they are now, sentiment may have existed in a less degree, or have been more ruled by judgment, it may have been calmer and more matter-of-fact; and yet Jane Austen, at the very end of her life, wrote thus. Her words seem to ring in our ears after they have been spoken. Anne Elliot must have been Jane Austen herself, speaking for the last time. There is something so true, so womanly about her, that it is impossible not to love her. She is the bright-eyed heroine of the earlier novels, matured, chastened, cultivated, to whom fidelity has brought only greater depth and sweetness instead of bitterness and pain.

What a difficult thing it would be to sit down and try to enumerate the different influences by which our lives have been affected—influences of other lives, of art, of nature, of place and circumstance,—of beautiful sights passing before our eyes, or painful ones: seasons following in their course—hills rising on our horizons—scenes of ruin and desolation—crowded thoroughfares—sounds in our ears, jarring or harmonious—the voices of friends, calling, warning, encouraging—of preachers preaching—of people in the street below, complaining, and asking our pity. What long processions of human beings are passing before us! What trains of thought go sweeping through our brains! Man seems a strange and ill-kept record of many and bewildering experiences. Looking at oneself—not as oneself, but as an abstract human being—one is lost in wonder at the vast complexities which have been brought to bear upon it; lost in wonder, and in disappointment perhaps, at the discordant result of so great a harmony. Only we know that the whole diapason is beyond our grasp: one man cannot hear the note of the grasshoppers, another is deaf when the cannon sounds. Waiting among these many echoes and mysteries of every kind, and light and darkness, and life and death, we seize a note or two of the great symphony, and try to sing; and because these notes happen to jar, we think all is discordant hopelessness. Then come pressing onward in the crowd of life, voices with some of the notes that are wanting to our own part—voices tuned to the same key as our own, or to an accordant one; making harmony for us as they pass us by. Perhaps this is in life the happiest of all experience, and to few of us there exists any more complete ideal.

And so now and then in our lives, when we learn to love a sweet and noble character, we all feel happier and better for the goodness and charity which is not ours, and yet which seems to belong to us while we are near it. Just as some people and states of mind affect us uncomfortably, so we seem to be true to ourselves with a truthful person, generous-minded with a generous nature; life seems less disappointing and self-seeking when we think of the just and sweet and unselfish spirits, moving untroubled among dinning and distracting influence. These are our friends in the best and noblest sense. We are the happier for their existence,—it is so much gain to us. They may have lived at some distant time, we may never have met face to face, or we may have known them and been blessed by their love; but their light shines from afar, their life is for us and with us in its generous example; their song is for our ears, and we hear it and love it still, though the singer may be lying dead.

Some women should raise and ennoble all those who follow after—true, gentle and strong and tender, whom "to love is a liberal education," whom to have known is a blessing in our past. Is not the cry of the children still ringing in our ears as when the poet first uttered her noble song?[1]

This little book, which has come out within the last few months, tells with a touching directness and simplicity the story of a good and gifted woman, whose name has long been a household word among us, but of whose history nothing was known until this little volume appeared. It only tells the story of a country lady, of days following days tranquilly, of common events; and yet the history is deeply interesting to those who loved the writer of whom it is written; and as we turn from the story of Jane Austen's life to her books again, we feel more than ever that she, too, was one of these true friends who belong to us inalienably—simple, wise, contented, living in others, one of those whom we seem to have a right to love. Such people belong to all human-kind by the very right of their wide and generous sympathies, of their gentle wisdom and loveableness. Jane Austen's life, as

---

[1]   Reference to Elizabeth Barrett Browning's "The Cry of the Children" (1850), written in response to a parliamentary report on child labor.

it is told by her nephew, is very touching, sweet, and peaceful. It is a country landscape, where the cattle are grazing, the boughs of the great elm-tree rocking in the wind: sometimes, as we read, they come falling with a crash into the sweep; birds are flying about the old house, homely in its simple rule. The rafters cross the whitewashed ceilings, the beams project into the room below. We can see it all: the parlour with the horsehair sofa, the scant, quaint furniture, the old-fashioned garden outside, with its flowers and vegetables combined, and along the south side of the garden the green terrace sloping away.

One may read the account of Catherine Morland's home with new interest, from the hint which is given of its likeness to the old house at Steventon, where dwelt the unknown friend whose voice we seem to hear at last, and whose face we seem to recognize, her bright eyes and brown curly hair, her quick and graceful figure. One can picture the children who are playing at the door of the old parsonage, and calling for Aunt Jane. One can imagine her pretty ways with them, her sympathy for the active, their games and imaginations. There is Cassandra. She is older than her sister, more critical, more beautiful, more reserved. There is the mother of the family, with her keen wit and clear mind; the handsome father—"the handsome proctor," as he was called; the five brothers, and the cousins driving up the lane. Tranquil summer passes by, the winter days go by; the young lady still sits writing at the old mahogany desk, and smiling, perhaps, at her own fancies, and hiding them away with her papers at the sound of coming steps. Now, the modest papers, printed and reprinted, lie in every hand, the fancies disport themselves at their will in the wisest brains and the most foolish.

It must have been at Steventon—Jane Austen's earliest home—that Mr. Collins first made his appearance (Lady Catherine not objecting, as we know, to his occasional absence on a Sunday, provided another clergyman was engaged to do the duty of the day), and here, conversing with Miss Jane, that he must have made many of his profoundest observations upon human nature; remarking, among other things, that resignation is never so perfect as when the blessing denied begins to lose somewhat of its value in our estimation, and propounding his celebrated theory about the usual practice of elegant females. It must have been here, too, that poor Mrs. Bennet declared, with some justice, that once estates are entailed, one can never tell how they will go; that Mrs. Allen's sprigged muslin and John Thorpe's rodomontades were woven; that his gig was built, "curricle-hung lamps, seat, trunk, sword-case, splashboard, silver moulding, all, you see, complete. The ironwork as good as new, or better. He asked fifty guineas ... I closed with him directly, threw down the money, and the carriage was mine."

"And I am sure," said Catherine, "I know so little of such things, that I cannot judge whether it was cheap or dear."

"Neither the one nor the other," says John Thorpe.

Mrs. Palmer was also born at Steventon—the good-humoured lady in *Sense and Sensibility*, who thinks it so ridiculous that her husband never hears her when she speaks to him. We are told that Marianne and Ellinor have been supposed to represent Cassandra and Jane Austen; but Mr. Austen Leigh says that he can trace no resemblance. Jane Austen is not twenty when this book is written, and only twenty-one when *Pride and Prejudice* is first devised. There is a pretty description of the sisters' devotion to one another; of the family party; of the old place where Jane Austen spends the first five-and-twenty years of her life—Steventon, where there are hedgerows winding, with green shady footpaths within the copse; where the earliest primroses and hyacinths are found. There is the wood-walk, with its rustic seats, leading to the meadows; the church-walk leading to the church, "which is far from the hum of the village, and within sight of no habitation, except a glimpse of the grey manor-house through its circling screen of sycamores. Sweet violets, both purple and white, grow in abundance beneath its south wall. Large elms protrude their rough branches, old hawthorns shed their blossoms over the graves, and the hollow yew-tree must be at least coeval with the church."

Cousins, as I have said, come on the scene—a young, widowed Comtesse de Feuillade, flying from the Revolution to her uncle's home. She is described as a clever and accomplished woman, interested in her young cousins, teaching them French (both Jane and Cassandra knew French), helping in their various schemes, in their theatricals in the barn. She eventually marries her cousin, Henry Austen. The simple family annals are not without their romance; but there is a cruel one for poor Cassandra, whose lover dies abroad, and his death saddens the whole family-party. Jane, too, "receives the addresses" (do such things as addresses exist nowadays?) "of a gentleman possessed of good character and fortune, and of everything, in short, except the subtle power of touching her heart." One cannot help wondering whether this was a Henry Crawford or an Elton or a Mr. Elliot, or had Jane already seen the person that even Cassandra thought good enough for her sister?

Here, too, is another sorrowful story. The sisters' fate (there is a sad coincidence and similarity in it) was to be undivided; their life, their experience was the same. Some one without a name takes leave of Jane one day, promising to come back. He never comes back: they hear of his death. The story seems even sadder than Cassandra's in its silence and uncertainty, for silence and uncertainty are death in life to some people.... And yet to Jane Austen there can have been no death in life. Her sunny temper and loving heart, even though saddened, must have reflected all the love and all the sunshine in her way.

There is little trace of such a story in Jane Austen's books—not one morbid word is to be found, not one vain regret. Hers was not a nature to fall crushed by the overthrow of one phase of her manifold life. Hers seems to have been a natural genius for life, if I may so speak; too vivid and genuinely unselfish to fail her in her need. She could gather every flower, every brightness along her road. Good spirit, content, all the interests of a happy and observant nature were hers. Her gentle humour and wit and interest cannot have failed.

It is impossible to calculate the difference of the grasp by which one or another human being realizes existence and the things relating to it, nor how much more vivid life seems to some than to others. Jane Austen, while her life lasted, realized it, and made the best use of the gifts that were hers. Yet, when her life was ending, then it was given to her to realize the change that was at hand; and as willingly as she had lived, she died. Some people seem scarcely to rise up to their own work, to their own ideal. Jane Austen's life, as it is told by her nephew, is beyond her work, which only contained one phase of that sweet and wise nature—the creative, observant, outward phase. For her home, for her sister, for her friends, she kept the depth and tenderness of her bright and gentle sympathy. She is described as busy with her neat and clever fingers sewing for the poor, working fanciful keepsakes for her friends. There is the cup and ball that she never failed to catch; the spillikens lie in an even ring where she has thrown them; there are her letters, straightly and neatly folded, and fitting smoothly in their creases. There is something sweet, orderly, and consistent in her character and all her tastes—in her fondness for Crabbe and Cowper,[1] in her little joke that she ought to be a Mrs. Crabbe. She sings of an evening old ballads to old-fashioned tunes with a low sweet voice.

Further on we have a glimpse of Jane and her sister in their mobcaps, young still, but dressed soberly beyond their years. One can imagine "Aunt Jane," with her brother's children round her knee, telling her delightful stories or listening to theirs, with never-failing sympathy. One can fancy Cassandra, who does not like desultory novels, more prudent and more reserved, and somewhat less of a playfellow, looking down upon the group with elder sister's eyes.[2]

. . .

A certain Mrs. Stent comes into one of these letters "ejaculating some wonder about the cocks and hens." Mrs. Stent seems to have tried their patience, and will be known henceforward as having bored Jane Austen.

They leave Steventon when Jane is about twenty-five years of age and go to Bath, from whence a couple of pleasant letters are given us. Jane is writing to her sister. She has visited Miss A., who, like all other young ladies, is considerably genteeler than her parents. She is heartily glad that Cassandra speaks so comfortably of her health and looks: could travelling fifty miles produce such an immediate change? "You were looking poorly when you were here, and everybody seemed sensible of it." Is there any charm in a hack postchaise? But if there were, Mrs. Craven's carriage might have undone it all. Here Mrs. Stent appears again. "Poor Mrs. Stent, it has been her lot to be always in the way; but we must be merciful, for perhaps in time we may come to be

---

[1] George Crabbe (1754–1832) and William Cowper (1731–1800), English poets.
[2] Ritchie here quotes extracts from an 1800 letter from Austen.

Mrs. Stents ourselves, unequal to anything and unwelcome to every-body. Elsewhere she writes, upon Mrs. ——'s mentioning that she had sent the *Rejected Addresses*[1] to Mr. H., "I began talking to her a little about them, and expressed my hope of their having amused her. Her answer was, 'Oh dear, yes, very much; very droll indeed; the opening of the house and the striking up of the fiddles!' What she meant, poor woman, who shall say?"

But there is no malice in Jane Austen. Hers is the charity of all clear minds, it is only the muddled who are intolerant. All who love Emma and Mr. Knightly must remember the touching little scene in which he reproves her for her thoughtless impatience of poor Miss Bates's volubility.[2]

. . .

Mr. Knightly's little sermon, in its old-fashioned English, is as appli-cable now as it was when it was spoken.... How alive they all are; with what grace and spirit they play their parts—all these people who were modestly put away for so many years.

Mr. Austen died at Bath, and his family removed to Southampton. In 1811, Mrs. Austen, her daughters, and her niece, settled finally at Chawton, a house belonging to Jane's brother, Mr. Knight (he is adopted by an uncle, whose name he takes), and from Chawton all her literary work was given to the world. *Sense and Sensibility, Pride and Prejudice*, were already written; but in the next five years, from thirty-five to forty, she set to work seriously, and wrote *Mansfield Park, Emma*, and *Persuasion*. Any one who has written a book will know what an amount of labour this represents.... One can picture to oneself the little family scene which Jane describes to Cassandra. *Pride and Prejudice* just come down in a parcel from town; the unsuspicious Miss B. to dinner; and Jane and her mother setting to in the evening and reading aloud half the first volume of a new novel sent down by the

---

[1]   Book of parodies of contemporary poets (1812) by James (1718–1839) and Horatio (1779–1849) Smith.

[2]   Ritchie here quotes passage from volume 3, chapter 7 of *Emma*.

brother. Unsuspicious Miss B. is delighted. Jane complains of her mother's too rapid way of getting on; "though she perfectly understands the characters herself, she cannot speak as they ought. Upon the whole, however," she says, "I am quite vain enough and well-satisfied enough." This is her own criticism of *Pride and Prejudice*.—"The work is rather too light, and bright, and sparkling. It wants shade. It wants to be stretched out here and there with a long chapter of sense, if it could be had; if not, of solemn specious nonsense about something unconnected with the story—an essay on writing, a critique on Walter Scott or the *History of Bonaparte*."

And so Jane Austen lives quietly working at her labour of love, interested in her "own darling children's" success; "the light of the home," one of the real living children says afterwards, speaking in the days when she was no longer there. She goes to London once or twice. Once she lives for some months in Hans Place, nursing a brother through an illness. Here it was that she received some little compliments and messages from the Prince Regent, and some valuable suggestions from Mr. Clarke, his librarian, respecting a very remarkable clergyman. He is anxious that she should delineate one who "should pass his time between the metropolis and the country, something like Beattie's minstrel,[1] entirely engaged in literature, and no man's enemy but his own." Failing to impress this character upon the authoress, he makes a different suggestion, and proposes that she should write a romance illustrative of the august house of Coburg. "It would be interesting," he says, "and very properly dedicated to Prince Leopold."

To which Miss Austen replies: "I could no more write a romance than an epic poem. I could not seriously sit down to write a romance under any other motive than to save my life; and if it were indispensable for me to keep it up, and never relax into laughing at myself or other people, I am sure I should be hung before the first chapter."

There is a delightful collection of friends' suggestions which she has put together, but which is too long to be quoted here. She calls it, "Plan of a Novel, as suggested by various Friends."

---

[1] James Beattie (1735–1803), Scottish philosopher and poet; *The Minstrel* was published 1771–74.

All this time, while her fame is slowly growing, life passes in the same way in the old cottage at Chawton. Aunt Jane, with her young face and her mob-cap, makes play-houses for the children, helps them to dress up, invents imaginary conversations for them, supposing that they are all grown up the day after a ball. One can imagine how delightful a game that must have seemed to the little girls. She built her nest, did this good woman, happily weaving it out of shreds, and ends, and scraps of daily duty, patiently put together; and it was from this nest that she sang the song, bright and brilliant, with quaint thrills and unexpected cadences, that reaches us even here through fifty years. The lesson her life seems to teach us is this: don't let us despise our nests—life is as much made of minutes as of years; let us complete the daily duties; let us patiently gather the twigs and the little scraps of moss, of dried grass together; and see the result!—a whole, completed and coherent, beautiful even without the song.

We come too soon to the story of her death. And yet did it come too soon? A sweet life is not the sweeter for being long. Jane Austen lived years enough to fulfil her mission. It was an unconscious one; and unconscious teachers are the highest. They teach by their lives, even more than by their words, and their lives need not reach three-score years and ten to be complete. She lived long enough to write six books that were masterpieces in their way—to make a thousand people the happier for her industry. She lived long enough to be loved by all those of her home.

One cannot read the story of her latter days without emotion; of her patience, her sweetness, and gratitude. There is family trouble, we are not told of what nature. She falls ill.

Her nieces find her in her dressing gown, like an invalid, in an arm-chair in her bed-room; but she gets up and greets them, and, pointing to seats which had been arranged for them by the fire, says: "There is a chair for the married lady, and a little stool for you, Caroline." But she is too weak to talk, and Cassandra takes them away.

At last they persuade her to go to Winchester, to a well-known doctor there.

"It distressed me," she says, in one of her last, dying letters, "to see Uncle Henry."

"And William Knight, who kindly attended us, riding in the rain almost the whole way. We expect a visit from them to-morrow, and hope they will stay the night; and on Thursday, which is a confirmation and a holiday, we hope to get Charles out to breakfast. We have had but one visit from him, poor fellow, as he is in the sick room.... God bless you, dear E., if ever you are ill, may you be as tenderly nursed as I have been ...."

But nursing does not cure her, nor can the doctor save her to them all, and she sinks from day to day. To the end she is full of concern for others.

"As for my dearest sister, my tender, watchful, indefatigable nurse has not been made ill by her exertions," she writes. "As to what I owe her, and the anxious affection of all my beloved family on this occasion, I can only cry over it, and pray God to bless them more and more."

One can hardly read this last sentence with dry eyes. It is her parting blessing and farewell to those she had blessed all her life by her presence and her love. Thank God that love is beyond death; and its benediction, still with us, not only spoken in words, but by the signs and the love of a lifetime, that does not end for us as long as we ourselves exist.

They asked her when she was near her end if there was anything she wanted.

"Nothing but death," she said. Those were her last words. She died on the 18th of July, 1817, and was buried in Winchester Cathedral, where she lies not unremembered.

SOURCE

Cornhill Magazine 24 (August 1871).

SELECTED SECONDARY READING

Gérin, Winifred. *Anne Thackeray Ritchie: A Biography.* Oxford: Oxford University Press, 1981.

STYLE AND MISS AUSTEN
(DECEMBER 1884)

Mary Augusta (Mrs. Humphry) Ward

MARY ARNOLD (1851–1920) was born in Hobart Town, Tasmania, to a then-school inspector and eventual history lecturer at Oxford and his wife. On the paternal side, Mary's family was the picture of propriety: she was the granddaughter of the famous headmaster of Rugby and the niece of poet and critic Matthew Arnold. On the maternal side, things were much more complicated, as her mother's family, the Kemps and Sorells, had a long history of mésalliances. After her father reconverted (for a time) from Roman Catholicism to Anglicanism, the family moved to Oxford, where Mary was able to improve on her boarding-school education by reading in the Bodleian Library, eventually becoming an expert in Spanish literature and history. She began publishing literary criticism in 1871, with an article on El Cid in *Macmillan's Magazine*.

In 1872 she married Thomas Humphry Ward, a tutor at Brasenose College, and from this point on published almost exclusively under the name "Mrs. Humphry Ward." Her three children were born over the next decade, during which time she became a founding member of an organization aimed at opening Oxford to women students and also became the first secretary of Somerville College, activities that her later anti-suffrage efforts would somewhat obscure. After the family moved to London, she and her husband both began writing for the *Times*, and Ward also wrote for a number of other periodicals, including the *Saturday Review* and the *Pall Mall*

Gazette. In 1888, her second novel, *Robert Elsmere*, secured her reputation. In later life she continued as an active novelist but also channelled her energies into anti-suffrage work, serving as the editor of the *Anti-Suffrage Review* from 1908, into support for the war effort during World War I, and into philanthropic work, especially on behalf of children. She received a CBE in 1919 and an honorary degree from Edinburgh University shortly before her death in 1920.

The following review essay was inspired by the publication in 1884 of the first edition of Jane Austen's letters, edited by her great-nephew Edward Knatchbull-Hugessen, Lord Brabourne. The first biography of Austen, by her nephew James Edward Austen Leigh, had appeared in 1871. Ward takes the opportunity of reviewing the new book to reflect not only on the state of contemporary biography but also to comment on Austen's characteristic style and subject matter. While Ward finds the letters of little interest, literarily or otherwise, she uses them as a vehicle for proactively defending Austen against charges that because she was not a political writer, she was not an important writer. Austen may seem to have lived through "the stormiest period of modern European history without being touched by any of the large fears and hopes, or even strongly impressed by any of the dramatic characters or careers in which it abounded," Ward acknowledges, but that was because her gift was one of condensation, not of expansion. Austen needs to be appreciated as an artist whose genius lay in her ability to seize "at once upon the most effective image or detail and realise at a glance how it will strike a reader."

BY THIS PUBLICATION OF a newly-discovered collection of Miss Austen's letters, Miss Austen's great-nephew has done her as ill a turn as it is in anybody's power to do to the author of *Pride and Prejudice*. The name of one of the nimblest, quickest, and least tiresome of mortals has been perforce associated with two volumes of half-edited matter, with letters of which she herself would never have authorised the publication, with family pedigrees of which she would have been the first person to feel the boredom and the incongruity, and literary criticisms of a kind to have set that keen wit of hers moving in its most trenchant fashion. When Lord Brabourne came into possession of those bundles of his great-aunt's letters which Mr. Austen Leigh, her first biographer, believed to have been lost, the temptation to make use of them in some way was no doubt irresistible. The virtue of literary reticence is fast becoming extinct; we have almost indeed forgotten that it is a virtue at all. To be able to persuade oneself that the world could possibly do without information which it is in one's power to give it, implies now a strength of mind so abnormal and so rare, that a modern instance of it is scarcely to be found. And the old distinction between public and private life, which still held firmly in the days when Jane Austen and Miss Ferrier[1] refused to give their names to any production of their pens—the old personal reserve, which still forms part of the continental idea of the typical Englishman—have been so rapidly swept away during the last generation, that it would be absurd nowadays to expect of any inheritor of a great writer's correspondence that he should form the same sort of strict judgment on its claims to publication which would have been natural and possible a hundred or even fifty years ago. Taste is laxer, the public easier to please, and book-making more profitable. A modern editor of unpublished documents, by the nature of things, approaches his task in a more prodigal frame of mind. The whole mood of the present day is one of greater indulgence towards what may be called the personal side of letters than used to be the case with our grandfathers; and the seven volumes which Mr. Froude has devoted to the Carlyles,[2] and which, under all the circumstances, would have been a scandal in the days of Southey and Scott, will perhaps be accepted later on as marking the highest point of a

---

[1] Susan Edmonstone Ferrier (1782–1854), Scottish novelist; Ward later discusses her novels *Marriage* (1818) and *Inheritance* (1824).

[2] Historian J.A. Froude (1818–94) published several biographical works on his close friends, Thomas and Jane Welsh Carlyle, from 1882 on.

tendency which has been long gathering strength and may not improbably soon have to fight against reaction.

Lord Brabourne, then, hardly deserves serious blame for not deciding as Mr. Austen Leigh would have probably decided twenty years ago, that the newly-discovered correspondence threw practically no fresh light on Miss Austen's personality, and, with half-a-dozen exceptions, which might have seen the light in a review, had therefore better be reserved for that family use for which it was originally intended; but he might at least have set some bounds to his confidence in the public. One small volume of these letters, carefully chosen and skilfully edited, would have been pleasant reading enough. They might have been used as illustrations of the novels, of the country society or the class relations of eighty years ago, and a few short explanations of the identity of the persons most frequently mentioned in them would have made them sufficiently intelligible to the general reader. As it is, the letters of the last fifteen years of Jane Austen's life dull the edge of whatever gentle enjoyment the reader may have derived from the sprightliness of the earlier ones, while the one literary merit which the collection possesses, its lightness and airiness of tone, is lost in the ponderous effect of the introductory chapters, with their endless strings of names and wandering criticisms on the novels. Such editorial performance as this makes one sigh once more for a more peremptory critical standard than any we possess in England. What English *belles-lettres* of the present day want more than anything else is a more widely diffused sense of *obligation* among the cultivators of them—obligation, if one must put it pedantically, to do the best a man can with his material, and to work in the presence of the highest ideals and achievements of his profession.

There are, however, in these volumes a few letters which were worth printing, and which do help to complete the picture already existing of Jane Austen. These are the letters written between 1796 and 1799, that is to say, during the period which witnessed the composition of *Pride and Prejudice, Sense and Sensibility,* and *Northanger Abbey.* Jane Austen at the time was a pretty, lively girl, very fond of dancing, deeply interested in dress, and full of the same *naïf* interest in the other sex with which Catherine Morland started on her Bath travels. The whole tone indeed of this early correspondence with her sister reminds one of an older and shrewder Catherine, and the ways of seeing and describing to which they bear witness are exactly those to which we owe the unflagging liveliness and gaiety of the two famous books in which the adventures of Catherine and Elizabeth Bennett are set forth. *Northanger Abbey* especially, gay, sparkling, and rapid as it is from beginning to end, is the book in which the bright energy of Jane Austen's youth finds its gayest and freshest expression. *Pride and Prejudice* is witty and sparkling too, but it probably went through many a heightening and polishing process during the fifteen years which elapsed between the time when it was written and the time when it appeared in print; and although a great deal of it may represent the young Jane Austen, the style as a whole bears marks certainly of a fuller maturity than had been reached by the writer of *Northanger Abbey*. It is in the story of Catherine Morland that we get the inimitable literary expression of that exuberant girlish wit, which expressed itself in letters and talk and harmless flirtations before it took to itself literary shape, and it is pleasant to turn from the high spirits of that delightful book to some of the first letters in this collection, and so to realise afresh, by means of such records of the woman, the perfect spontaneity of the writer. Any one who has ever interested himself in the impulsive little heroine, who was as nearly plain as any heroine dared to be before Jane Eyre, but whose perfect good-humour and frankness won the heart of her Henry, will feel that in one or two of these newly-printed letters he comes very near to the secret of Catherine's manufacture.

Here, for instance, is a picture, pieced together from passages of different dates, of Jane Austen in a frame of mind which has something of Catherine Morland and something of Elizabeth Bennett in it, though it is a little too satirical and conscious for the one, and perhaps a trifle too frivolous for the other. Tom Lefroy, the hero of the little episode, lived to be Chief Justice of Ireland, and only died in 1854.

The first extract occurs in a letter written from Steventon in January, 1796:—

> You scold me so much in the nice long letter which I have this moment received from you, that I am almost afraid to tell you

how my Irish friend and I behave. Imagine to yourself everything most profligate and shocking in the way of dancing and sitting down together. I *can* expose myself, however, only once more, because he leaves the country soon after next Friday, on which day we *are* to have a dance at Ashe after all. He is a very gentlemanly, good-looking, pleasant young man, I assure you. But as to our having ever met, except at the three last balls, I cannot say much; for he is so excessively laughed at about me at Ashe, that he is ashamed of coming to Steventon, and ran away when we called on Mrs. Lefroy a few days ago....

After I had written the above, we received a visit from Mr. Tom Lefroy and his cousin George. The latter is really very well-behaved now; and as for the other he has but *one* fault, which time will, I trust, entirely remove—it is that his morning coat is a great deal too light. He is a very great admirer of Tom Jones, and therefore wears the same coloured clothes, I imagine, which *he* did when he was wounded.... Our party to Ashe to-morrow night will consist of Edward Cooper, James (for a ball is nothing without him) Buller, who is now staying with us, and I. I look forward with great impatience to it, as I rather expect to receive an offer from my friend in the course of the evening.

I shall refuse him however, unless he promises to give away his white coat.... Tell Mary that I make over Mr. Heartley and all his estate to her for her sole use and benefit in future, and not only him, but all my other admirers into the bargain, wherever she can find them, even the kiss which C. Powlett wanted to give me, as I mean to confine myself in future to Mr. Tom Lefroy, for whom I don't care sixpence. Assure her also as a last and indubitable proof of Warren's indifference to me that he actually drew that gentleman's picture for me, and delivered it to me without a sigh!

Friday (the day of the Ashe ball). At length the day has come on which I am to flirt my last with Tom Lefroy, and when you receive this it will be over. My tears flow as I write at the melancholy idea.

Slight, however, as the relation was, it seems to have been more durable than the signs of frail vitality about it would have led one to expect. It is not till two years later that Jane Austen herself gives it its *coup de grace* in her light characteristic way. She describes a visit paid by Tom Lefroy's aunt to Steventon, in which the nephew's name was never once mentioned to Jane herself, "and I was too proud to make any inquiries; but on my father's asking where he was, I learnt that he was gone back to London, on his way to Ireland, where he is called to the bar, and means to practise." And then—alas! for the faithfulness of woman—she flies off to describe the position in which things are with regard to an unnamed *friend* of Mr. Lefroy's, who had evidently taken his place in her thoughts, and was rapidly succeeding to that full measure of indifference which appears to have been the ultimate portion of all Jane's admirers. "There is less love and more sense in it than sometimes appeared before," she says provokingly, describing a letter from this unknown aspirant—"and I am very well satisfied. It will all go on exceedingly well, and decline away in a very reasonable manner."

There are a good many other touches in these girlish letters that give one glimpses, as it were, into the workshop which produced the novels. "Mr. Richard Harvey," she says on one occasion, "is going to be married; but as it is a great secret, and only known to half the neighbourhood, you must not mention it. The lady's name is Musgrave." Again, "We have been very gay since I wrote last, dining at Hackington, returning by moonlight and everything quite in style, including Mr. Claringbould's funeral which we saw go by on Sunday." Or, "If you should ever see Lucy, you may tell her that I scolded Miss Fletcher for her negligence in writing, as she desired me to do, but without being able to bring her to any proper sense of shame; that Miss Fletcher says in her defence, that as everybody whom Lucy knew when she was in Canterbury has now left it, she has nothing at all to write to her about. By *everybody*, I suppose Miss Fletcher means that a new set of officers has arrived there. But this is a note of my own." Or again, with mocking reference to some of those pomposities of authorship which she ridicules in *Northanger Abbey*—"I am very much flattered by your commendation of my last letter, for I write only for fame, and without any view to pecuniary emolument." Her lively pen touches everybody in turn. One feels there may have been something formidable in a daughter who could put together with a few strokes so suggestive an outline as this:—"My mother continues hearty; her appetite and nights are very good, but she sometimes complains of an asthma, a dropsy, water in her chest and a liver disorder." And it is characteristic that even her letters of grief, after the death of a favourite sister-in-law, are broken within the first fortnight by some flashes of terse satire on the affairs of the neighbourhood.

Some little pleasure and entertainment then may be gleaned, by those who already know their Miss Austen, from the first dozen letters or so of this collection. They fill up a gap in Mr. Austen Leigh's book. The turn of phrase is generally light and happy; and they enable us to realise something of that buoyant and yet critical enjoyment of life, of which the six novels were the direct outcome. But after all, there is very little personal or literary distinction in them; the judgment of an unfriendly Frenchman would probably find that note of "common-ness" in them which Madame de Staël[1] insisted in attributing to *Pride and Prejudice*. And commonness indeed there is, using the word, that is to say, not in any strong or disagreeable sense, but simply as opposed to distinction, charm, aroma, or any of those various words by which one tries to express that magical personal quality of which Madame de Sévigné[2] is the typical representative in literature. And even the gaiety and moderate felicity of phrase which beguiled on through the earlier letters disappears from the later correspondence. The writer of it indeed is the same kindly, blameless, and gently humorous person as the Jane Austen of 1796, but whereas at twenty-one Jane Austen's letters were like her novels, and therefore may be said to possess some slight claim to belong to literature, by thirty-one they had become the mere ordinary chit-chat of the ordinary gentlewoman, with no claims whatever to publication or remembrance beyond the family circle. Lord Brabourne's book indeed only impresses upon us with fresh force what was already fairly well-known—that broadly speaking, the

---

[1] Germaine de Staël (1766–1816), French-Swiss essayist and novelist. Her most popular novel was *Corinne* (1807).

[2] Marie de Rabutin-Chantal, Madame de Sévigné (1626–96), French letter-writer.

whole *yield* of Jane Austen's individuality is to be found in her novels. There are a certain number of facts about her which help to explain her books, and which are of use to the student of the psychological side of letters, but these were already within everybody's reach, so that the collection printed by Lord Brabourne is as a whole neither amusing nor sufficiently instructive to make it worth publication.

The triviality of the letters is easily explained. No circumstances were ever less favourable than Jane Austen's to good letter-writing. She possessed one literary instrument which she used with extraordinary skill and delicacy—the instrument of critical observation as applied to the commoner types and relations of human life. Within the limits fixed for her by temperament and circumstances she brought it to bear with unrivalled success, success which has placed her amongst English classics. But she was practically a stranger to what one may call, without pedantry, the world of ideas. The intellectual and moral framework of her books is of the simplest and most conventional kind. The author of *Corinne*, placed as she was in the very centre of the European stress and tumult, might well think them too tame and commonplace to be read. Great interests, great questions, were life and breath to Madame de Staël as they were to her successor George Sand.[1] She realised the continuity of human history, the great fundamental laws and necessities underlying all the outward tangle and complication. And it was this insight, this far-reaching sympathy, which gave her such power over her time, and made her personality and her thoughts "incalculably diffusive." Meanwhile Jane Austen, in her Hampshire home, seems to have lived through the stormiest period of modern European history without being touched by any of the large fears and hopes, or even strongly impressed by any of the dramatic characters or careers in which it abounded. Though the letters extend from 1796 to 1817, there is barely a mention of politics in them, except in some small personal connection, and of the literary forces of the time—Goethe, Byron, Wordsworth—there is hardly a trace. Even when she comes to London, though we have an occasional bare record of a visit to a theatre, we still hear of nothing

---

[1]   Pen name of Amandine-Aurore-Lucile Dupin (1804–76), French novelist.

except sisters, cousins, neighbours, the price of "Irish," and the new fashions in caps. And for the rest, Kent and Hampshire, with their county families, their marryings and christenings, their dancings and charities, are the only world she knows or cares to know. She never seems to have had a literary acquaintance, or to have desired to make one. While Miss Ferrier's wits were quickened by the give and take of Edinburgh society in its best days, and Miss Edgeworth[1] found herself welcomed with extravagant flattery on the Continent as the representative of English culture, all the literary influence that Jane Austen ever experienced was due to her father, and all the literary influence she ever personally exerted was brought to bear upon a novel-writing niece. No doubt if she had lived a little longer things would have been different. When she died, at the age of forty-one, her books had already brought her some fame, and friends would have followed. As it was, her circle of interests, both intellectual and personal, was a narrower one than that of any other writer we can remember with the same literary position.

In spite, however, of her narrow *Weltanschauung,* and her dearth of literary relationships, Jane Austen is a classic, and *Pride and Prejudice* will probably be read when *Corinne,* though not its author, is forgotten. Her life is a striking proof that a great novelist may live without a philosophy, and die with out ever having belonged to a literary *coterie.* But out of the stuff of which the life was composed it was impossible to make a good letter-writer. To be a good letter-writer a man or woman must either have ideas, or sentiments strong enough to take the place of ideas, or knowledge of and contact with what is intrinsically interesting and important. Jane Austen had none of these. The graphic portraiture of men and women seen from the outside, in which she excelled, was not possible in letters. It required more freedom, more elbow-room than letters could give. Jane Austen, in describing real people, found herself limited by the natural scruples of an amiable and gentle nature. There was a short time when the exuberance of her talent overflowed a little into her correspondence. But it soon came to an end, and for the rest of her life Jane Austen's letters were below rather than above the average in interest, point and charm.

---

[1] Maria Edgeworth (1768–1849), Irish novelist.

Miss Austen's novels are a well-worn subject. We have all read her, or ought to have read her; we all know what Macaulay[1] and what Scott thought of her; and the qualities of her humour, the extent of her range have been pointed out again and again. Perhaps, after all, however, it may be still worth while to try and face the question which these disappointing letters bring home to one. How was it that, with all her lack of knowledge and of ideas, and with her comparative lack of passion, which so often supplies the place of both, Jane Austen accomplished work so permanent and so admirable? What is it, in a word, which makes *Pride and Prejudice* and *Northanger Abbey* English classics, while the books of her contemporaries, Miss Ferrier and Miss Edgeworth, have practically lost their hold upon our sympathies, and are retreating year by year into a dimmer background? There are two kinds of qualities which go to the making of a classic. There are the qualities of expansion and the qualities of concentration. The great books of the world are rich in both. If you compare Chaucer's and Gower's treatment of the same theme—the subject of the *Man of Lawes Tale*,[2] for instance—you will see not only that Chaucer's treatment is light and rapid where Gower's is heavy and prolix, but that Chaucer knew where, as the French would say, to "lean," where to dwell, where to expand. You may trace this poetic expansion at work in all the great moments or crises of the story. Gower plods on through the trial of Constance for the murder of Dame Hermengild, and through the various incidents which accompany it, with no variation of tone or pace. Chaucer, when he has brought Constance face to face with her enemies, pauses, as any true poet would, and lets the tragedy of the situation penetrate himself and his readers.

> Have ye not seyn sometyme a palë face
> Among a prees, of him that hath be lad
> Toward his deth, wher as him gat no grace,
> And swich a colour in his face hath had,
> Men mightë knowe his face, that was bistad

---

[1] Thomas Babington Macaulay (1800–59), historian and MP.

[2] "The Man of Law's Tale" is the fifth of Chaucer's *Canterbury Tales* (ca. 1387). The story is also told in John Gower's (1330–1408) *Confessio Amantis* (ca. 1390s). Ward goes on to mention other works by Chaucer.

Amongës alle faces in that route:
So stant Custance, and looketh hir aboute.

O queenës, lyuinge in prosperitee
Duchesses, and ladyës euerich one
Haueth some rewthe on hir aduersitee;
An emperourës doughter stant allone;
She hath no wight to whom to make hir mone.
O blood roial! that stondest in this drede,
Fer ben thy frendës at thy gretë nede!

And a little further on there is a still more striking instance of it, in the exquisite scene between Constance and her child before she is turned adrift on the Northumbrian coast. As for the qualities of condensation they may be traced in the *Troilus and Cressid* as compared with the *Filostrato* and in the *Knightes Tale*, and elsewhere. But the qualities of expansion develop first in the literary history of the world; those of concentration come later, and the human mind takes longer to fashion the instruments which fit and display them. Although a great writer will have both in some measure, the proportion in which he possesses them will depend upon his date. The progress of literary expression during the last two hundred years has on the whole, and making due allowance for the vast stores of new material which have found their way into literature since Rousseau, been a progress towards concentration. Literature tends more and more to become a kind of shorthand. The great writers of this generation take more for granted than the great writers of the last, and the struggle to avoid commonplace and repetition becomes more and more diffused. The mind of the modern writer is on the whole most anxiously concerned with this perpetual necessity for omission, for compression. It will never describe if it can suggest, or argue if it can imply. The first condition of success in letters is nowadays to avoid vapouring, and to wage war upon those platitudes we all submit to with so much cheerful admiration in our Richardson or our *Spectator*.[1]

---

[1] Samuel Richardson (1689–1761), English novelist. *The Spectator* was a popular daily periodical published in 1711–12 and 1714.

It was her possession of the qualities of condensation that made Jane Austen what she was. Condensation in literary matters means an exquisite power of choice and discrimination—a capacity for isolating from the vast mass of detail which goes to make up human life just those details and no others which will produce a desired effect and blend into one clear and harmonious whole. It implies the determination to avoid everything cheap and easy—cheapness in sentiment, in description, in caricature. In matters of mere language it means the perpetual effort to be content with one word rather than two, the perpetual impulse to clip and prune either than expand and lengthen. And if to this temper of self-restraint you add the imagination which seizes at once upon the most effective image or detail and realises at a glance how it will strike a reader, and a spontaneous interest in men and women as such, you have arrived at the component parts of such a gift as Jane Austen's. Nothing impresses them more strongly upon the reader than a comparison of her work with that of her slightly younger contemporary, Miss Ferrier. Miss Ferrier had a great deal of humour, some observation, and a store of natural vigour which made her novels welcome to the generation of Scott and Byron. Stronger expressions of praise were used to her and about her than ever seem to have suggested themselves to any contemporary admirer of Miss Austen, and the author of *Marriage* was encouraged to believe that her work would rank with that of Scott as a representation of Scottish life and manners. But we who read Miss Ferrier with an interval of fifty years between us and her can judge the proportions of things more clearly. Miss Ferrier is scarcely read now, except for the sake of satisfying a literary curiosity, and will gradually drop more and more out of reading. And it is very easy to understand why, if one does but approach her books with these qualities of expansion and concentration which go to make up a classic in one's mind. She has little or no faculty of choice, nothing is refused that presents itself; reflections, love-making, incident, are all superabundant and second rate. Everything is done to death, whether it is Miss Pratt's bustle, or Lady Julianna's finery, or Mr. McDow's brutality, and as for the sentiment—these reflections from the first volume of the *Inheritance* are a fair average specimen of it.

"Ah," thought Gertrude, "how willingly would I renounce all pomp of greatness to dwell here in lowly affection with one who would love me and whom I could love in return. How strange that I, who could cherish the very worm that crawls beneath my feet, have no one being to whom I could utter the thoughts of my heart, no one on whom I could bestow its best affections!" She raised her eyes, swimming in tears to heaven, but it was in the poetic enthusiasm of feeling, not in the calm spirit of devotion!

There is no particular reason why writing of this kind should ever stop; there is nothing intimate and living in it, none of that wrestle of the artist with experience which is the source of all the labours and all the trials of art; it is all conventional, traditional, *hearsay* in fact. The qualities of concentration are altogether wanting. But now, put side by side with Gertrude's sentiment or Mrs. Sinclair's remorse, some of the mental history of Jane Austen's *dramatis personae*, and the gulf which this marvellous choosing faculty digs between one writer and another will be plain at once. Anne Eliot, in *Persuasion*, has arrived at the critical moment of her fate. The man whom she had rejected seven years before has reappeared upon the scene, and as soon as she is brought in contact with him all lesser affections and inclinations, which had been filling up the time of his absence, disappear. Others might have had a chance if he had remained away, but his return, his neighbourhood, rouses a feeling which sweeps all before it. This is the situation. We may imagine, if Miss Ferrier had had to deal with it, how she would have spun it out; with what raptures, what despairs, what appeals to heaven she would have embroidered it! But Jane Austen at once seizes upon the vital points of it, and puts them before us, at first with a sober truth, and then with a little rise into poetry, which is a triumph of style.

"There was much regret," she says, in her analysis of Anne's feelings towards the man she had resolved to sacrifice to her old lover. "How she might have felt had there been no Captain Wentworth in the case is not worth inquiring; for there was a Captain Wentworth, and be the conclusion of the present suspense good or bad, her affection would be his for ever. Their union, she believed, could not divide her more from other men than their final separation. Prettier musings of high-wrought love and eternal constancy could never have passed along the streets of Bath than Anne was sporting with from Camden Place to Westgate Buildings. It was almost enough to spread purification and perfume all the way." How terse it is, how suggestive, how free from vulgarity and commonplace!

Another striking instance of this choosing instinct of hers is the description of Darcy's place, Pemberley, in *Pride and Prejudice*. There, although there is scarcely any description at all, every stroke of the pen is so managed that any reader with ordinary attention may realise, if he pleases, the whole lie of the park, the look of the house, as Elizabeth surveyed it from the opposite side of the ravine above which it stood, the relative positions of the lawns, stables, and woods. Anybody with a turn that way could sketch it with ease, and yet there is no effort, no intention to describe, nothing but a clear and vivid imagination working with that self-restraint, that concentration, which is the larger half of style. This self-restraint indeed is her important, her determining quality. In other ways she has great deficiencies. For fine instances of the qualities of expansion we must go elsewhere than to Jane Austen. Emotion, inspiration, glow, and passion are not hers; she is a small, thin classic. But classic she is; for her work is a typical English embodiment of those drier and more bracing elements of style in which French literature has always been rich, and our own perhaps comparatively poor.

SOURCE

Macmillan's 51 (December 1884).

SELECTED SECONDARY READING

Sutherland, John. *Mrs. Humphry Ward: Eminent Victorian, Pre-Eminent Edwardian*. Oxford: Clarendon Press, 1990.

WOMEN'S BOOKS—A POSSIBLE LIBRARY
(MAY 1889)

Helen Blackburn

HELEN BLACKBURN (1842–1903) was born in County Kerry, Ireland, and moved to London with her parents in 1859. Her father was a civil engineer who in 1877 patented a forerunner of the automobile. She first became involved with the women's rights movement, centred around Barbara Leigh Smith Bodichon and Bessie Rayner Parkes at Langham Place in London, in her twenties. By the 1870s she was an active participant, serving as secretary of the National Women's Suffrage Society from 1874 to 1895 and of the Bristol and West of England Suffrage Committee from 1880 to 1895. She was also a founding member, with Lydia Becker, of the Liberty and Property Defence League. Blackburn's 1902 book, *Women's Suffrage*, is a standard text about the early years of the British women's movement, and her library, which she bequeathed to Girton College, Cambridge, is a vital repository of original documents.

In 1881, after having first contributed a number of articles and reviews, Blackburn became the third editor of the *Englishwoman's Review*, a successor of the respected and influential *English Woman's Journal*. The *Englishwoman's Review*, published from 1866 to 1910, was founded by Jessie Boucherett with an unabashedly feminist agenda. In her first editorial column on "The Work We Have to Do," Boucherett had declared that a periodical was "imperatively required" that would examine "the sources whence spring the evils

which oppress women ... as well as the evils themselves"
(October 1866). Blackburn continued Boucherett's
program, documenting the progress of the women's movement and exhorting women to "look not backward, but
rather forward" (January 1890). She continued to edit the
journal until she left to care for her dying father in 1895.

"Women's Books—A Possible Library" was published in
1889, just two years before Blackburn assumed the editorship
of the *Englishwoman's Review*. In this article, Blackburn cata-
logues notable British women writers from the fifteenth
century on. Her project is twofold. First, she wishes to establish the significant literary achievements of women, especially
her near contemporaries, and to demonstrate that women
have established themselves in fields other than fiction and
poetry—being careful to include "those who edit." But
second, Blackburn also wants to defend women writers from
charges of inferiority. Thus, a full generation before Virginia
Woolf, Blackburn is engaged in the kind of feminist recovery
project represented by *A Room of One's Own* (1929) and that
second-wave feminists would resume in the 1970s.

WHAT IS THE IMPRESSION WHICH a library composed
exclusively of books written by women would make on the mind?
Would there be anything gained by collecting the works of women
apart from the works of men? Would a sense of despondency creep
over us at the comparatively small space such a library would occupy
in the world's literature, or would it create a sense of surprise, that
cut off as women have been from so much of the world's culture,
they have added so much to its literature? Should we be struck most
by the amount of useless and ephemeral, or by the amount of good
and sterling work?

Such questions as these are suggested by the plan lately set on foot
in Paris to form a library of women's books. We might be able to
answer them to some extent by imagining ourselves in a library

wherein should be gathered together all the books written by women in the British Isles.

Let us look round. What an over-weening number of novels will first strike the eye—many three-volumed sets rapidly becoming invisible in the dust of oblivion, but not all; a goodly array are fresh and clean with the light of daily use. English classics cannot afford to lose their Jane Austen, thrilling the dullest commonplace existence with a sense of living reality; nor their Brontë's vivid power; nor the pitiless dissection of human motive of their George Eliot; and the youth of the land cannot spare, and long may they be unable to spare, the healthful experience of life and the recreation from work which those goodly rows of Mrs. Gaskell, Mrs. Craig, Miss Yonge, Miss Thackeray, Mrs. Oliphant, Mrs. Marshall[1] afford them. Let us not miss either that dear old friend, *The Cottagers of Glenburnie*, nor our newer friend, *That Lass o' Lowrie's*;[2]—surely these, and more than these, will defy the sedulous dust for many a day.

And next we may look for the poets: Mrs. Hemans, L.E.L., their sweet songs grow dusty, and Joanna Baillie; but not till each has set her mark on her day, though it be a less enduring niche than those carved by the strong strains of Elizabeth Barrett Browning, or by the deep pathos of Adelaide Ann Proctor,[3] or by the dramatic force of some who yet live and write amongst us.

No Shakespeare though, mutters the critic. How many Shakespeares, sir critic, has the world yet seen that you expect his rival to appear already? Patience please, and let us proceed. Here we come to travels, for women have shared many opportunities of travel, and travelling they have observed much to record, and recording they have displayed power of description which will make these volumes often valued sources, not only of entertainment, but of knowledge. Sorry, indeed,

---

[1] Popular English and Scottish novelists: Elizabeth Gaskell (1810–65), Dinah Mulock Craik (1826–87), Charlotte Yonge (1823–1901), Anne Thackeray Ritchie (1837–1919), Margaret Oliphant (1828–97), and Emma Marshall (1830–99).

[2] Novels published in 1808 and 1877 by Scottish novelist Eliza Hamilton (1758–1816) and American-born Frances Hodgson Burnett (1849–1924).

[3] Popular Romantic and Victorian poets: Felicia Hemans (1793–1835), Laetitia Elizabeth Landon (1802–38), Joanna Baillie (1762–1851), Elizabeth Barrett Browning (1806–61), and Adelaide Anne Procter (1825–64).

would our literature be to miss Lady Duff Gordon's *Letters from the Nile,* or Miss Edwards' *Thousand Miles down the Ancient River,* or Miss Gordon Cumming's oceanic experiences;[1] or—but we must not attempt to enumerate, but pass on from descriptions of external scenes to descriptions of the lives of fellow-men and women—memoirs edited, perhaps, by the wife who had shared the life she now records—and here spring to memory a Baroness Bunsen, a Mrs. Kingsley[2]—or edited for friendship's or for admiration's sake—and we look for Mrs. Gaskell's *Life of the Brontës,* Mrs. Butler's *St. Catherine,* Mrs. Oliphant's *St. Francis,* Mrs. Venturi's *Mazzini,*[3] and then insensibly we find ourselves at the shelves of history; Miss Strickland's *Lives of the Queens of England,* Mrs. W.H. Green's recent Henry II.:[4] nor let us omit the labours of those who edit. Shall not our library contain amongst the works of women those calendars of State papers which Mrs. Everett Green has so laboriously and carefully edited for the benefit of historical students,[5] and periodical literature where women editors store facts for the historians of the future, amongst which the ENGLISHWOMAN'S REVIEW itself (permit the personal remark, dear editor) should find a place.

---

[1] Travel writer and translator Lady Lucie Duff Gordon (1821–69) published several volumes of letters about her travels in Africa; Blackburn probably refers to her *Letters from Egypt* (1865). Novelist and Egyptologist Amelia Edwards (1831–92) published *A Thousand Miles Up the Nile* in 1877. Scottish journalist and Church Missionary Society worker Constance Gordon-Cumming (1837–1924) published numerous articles in *Blackwood's Edinburgh Magazine* and elsewhere, including "Across the Yellow Sea" (1882).

[2] Frances, Baroness Bunsen (1791–1896) published a memoir of her husband Christian Carl Josias von Bunsen (1791–1860), ambassador to Britain from the court of Friederich Wilhelm IV, king of Prussia; Frances Eliza Grenfell Kingsley (1814–91) edited the *Letters and Memories* (1877) of her husband, novelist Charles Kingsley (1819–75).

[3] Gaskell's *Life of Charlotte Brontë* was published in 1857. Social activist and journalist Josephine Butler's (1828–1906) *Catharine of Sienna* appeared in 1878. Oliphant's *Francis of Assisi* (1870) was just one of many biographies she wrote or edited. Emilie Ashurst Venturi (d. 1893) published several books, translations, and articles on the Italian patriot Giuseppe Mazzini (1805–72), including an 1872 biography.

[4] Agnes Strickland (1796–1874) published 12 volumes of *Lives of the Queens of England* between 1840 and 1848, with significant contributions from her sister Elizabeth (1794–1875). Irish historian Alice Stopford (Mrs. J.R.) Green's (1848–1929) *Henry the Second* was published in 1888; Blackburn seems to have confused Green's husband with the biblical scholar William Henry Green.

[5] Archivist Mary Anne Everett Green (1818–95) edited the first ten volumes of the *Calendar of State Papers* of the Public Record Office (1860).

Translations will also have their place assigned—translations from many tongues, ancient and modern; Miss Swanwick's Aeschylus will be there, and Mrs. Webster's Euripides and Miss Martineau's abridgment of the positive philosophy.[1] The name of Harriet Martineau suggests not only philosophy, but history and political economy; and this again recalls Mrs. Marcet's volumes—those conversations on political economy and on chemistry to which many of the generation now grown old owe their first interest in these great subjects—as do many of the now rising generation owe theirs to Mrs. Fawcett's *Handbook of Political Economy*, and Miss Buckley's *Fairy Tales of Science*.[2] Mrs. Somerville will fill the place of honour in these shelves—and beside her Miss Clerk, bringing the newest knowledge of the starry firmament to the attention of the readers of to-day.[3] If none of the greatest original discoveries are associated with women, they have assuredly filled an important part in popularizing the results of the labours of discoverers. From science to art seems a natural transition, and here what grateful memories rise to many of us at the sight of Mrs. Jameson's *Sacred and Legendary Art*, and the companion volumes which have taught us appreciation of the beauties and sympathy with the feelings of early continental art; and fitly by the side of Mrs. Jameson stand Miss Stokes' labours on Celtic art.[4] Next we shall reach philosophy—philosophy of the ideal with Miss Cobbe's ethics; philos-

---

[1] Anna Swanwick (1813–99) published her translation of Aeschylus's plays in 1873 and also translated Goethe's works; poet and playwright Augusta Webster's (1837–94) translation of *Medea* was published in 1868; Martineau's condensed translation of Auguste Comte's *Positive Philosophy* appeared in 1852–53.

[2] Martineau's *Illustrations of Political Economy* (1832–34) was instrumental in popularizing economic theory. Jane Haldimand Marcet (1769–1858) published a "Conversations on" series of scientific and philosophical books for children; suffragist Millicent Garret Fawcett's (1847–1929) *Political Economy for Beginners* was published in 1870; Arabella Burton Buckley (1840–1929) published *The Fairy-Land of Science* in 1879 and was the author of other educational books for children.

[3] Scottish mathematician and scientist Mary Fairfax Greig Somerville (1780–1872) published a number of highly respected scientific texts between 1831 and 1868; physicist Agnes Mary Clerke (1842–1907) published a number of works in astronomy, including *A Popular History of Astronomy During the Nineteenth Century* (1886).

[4] Art historian and critic Anna Jameson's (1794–1860) *Sacred and Legendary Art* was published in 1848; Margaret Stokes (1832–1900) wrote and edited a number of works on Irish art and architecture.

ophy of the practical work of the philanthropist, with Miss Carpenter's *Juvenile Delinquents,* and the Misses Davenport Hill's *Children of the State.*[1] Yet still what diverse subjects remain—papers and short studies exhumed from transactions; pamphlets, reports and blue books should be gathered here, to say nothing of the important province of education and children's literature to which so many of the best women have contributed of their best powers.

But we must pause—for suddenly we notice that every book referred to hitherto has been written within the present century, most within the present reign, and our library should be for all centuries.

Let us change our point of view, and instead of passing from subject to subject, pass from century to century. The shelves for all the previous centuries put together will be few compared to those of the nineteenth century, flooded as it is by the printer's art; but though the elder works be few their subjects will be various. Perhaps the oldest book of all will be the *Treatise on Hawking and Fishing,* written by Juliana Berners, Prioress of Sopwell[2]—a curious subject from which to start, but suggesting that in the fifteenth century men and women had some common share in recreative pursuits. We shall not find much else for that century, but the sixteenth should be represented by a fair number of the translations—from Italian, French and the classics—on which the scholarly women of the Tudor period exercised their learning rather than on original writings. The seventeenth century, when the lack of the educational endowments swept away by the Reformation, had begun to make itself seriously felt and education had sunk to its lowest ebb, will yield but scanty contribution. The Duchess of Newcastle's dramas and Mary Astell's various essays, urging

---

[1] Feminist journalist Frances Power Cobbe (1822–1904) published an *Essay on Intuitive Morals* (1855) and *Darwinism in Morals* (1872), as well as numerous books and pamphlets on women's rights; Mary Carpenter's (1807–77) *Juvenile Delinquents* (1855) directly shaped legislation on juvenile offenders. Florence Davenport Hill (1829–1919) published *Children of the State* in 1868; Blackburn either mistakenly attributes the work as a joint effort of Florence and her sister Rosamond (1825–1902) or assumes social worker Octavia Hill (1838–1912) is another sibling.

[2] Juliana Berners (b. ca. 1368) probably was not the prioress of Sopwell Abbey, but she does appear to have contributed the hawking and hunting sections to the 1486 *Book of St. Albans.*

a more serious estimate of the place of women in life, will redeem it from vacuity,[1] and thanks perhaps to these, the eighteenth century will be less poverty-stricken—at any rate we shall have Miss Elizabeth Elstob's *Anglo-Saxon Grammar*, Lady Mary Wortley Montagu's *Letters from the East*, and Lady Pakington's *Whole Duty of Man*—for though attributed to several learned divines, the evidence points rather to that lady's authorship.[2] And then, as the century grows older, we shall come to a remarkable trio of women—women who each in her own line ushered in that new order which is fulfilling itself in the life of our own day. Hannah More, the pioneer of the practical philanthropy which is so distinctive a feature of the present century, published her first poem in 1773.[3] Mary Wollstonecraft championed the wider lives of women by her *Vindication of the Rights of Women* in 1791, giving the impetus which has gone forward ever since.[4] Maria Edgeworth published in 1798 the earliest of the long series of books which have won for her the earliest niche of enduring fame amongst the women novelists of the British Isles.[5]

Slight as this sketch is, touching as with mere finger tips salient books here and there, yet it may suffice to indicate the broad general impressions our imagined library might convey; how the value of the work done by women in literature bears a steady proportion to the position attained in means of culture. Thousands of women must have been originals in the sense of finding out thoughts, facts, ideas for themselves; few can be original as the world reckons originality,

[1] Poet and playwright Margaret Cavendish, Duchess of Newcastle (1623–74) published two volumes of plays in the 1660s; writer Mary Astell (1666–1731) established her reputation with *A Serious Proposal to the Ladies* (1694).

[2] Elizabeth Elstob's (1683–1758) *Rudiments of Grammar for the English-Saxon Tongue* was published in 1715; poet Lady Mary Wortley Montagu's (1689–1762) *Embassy Letters* were published in 1763. First published in 1658, the authorship of the devotional book *The Whole Duty of Man* is still uncertain, although it has been variously attributed to clergymen Richard Allestree (1619–81) and Richard Sterne (1596–1683) and to Lady Dorothy Coventry Pakington (d. 1679), who was noted for her piety.

[3] Poet and religious writer Hannah More (1745–1833), best known for her writings on abolition and female education and for her *Cheap Repository Tracts* (1795–98).

[4] Pioneering English feminist Mary Wollstonecraft (1759–97).

[5] Anglo-Irish novelist Maria Edgeworth (1767–1849) also published works on female education and didactic tales for children.

that is finding out or doing what has never been known or done before, for such originality is only possible when you first know all that has been already discovered. Then and then only can man or woman have an appreciable chance of forming a combination of ideas which shall be new for the world as well as for the individual. This chance, rare at best, is of necessity rarest for those whose access to knowledge has been barred more or less—generally more rather than less—throughout historic time.

Again, our library indicates that the works produced by women in this quarter of a century alone contain more of intrinsic worth than all the previous generations, from Juliana Berners to Hannah More. Such an indication as this should tend to heighten the increasing respect for women's capacities, increase respect for their latent powers in the hearts of women themselves, and respect for the value of women's work in the hearts of men.

SOURCE

Englishwoman's Review 20 (15 May 1889).

SELECTED SECONDARY READING

Davies, Stephen. *Libertarian Feminism in Britain, 1860–1910.* Libertarian Alliance Pamphlet 7. London: Libertarian Alliance/British Association of Libertarian Feminists, 1987.

Lacey, Candida Ann, ed. *Barbara Leigh Smith Bodichon and the Langham Place Group.* New York: Routledge, 1986.

Robinson, Solveig C. "'Amazed at Our Success': The Langham Place Editors and the Emergence of a Feminist Critical Tradition." *Victorian Periodicals Review* 28.2 (1995): 159–72.

LITERATURE: THEN AND NOW
(APRIL 1890)

Eliza Lynn Linton

ELIZA LYNN (1822–98) was born in Crosthwaite, Cumberland, the youngest of 12 children of an Anglican clergyman and his wife. Eliza's mother, who was the daughter of the Bishop of Carlisle, died when Eliza was an infant. Neglected by her father and tormented by her elder siblings, Eliza retreated into books, teaching herself French, Italian, German, and Spanish, as well as some Greek and Latin. At age 23, she convinced her father to allow her to go to London to establish a career as a writer. After publishing two historical novels—*Azeth the Egyptian* (1846) and *Amymone* (1848)— in 1849 she secured a job with the *Morning Chronicle*, becoming the first salaried woman newspaper journalist in Britain. She left the post after two years and worked for awhile as a foreign correspondent in Paris, in the meantime publishing her first contemporary novel, *Realities* (1851). In 1853 she began writing for Dickens's *Household Words*.

In 1858 she married the radical engraver William James Linton, a widower with a large family. The marriage seems to have been largely one of convenience, and it ended in a separation. William emigrated to the United States in 1867, although several of his children remained in Eliza's care. To support her new family, Lynn Linton increased her literary output. She was invited by the former editor of the *Morning Chronicle*, John Douglas Cook, to join the staff of the *Saturday Review*, and throughout the 1860s and 1870s she published a series of highly entertaining essays of social and literary criticism, most notably the scathing "Girl of the Period" (1868), which was reissued under her own name in 1883. She also wrote regularly for the *Fortnightly Review* and other periodicals.

The anti-feminist theme of her "Girl of the Period" essay recurs in many of Lynn Linton's novels, including *The Rebel of the Family* (1880) and *The One Too Many* (1894). Her ambiguous feelings about her sexuality and her contradictory attitudes about professional women are explored in her fictional autobiography, *The Autobiography of Christopher Kirkland* (1885), in which she assumes a male persona, and in her posthumous memoir, *My Literary Life* (1899).

In addition to its anti-feminism, an identifying element of Lynn Linton's writing is her relative conservatism, both social and literary. In "Literature: Then and Now," which originally appeared in the *Fortnightly Review*, Lynn Linton compares the past to the present—and the present, as ever, comes up short. In earlier times, Lynn Linton asserts, literature may already have been "a profession," but its practitioners were "gentlemen and scholars—men who neither sold their conscience nor prostituted their talents." Furthermore, literary critics were conscientious defenders of standards and principles. By contrast, the writers and critics of the late nineteenth century are characterized by Lynn Linton as mere self-serving hacks, producing "frothy" literature and partisan criticism. Lynn Linton's own highly allusive style—a style explicitly directed towards educated readers—clearly indicates her affiliation with the previous generation, those "representatives of the grand old philosophers," and the literary standards she believes should be reintroduced.

LITERATURE, AMONG OTHER THINGS, has passed through phases so different as to be in themselves transformations. From the time when the Roman man of letters assembled his friends to hear him read from his own manuscript a new treatise on the Nature of the Gods, or his last new ode of perfect polish and completeness, up to now when we go to first nights to support a friend's play, or give private invitations for a drawing-room recital, there have been changes in method and distribution, as well as in subject, which have revolutionised the world. That which was once select and eclectic has now become generalised and common, and those things which once ranked as among the best treasures a man could possess, are now sold by the hundredweight as so much rubbish to be reconstructed and reformed.

When a Pope sent emissaries to beg from a more fortunate holder a copy of *Cicero's De Oratore*,[1] as he might have begged for a costly jewel, and Bibles were lent and borrowed by churches and monasteries as friendly housekeepers lend their plate and glass on grand occasions— when a library of a hundred and fifty volumes was more than a princely possession, and represented cost, painstaking, and success in search of a monumental kind—rarity bred an almost superstitious respect, and books were valued as "things-in-themselves" quite as much as for what they taught. They were valued even more than gold and silver, and their bestowal ranked as a good work of extraordinary merit. The bequest of a book to a religious house ensured eternal salvation and was paid for by a daily mass in perpetuity for the soul of the pious donor. The shadow of this splendour was the irrevocable sentence of damnation pronounced against him who should purloin, conceal, or even obliterate the title of—say, that Latin translation of Aristotle's *Physics*[2] at Rochester—so great was the store set by the treasure and so unbounded the veneration for the author. In those pre-printing days a new book was a phenomenon of more importance than is now the discovery of a new planet. Cowled scribes copied and recopied the manuscript, adding illuminated headings and marginal illustrations of perhaps greater worth than the text, and throwing into their work a love, an enthusiasm, a singleness of devotion of which even collectors of first editions and unique copies fall short. From these exclusive

---

[1] Marcus Tullius Cicero (106–43 BC), Roman statesman and scholar. His *De Oratore* is a treatise on public speaking.
[2] Aristotle (384–322 BC), Greek philosopher.

times, when the man of letters, such as he was, was part priest, part monarch, having absolute power so far as his realm extended—but that realm including only the chosen few—up to the present state of circulating libraries and overflowing publications, we strike the whole chord of social change and political revolution. What literature was—thought, morals, and society were. What literature is—these are.

Even in those early days, when literature had its crown of stars, the man of letters was of the two kinds—the respectable and the Bohemian. In his quiet cell the cloistered scribe copied and recopied his favourite manuscripts as the lighter fringes of the religious life to which he had dedicated himself. In the hall, the bard, who was also a vassal, celebrated his seigneur's valiant deeds as part of the service he owed for protection. Or men of honourable status, like Froissart, wrote of what they had seen and heard, and took their place by Herodotus and Tacitus[1] for all time to come. But out of doors the free-living Troubadours roamed far and wide with jongleurs and glee-maidens, chanting their lady's charms to the world outside her bower, or vaunting the lighter loves which brought no pain and left no sorrow, and were worn as transiently and lost as gaily as the roses of Provence—the May-blossom of England. Bedouins of literature—wild asses of the desert, unbitted and unbridled—this class has ever been from the first up to now—from the masterless men who wandered from castle to castle, harping for meat and lodging, onward through Villon and Savage,[2] and up to the *rois de Bohème* of Balzac's time,[3] and the unkempt, impecunious, irresponsible Geniuses of our own. For the poet, the singer, is the father and grandfather of the literary tribe. All literature begins in the rhymed ballad, the rhythmic fable, the alliterative saga, the rude dramatic carpentry of the "mystery play," whatever the God to be honoured in the representation. Prose is a later development; and in prose the spoken oration comes before the

---

[1]   Jean Froissart (ca. 1333–1400), French poet and historian; Herodotus (ca. 484–430 BC), Greek historian; Tacitus (ca. 56–120), Roman historian.

[2]   François Villon (ca. 1431–63), French lyric poet; Richard Savage (ca. 1697–1743), English poet.

[3]   "Kings of Bohemia," or artists and their hangers-on; Honoré de Balzac (1799–1850), French realist novelist.

written essay. But the poet, the rhymer, the singer, was the ancestor of the whole grand race; and if on the one side he touched the priest and the seer, on the other he was but a wild ass of the desert, doing no good to himself or anyone else.

A whole treatise might be written on the dedications of books. These, like the books themselves, have undergone transitions which have changed their original character. In the earliest times they were the expression not so much of servile fawning as of genuine loyalty. They were part of the service spoken of above—part of the badge, the livery, which proclaimed a man's clanship and vassalage. They were the transfer into human life of that dedication to the God which made men offer the first fruits of their flocks and fields to Jehovah, Zeus, Jove—which made the virgin bride carry her hair to Artemis, and all who were in dread of sorrow and afraid of dark days seek to propitiate the Fatal Sisters.[1] This simplicity of intention redeemed the ofttimes too great abasement of the words. Language was then fuller of verbal submission than it is now, because the gradations of society were sharper, and the grip of the higher on the lower was stronger. The fact of submission was infinitely potent and universal; so that the seigneur was in very truth a minor kind of god in the sight of heaven, and a very real one in his dealings with men.

This habit of dedicating books survived the religiousness of the informing spirit which made it a gift of good things from the inferior to the superior—a toll paid for love and reverence and gratitude for past favours and humble trust in favours still to come, without which life would be but a shipwreck on a desert shore. It survived the honesty and the reality of the feudal spirit which had inspired them. When, through Gutenberg and Caxton, literature became more democratic and less exclusive, the hanger-on had then displaced the vassal, and the patron was the seigneur in a more modern form. And then the dedications grow to be servile and fawning and flattering. It was all the difference between the payment of a duty, willingly paid and counted into the

---

[1] Jehovah, Zeus, and Jove are all names for supreme gods. Artemis was the Greek goddess of the moon and the hunt; she presided over rituals pertaining to life changes for women. In classical mythology, the Fatal Sisters are the three goddesses who determine the length and course of human life.

service, and currying favour from one who could give or withhold at pleasure. As it ever is, the transition time was bad for all concerned. It was specially bad for the man of letters, who by degrees sank to the lowest depths to which he could fall. When private patrons grew scarce, and the public had not yet discovered it had an intellect which wanted feeding, the poor author was at the bottom of the social scale. He was essentially of the class of rogues and vagabonds—the constant inmate of the debtors' prison and the sponging-houses—unclean, immoral, without self-respect or social standing, contemptible and justly despised. But there have always been the ten just men who have saved the city;[1] and, together with rufflers and roysterers, drunkards and booksellers' hacks, were men of birth and breeding, of profound scholarship and absolute independence, whose lives ennobled literature as much as literature ennobled them. The works of these men redeemed the profession from the vileness that threatened to destroy it, just as they themselves redeemed that wretched creature who, like the domestic chaplain, if admitted to the table of his patron, sat below the salt, left before the pudding, drank nothing better than small beer, and was perhaps rewarded for his flattery with an Abigail of damaged virtue for his wife. So the balance hangs. On the one side we see the self-abasement and shameful poverty of Grub Street, with some of our best classics written to pay a gambling debt or a tavern score; on the other, the splendid achievements of scholars and poets who were men of birth and fortune, honour and good conduct, loving literature for its own sake, and following it as faithfully, as devotedly, as a knight of old served his mistress.

In our own century we have had a period of high honour and fine feeling when men wrote for money, truly, and made literature a profession by which their families were to be supported, but when they were gentlemen and scholars—men who neither sold their conscience nor prostituted their talents, and who abided steadfastly by their convictions, not counting the cost. Literature was to them a noble calling, and they felt all its responsibilities. They followed it in the quiet dignity of home, and they did not stand in the open market touting for

---

[1] Reference to Genesis 18, in which God promises Abraham not to destroy the city of Sodom if ten righteous men can be found among the wicked.

bidders and buyers. When they came up to London once in three or four years or so, it was to meet with their peers, look after new books, pick up old ones, and gather fresh materials for the tale of bricks they had undertaken to deliver. They did not come to get hold of smart young reviewers or impressible editors, and so to dip their fingers into the honey-pot of undeserved praise. There was then no self-advertisement and no organised racket. The work was done, and all pains were taken in the doing. Then it was left to make its own mark unaided by the arts which are essential to a showman's success—and good at that—but which are as derogatory to the true dignity of literature as is the advertising quack to the true dignity of medicine. No one then attempted to "nobble the press"; and they would not have succeeded if they had. Such men as Southey and Wordsworth[1]—to name no others—wrote honestly as they thought; the one from books rather than from cogitation, the other from cogitation rather than from books; but each with as much pride and dignity as the other; and of all the men whose names are clustered together like a constellation in the first half of this century no one touted and no one bribed. Lady Morgan[2] was perhaps the first author who foreshadowed the purely modern spirit of self-advertisement and the "flurry," so dear to present writers. Her success was greater than her reputation; for the two are not identical. Mrs. Gore was the fashionable woman of society whose drawing-room helped her books; and Moore touched the golden fringe as much by favour as by merit.[3] But the nobler form of faithful work, personal modesty, and professional self-respect existed up to the later half of the present century. And while the new journalism was the cockatrice still in the egg, that personal modesty and professional self-respect formed the rule and not the exception. With the new journalism—all its sensationalism, all its rant, and all its personality—literature has changed its character; and the virtues of the past are emphatically the clogs and fetters of the present.

---

[1] Robert Southey (1774–1843) and William Wordsworth (1770–1850), English Romantic poets and Poet Laureates.
[2] Sydney Owenson, Lady Morgan (1776–1859), Irish novelist.
[3] Catherine Gore (1799–1800), English novelist and playwright; Thomas Moore (1779–1852), Irish poet.

In those days, too, reviewing was a distinct branch of the profession demanding certain qualifications as absolutely essential;—and it was done faithfully and without fear or favour. Naturally the reviewer's own principles tinged all he wrote, but he wrote according to his conscience. He might have the narrow mind of a partisan; he had not the petty spite of a jealous enemy—inimical because jealous. Macaulay and Croker and Hayward carried on the best traditions of the reviewer's office.[1] They clothed in triumphal robes those of whom they approved. They broke the heads, and sometimes the hearts, of those whom they opposed. The *Edinburgh's* buff and blue was a flag that heralded a different political verdict from that of the *Quarterly's* more sober-suited livery; but the judges in either case were honest towards literature so far as prepossession and party politics can leave men honest; and in neither camp was there the venality, the corruption, the falsehood, or the close ring of a "mutual admiration" society.

The same manly impartiality of management, subject only to the private judgment of the reviewer, characterized the old *Saturday Review*. If the most formidable, it was also the freest paper of its time. When John Douglas Cook, and after his death Philip Harwood,[2] held the helm of that dashing fire-ship, the only indication of any kind given to a reviewer was, by rare chance, a private note accompanying the books, saying that, if the work in question could not be conscientiously praised, the editor preferred not to notice it at all. If it was the first book sent to this special reviewer of an author who had already been reviewed in the journal, then the management sent the former notice to prevent a possible fiasco of contradiction. For the rest, all was left to the judgment, honour, and independence of the reviewer. The person who should have sought to gain influence with the editor would have had to eat a mighty peck of the dust of humiliation; and the golden stairs, or the flowery, sought to have been built, would have been pulled about

---

[1]   Thomas Babington Macaulay (1800–1859), historian and essayist for the *Edinburgh Review*; John Wilson Croker (1780–1857), politician and contributor to the conservative *Quarterly Review*; Abraham Hayward (1801–84), man of letters and frequent periodical contributor.

[2]   John Douglas Cook (1808–68), editor of the *Saturday Review* from 1855 to 1868; Philip Harwood (1809–87), an assistant editor under Cook, took over the *Review* after Cook's death.

his ears before he knew where he was. Sharp-tongued and hard-hitting as the journal was, and by no means sensitive to tender skins, it was absolutely and proudly independent. No clique owned it; no outsider was mishandled because an outsider; and its praise or blame flowed undeflected by any venal influence or base intrigues.

At this present day the work of reviewing has fallen into comparatively few hands. A small knot of men hold the success or failure of many—making or marring reputations according to the word of command and the rights of affiliation. Of a work lately published, one man alone wrote sixteen reviews. The author was his friend; and in sixteen different "vehicles" he carried the flag of his friend's triumph and success. He could have blackballed and kept back to the same extent one who had not paid tribute to the clique, or who was an outsider against whom it was good fun to heave the traditional brick. This is the secret of certain suddenly attained literary honours—those which have been gained by consentaneous acclamation following a mediocre production, rather than by the steadily rising, gradually increasing chorus of praise consequent on the repeated output of good work. Then, if you like, comes an apparently sudden burst, and the young writer is borne shoulder-high to the front. But this is very different from the *claque* which gives sixteen reviews of one work by the same hand and so ensures at least the temporary success of what may not be worth the paper it is printed on. These "made" reputations—made, not earned—have the trick of crumbling to pieces by use, like Rübezahl's fairy gold of the evening passing into withered leaves in the morning—or the Algonquin rabbit's bower of refuge and delight, showing nothing but sticks and straws and thorns and brushwood when the glamour passed.[1]

One of the odd things of the present time is the incompetency of those who write for the instruction of others. To say that half the novel-writers, for instance, do not know their own language, and are often

---

[1]   In German folklore, Rubezahl is a gnome who tries to win a princess; when she deserts him, he destroys the magic palace and riches he has created from the air for her. In Algonquin folklore, the lazy rabbit Ableegumooch thinks other animals have an easier time gathering food; when he tries to imitate them, he finds that only his own ways work for him.

deficient in even elemental grammar, is to say what every one who reads can see for himself. To say, too, that critics have more words than matter is again a thing too patent to be denied. When a really deep and learned book appears, there are but three or four men in the kingdom capable of reviewing it. The rank and file try their hands at it and jump on it with hobnailed boots, pounding at the outside but not touching the kernel. Being beyond them, they fall foul of it as obscure or unintelligible. The rasher kind fling their boomerang at a matter of fact of which they think they can judge as well as the "fuzzy-wuzzy" of the tropics can judge of the ice and snow of the Arctic regions. But the boomerang justifies its lines and comes back on the head of him who cast it so gaily into the void; and the would-be smiter is sorely smitten, to the vindication of the law of reprisals. Sometimes a book is beyond even the leaders of literature and has to be let alone—no man found able to bend that bow. I believe I am right in saying this was the case with Sir Richard Burton's *Book of the Sword*.[1] This extraordinary work has remained practically unreviewed to this day; no man on the press having the varied information necessary for a competent criticism of such a strange mass of learning, and editors having the wisdom to set aside a marvel which might prove a snare and a trap.

It takes, however, knowledge to understand one's own ignorance. With that knowledge one can avoid those pitfalls which are sometimes dug for the rash and unwary—those lines of impossible Latin and non-existing Greek, for example, over which more than one somersault has been made—head and heels coming to the ground together—while the cruel joker stood by laughing in his sleeve as the wig fell off and the stuffing came out.

If the editor of to-day is not always the well-read scholar his predecessors mostly were, the young lions who roar in his columns and pages are even less well equipped with what used to be considered necessary literary plenishing. The smart young men who know their way about, who have seen more than they have read and observed more than they have thought or felt—look on the old-time erudition,

---

[1] Sir Richard Francis Burton (1821–90), explorer and linguist. His *Book of the Sword* (1884) tells the story of swords and swordplay from prehistory to Roman times; because of poor sales, further volumes were never published.

with all its classical impedimenta and dusty mediaeval scholasticism, as so much rubbish to be flung-into the waste-paper basket. What has the Lydian lyre or the Phrygian flute[1] to do with a rattling article on the modern music-hall? Who cares for the Doctors, "cherubic," "angelic," or otherwise, who has to review a sporting novel? Like to like, if it is not always that like cures like. As the literature, so the reviewer; and a mighty poor dish is made of it between them; for perhaps there was never a time in literature when there was less education among the *literati* than at present. Contrast this smart young man, with his flow of words and wallet-full of superficial facts, with a steady-going ordinarily educated man of middle age who was nourished on the classics of such languages as he knows. He can put his finger on the source of almost all the allusions and quotations he meets with, while the smart young man is hopelessly abroad. Dante and Tasso and Ariosto[2] are household words to the one—to the other names without point or meaning. Montaigne and Rochefoucauld, Voltaire and Rousseau, Racine and Corneille[3] the one, too, knows from end to end; but the other knows no more of them than he knows of Kant or Fichte, Goethe or Schiller.[4] He can reel you off a dozen Bab Ballads; he knows by heart the "Heathen Chinee" and "Jem Bludso";[5] he could pass an examination in Mark Twain and Ally Sloper.[6] So be it. Being of the time he must understand the conditions of the time and catch the froth as it rises. But it would not hurt him to know something more than he does, and so be able to dip his cup deeper than the froth—coming down to the purer springs where

---

1   Lydian and Phrygian are two of the classical Greek musical scales.

2   Dante Alighieri (1265–1321), Turquato Tasso (1544–95), and Ludivico Ariosto (1474–1533), Italian poets.

3   Michel de Montaigne (1533–92), François, Duke de Rochefoucauld (1613–80), Voltaire (pen name of François Marie Arouet, 1694–1778), Jean-Jacques Rousseau (1712–78), French philosophers; Jean Racine (1639–99), French playwright.

4   Immanuel Kant (1724–1804) and Johann Gottlieb Fichte (1762–1814), German philosophers; Johann Wolfgang von Goethe (1749–1832) and Friedrich Schiller (1759–1805), German poets.

5   The Bab Ballads are a series of comic poems written by W.S. Gilbert (1836–1911) and published in *Fun* magazine from 1861 to 1905; "The Heathen Chinee" (1870) is a comic poem by American writer Bret Harte (1836–1902); "Jim Bludso of the Prairie Belle" is a comic dialect poem by American poet John Hay (1838–1905).

6   *Ally Sloper's Half-Holiday* (1884–1916) was an extremely popular Victorian comic paper.

the thoughts of great men mix and mingle, and enrich the mind as
nothing else can.

But, indeed, our literature is too entirely frothy at the present day.
Nothing more superficial has yet appeared. We can read nothing that
takes time or trouble. Our science is got by reviews, and even these
have lately been boiled down to their bare bones. Expansion, illustration, exhaustive treatment generally, perfectness of arrangement,
beauty of style—all have gone by the board in favour of a terseness
which reduces literature to so many pages of algebraic signs or rows
of hieroglyphics. The telegraph has destroyed letter writing; the
condensation of the shorter reviews is ruining literature. Richardson's
nine volumes[1] have given place to the wide-spaced "shilling shocker."
A learned work which occupies a lifetime—say Spedding's *Bacon*[2]—
is like an aerolite in a field of cheap bricks, wondered at and admired,
but of no general use. The fine and sufficing reviews of the *Edinburgh*
and *Quarterly* are caviare to the general, if still a handful of the faithful appreciate them; while the glib skimmings of the clever handy-
man are taken as the gist of the matter, and nothing that he has left
out is considered worth insertion. We get our science chiefly by these
superficial skimmings, and even these are re-skimmed for the benefit of those who live fast and have no time for real thought or solid
learning. A few catchwords get adopted, and those who know
absolutely nothing of the source or the original context, pick up the
current phrases and apply them with liberality. This generalized adoption simply turns those pregnant phrases into cant and a kind of
respectable burgomaster slang. These phrases break out suddenly,
thick and "rash," as mushrooms on a dewy morning, and they are
flung about so profusely that you weary of their very echo. I well
remember the genesis of certain expressions like "the line of least
resistance," " the survival of the fittest," "environment," "differentia-
tion," "atavism," " heredity," "natural selection," &c., and how the
words caught on and were adopted by writers who knew no more

---

[1]   Samuel Richardson (1689–1761), English novelist; his novels typically ran to multiple
    volumes.
[2]   James Spedding (1808–81) collected and edited all of Francis Bacon's (1561–1626)
    works and issued them in new editions from 1857 to 1874.

about their birthplaces than the Egyptian fellah knows about the sources of the Nile. But they give a certain colour of erudition to the page where they appear; and colour goes a long way.

If some of the young lions on the press have suspiciously long ears, and if their roar is apt to degenerate into the familiar bray when dealing with things demanding thought and general culture, they are emphatically "all there" when put to the handling of matters congenial to the tastes of modern society. Their descriptions of functions, with the catalogue of guests and the kind of dresses worn by the ladies, leave nothing to be desired. They might boggle over Dante and find Burton's *Anatomy of Melancholy*[1] a tough morsel, but they are at home when they note who talks to whom, and whether "crushed strawberry" or "dead roseleaves" become the Beauty best. Also, they are great in interviews, where also they are more than a trifle offensive. Say that you decline to be interviewed on any subject whatever for a certain paper, but, because touched by a certain bit of cheap sentiment about his mother, you receive privately as a simple gentleman the man who wanted to draw you out on politics, religion, morals, and give to the world in the columns of penny paper the result of a life's difficulties and struggles. Your young interviewer comes, on the distinct understanding that there is to be no record of your conversation, and that he is received as a gentleman only. He keeps to the letter of the agreement, but he earns his Judas-pence by a coarse attack on your general manners and being, which he makes spicy by accusations of petty sins entirely foreign to your temperament and nature. He, too, is of the time—the time which, in literature at all events, has forgotten the old traditions of good faith and high breeding, and which rakes up its Judas-pence[2] by any act of treachery within its reach.

Another young lion of the time bursts into your room unannounced, unknown, uninvited. He comes on a self-appointed mission, seeking to entangle you in your talk concerning A. or B., that he may fasten on you materials for an action of libel. He works round his subject like a

---

[1] *The Anatomy of Melancholy* (1621) is a philosophical work by English writer Robert Burton (1577–1640).

[2] Reference to the Old Testament, in which the disciple Judas betrays Jesus to the legal authorities for a reward of 30 pieces of silver.

questing hound, his nose to the ground, sniffing the scent. He seeks to entrap you into an admission, to trip you up over an assertion, to make you blurt out the truth as contradiction to his lie. You have to be alert and alive, else, before you know your whereabouts, your unknown interviewer will have nailed you to a confession which will cost you more than you care to pay. That also comes into the code of honour of the present day. So, too, it comes into the idea of fitness and general harmony that you should be asked to submit yourself to the inquisitorial acumen of a girl young enough to be your granddaughter. The editor of such-and-such a paper writes to you requesting you to see a young lady, whom you knew when you were of middle age and she was a golden-haired child, and to answer her on such topics as she shall see fit to broach. The girl is a good girl, a clever girl, a pretty girl, and one whose literary career you would willingly help. But a certain feeling of self-respect and dignity, as well as regard for that general fitness of things, makes you decline. You have drunk deep of the waters of life, bitter and sweet; you have known love and sorrow and loss, difficulties of fortune and difficulties of faith; you have stood by the grave of your dead illusions and watched the last flicker of your futile love; you have touched every note of the chord and trodden the wine-press emphatically alone; and then you are asked to bare your soul, scarred and seamed and tear-stained as it is with sorrow and experience, to the gaze of a fresh young maid just entering life, who is to question you on such topics as she shall see fitting. Fancy any of the self-respecting men of the past generation receiving such a proposition! Fancy Walter Savage Landor on the gridiron of the interviewer, or Walter Scott, or Robert Southey, or Wordsworth, or even Coleridge,[1] though he was less reticent than those others! But even Coleridge would have chosen his interpreter according to his own dignity, and the smart young man, as well as the fresh young maid, would not have been in it.

It may be said that some slight line of relation exists between the modern interviewer and Boswell;[2] and that the jaunty presumption of

---

[1] Walter Savage Landor (1775–1864) and Samuel Taylor Coleridge (1772–1834), English poets. Linton was a great admirer and protegé of Landor.

[2] James Boswell (1740–95), Scottish writer best known for his biography and memoirs of English writer and lexicographer Samuel Johnson (1709–84).

the former finds its Prototype in the foolishness of the latter. But the line is very slight—the relation very wide. The modern interviewer stands as far below Boswell in comprehension of his subject, and in the faculty of making his readers comprehend it too, as the modern *littérateur* stands below Johnson himself in depth of thought and width of learning. Boswell might have been the germ, the embryo of the later development; but Lord! as he would have said, that later development has wandered wonderfully far from its original sketch! The full-grown creature is as unlike its embryo as the flower is unlike the seed.

All the same, the modern interviewer fits in exactly with the modern man, whether of action or of letters. Barnum's advice to all who have anything to sell has been taken to heart by our modern *literati*, and the art of self-advertisement is carried to the highest point of perfection.[1] In the days when literature respected itself and men of letters had their own "pundonor"[2] which they cherished, no man would have sent his book unsolicited to an influential stranger, or would have fished with a long line for subscribers. The presentation copy to a friend, or a brother worker even if unknown, was another matter. But to tout for a favourable notice, or indeed for any notice at all, was as impossible to the self-respecting *littérateur* as to tout for subscribers. Authors do both nowadays. They send you printed forms of subscription to fill up, for books perhaps as yet unwritten and in any case unpublished—books of the merits of which you have no means of forming the faintest opinion, but which you are expected to buy on trust. You are not necessarily a fellow-worker. If you were, the thing would not be so glaring, though even here, from a total stranger by no means in the forefront of the profession, the application is an impertinence. But those who try to get subscribers by this method do not confine themselves to their own craft. They sweep the seas with a net as wide as that of a hospital, an institution, a philanthropist, a money-lender. Catch or miss, it is an advertisement; and Barnum's advice was wise. It is part of the modern spirit of blare and bustle. No one is content to do good work quietly, trusting to the

---

[1] P.T. Barnum (1810–91), American entrepreneur and showman, reputed to have said "There's a sucker born every minute."

[2] Self-respect; self-esteem.

intrinsic merits of what he sends out, and disdaining the patter of the cheapjack as the showier arts of Dr. Dulcamara.[1] Every one must have his share of the drums and fifes which wake up the street; and the once proud and dignified Muse, who, like a second Egeria,[2] kept herself concealed while her work prospered and did good, now jigs along the highway like a hallelujah lass, shouting her loudest and dancing her lustiest. It may be all right. Perhaps in view of the close ring of reviewers, it is only another form of self-protection. Whether right or wrong, it is open to onlookers to pronounce the form ugly and the method hateful; and one need not be a fossil to regret the past days of quietness, reserve, and dignity.

Nothing can exceed the ingenuity in self-advertisement of the time, unless it be the ingenuity in ill-nature of attacks. An action for libel, carrying a farthing damages, is a splendid advertisement for a man whose work, left to itself and not floated by friendly gas, would sink like a stone to the bottom. A mare's-nest[3] found in the compound of a man of mark sells that issue clean off and the second edition after it. It "matters not a cherry stone" that the mare's-nest has to be demolished next day, and all the foals hatching in the eggs among the sticks and straws have to pass away in smoke. It answered its purpose while it lasted, and the proprietor of the journal reaped the benefit—which was all that was wanted. For, indeed, other flags beside dignity have died out of modern literature—truth and fairness among the rest. Our prize-fights might have been brutal; no one says they were not. But they were conducted according to their own laws, and a blow below the belt was "foul." Perhaps this was better than the indiscriminate hard hitting of the present day, when no rules are observed, and the fouler the blow the more it tells in the scrimmage; when a well-concocted lie, which looks so like the truth that it can never be quite sworn away, is held to be a legitimate weapon of attack; when the grossest betrayal of confidence, the meanest treachery in return for hospitality, is only one draggled feather the more in the battered cap

---

[1] Quack doctor who sells patent medicine in an 1866 burlesque by W.S. Gilbert.

[2] Egeria or Aetheria (ca. 380s) wrote about her pilgrimage to Jerusalem and the customs and religious practices she observed.

[3] Hoax or delusion; in this context, a false report or accusation.

of the literary mercenary. "Grub Street" and the "penny-a-liner" have been words of contempt universally accepted. We want a phrase, terse, inclusive, descriptive, which shall express the nature of the literary mercenary—the man who hires out his brains no matter to which side or what cause—who will assassinate an honourable reputation as soon as he will expose a pretender—find a mare's-nest as soon as scotch a snake; the man who has no law save that of making his journal sell—for whom the Ten Commandments are as obsolete as the Broad Stone of Honour—and to whom the *debâcle* to come, if his political principles ever take shape in parliamentary enactments, is on all fours with that famous, "Apres moi le déluge."[1]

When truth and honour, self-respect and sincerity have gone out of a profession, its life has gone. It has become then the "purry pome" of chivalry, and the sooner it is buried the better. From the dead self something better will spring up.

The democratic wave which has spread over all society—and washed down some things which had better have been left standing—has swept through the whole province of literature. The spread of education among the people demands literature cheap enough to at once suit their pockets and meet their wants. This naturally increases the output; and the output necessitates more hands. Among the hundreds who write where formerly was one, there must of necessity be a larger percentage of the incompetent. So we find it; and so every editor and every publisher and every author of any name at all prove it. The cartloads of absolute rubbish which are shot into the publishers' offices and laid on the tables of editors have their screenings and filterings in the private houses of authors. People who have nothing to say and who could not say it if they had, dance down the flowers of rhetoric and upset all the orderly arrangements of syntax—then send you the result. There is not a grammatical error, short of "they was," and "he were," that they do not commit. Their composition is as dislocated as a creature that has been broken alive on the wheel. All their carts go before all their horses and their prepositions are tin-tacked on to the wrong verbs. Their sentences are so many cats'-cradles

---

[1]   "After me, disaster"; attributed to French king Louis XV (1710–74).

where you seek in vain for the governing line—the guiding clue. Their epithets are simply repetitions one of the other—sticky drops of the same material agglutinated, and as void of suggestiveness as of beauty. There is not an original thought in the whole twenty pages of closely written manuscript—foolscap—and not a line of description drawn at first hand. They reproduce what they have read and warm up the stale dish into a still more unpalatable hash. The trashiest magazine, the most ignorant paper published, declines their work. The fence to be cleared with either is very low, very easy; but these halting aspirants have not been able to do even that.

Then they throw themselves on the mercy of some entire stranger, whom they know only by name, and beg for perusal, correction, sifting, and influence with some editor to get the one or two that he may choose out of the half-score sent him for his verdict accepted, published, and paid for. Their letters are as piteous as cries. You see and know the hard struggle that it all is, and you would, if you could, help them—but not to still further vitiate the public taste, and still more deeply degrade one of the noblest professions that man has made, by letting loose on the public the futile stuff they call their "work." Inadequate all through, you would rather pay for its suppression than help in its publication; but if you return it, declining to do anything to get it floated and deprecating further efforts, you are sure to be set down as jealous, grasping, obstructive, and without the feeling of comradeship. If you write with gingerly caution and intentional tenderness for possible sore places, you leave the door open for another inrush; and, time being valuable and eyesight precious, you have in all probability given yourself away. As an appalling amount of trash is printed, you cannot wonder nor condemn when these feeble folk say fatuously, "Why not we as well as others?" Judged by their own standard—always a flattering one—their work is not worse than what they have read, and maybe is better than some. And the money is so much wanted—which makes the whole sad tragedy! For all that, no one who respects his profession would help in the publication of trash which shows nothing, inspires nothing, teaches nothing, suggests nothing—which is just stale material very badly mixed and served. These impossible manuscripts are for the most part grotesque attempts at sensationalism or vapid sentimentalism. Sometimes they are essays of the cat's-cradle sort, where you look in vain for a central point or a leading line, and where there is neither orderly sequence of idea nor the sense of proportion.

Of all forms of fiction the sensational demands the most careful treatment. There is but one step from the sublime to the ridiculous, and to the sublime may be added the horrible, the eerie, the bloodcurdling, the sensational. That step is no wider than the bridge, itself no thicker than a hair, over which the True Believer passes on his way to heaven, with the pit yawning below. And just as many a peccant soul trips, stumbles, and falls, so do the sensational writers pass over the narrow line and plunge headlong into bathos. It becomes a trick as mechanical as the pea and the thimble, and is no longer a weird vision filling the imagination unbidden. It is pumped up; it does not flow naturally. It is a ghost made out of a turnip and a white sheet thrown about a hop-pole; it is not the silent spectre stealing between you and the moonlight—the formless Horror that, like another Gorgon's head, turns your very heart to stone. Murder and mystery and the wild phantasies of that region which is neither earth nor sky; tales of those peoples where the men are magicians and the women are superhuman in insight and understanding; crimes which have no name and sorrows which have no human source; the annals of Scotland Yard and the experiences of Bedlam, have all been ransacked and exhausted, and nothing is now left for the later hands but the barren gleaning of well-harvested fields and the jags and rags of worn-out garments. Sensationalism is played out, and the "shilling shocker" has run its course. But among all this chaff and rubbish we every now and then light on a bit of real gold—as in that wonderful piece of work, *A Village Tragedy*[1]—one of the strongest as well as one of the most subtle stories of these later days. For the most part, however, our fiction is not "epoch-making"; and the mantles of Scott, Dickens, Thackeray, and George Eliot still flutter above our heads, covering no man's shoulders. Some younger writers are forging ahead, and one in especial has found his way to the front—heartily welcome for the power and originality that he shows.

---

[1] Novel (1887) by English novelist Margaret L. Woods (1856–1945).

If we are not up to the highest mark in fiction, neither are we in one class of poems. We have idyls and dramas, and splendid concerted pieces like grand orchestral music, but we have no now songs which stir the nation's heart. Our music-hall songs, like our drawing-room ditties, are beneath contempt, and need not be spoken of. What we want are strong, stirring, wholesome songs, such as Dibdin wrote— songs which go down to the very roots of patriotism, and help, even more than set orations, to keep men faithful to law and country.[1] In this day of universal disintegration and the supremacy of fads, there are so many who would sacrifice the good of the country—the integrity of the empire—to some impracticable theory that looks like godly justice on paper and would be cruel wrong in practice. And we want "keying- up" again to the one central duty—the one passionate devo- tion—the patriotic love of Englishmen for England. Let them sneer as they will, these milk-and-water faddists, at the Jingo sentiment. The Jingo song was a godsend, and struck the right chord boldly and truly. We want more of the same character if on another topic. The times are ripe, the work is waiting to be done, and a new Dibdin would be of priceless value. This, too, would be a return of the Now to the Then, and one which would do more public good than even the fitting of Scott's mantle or the gift of Thackeray's. The songs of a nation both show more and sink deeper than would seem at first sight. The minds which appreciated "Drink to me only with thine eyes," and "Bid me to live and I will live,"[2] were of a different cast and mould in all concern- ing love than are those which find pleasure in luscious insipidity or sensual vulgarity. Dibdin's songs roused quite different feelings from those which are touched by "Tommy make Room for your Uncle," or "A Pair of Lovely Black Eyes";[3] and the fact that patriotic songs are seemingly dead and done with is in itself a revelation of public feeling. All that used to be patriotism seems to have gone into a slashing kind of religiosity, where Heaven replaces the country and the devil swallows

---

[1] Charles Dibdin (1745–1814), English songwriter who specialized in patriotic and senti- mental songs.

[2] First lines from songs by English poets Ben Jonson (1572–1634) and Robert Herrick (1591–1674).

[3] Popular songs of the 1870s.

up all the other enemies. The effect of these songs and hymns on the congregations is a measure of what might be done by a little manly vigour and working patriotism.

In every direction we come to the same patent fact—the need of reorganisation in literature. There are too many writers because some of them are so ineffably weak and bad. There is too little good work of real sound scholarship, and too much worthless froth—bright, sparkling, iridescent, what you will—but only froth when all is said that can be said of it. Writers themselves have lost their old self-respecting quiet dignity. They are no longer the representatives of the grand old philosophers, thinking before they spoke and learning before they taught; the majority of them are mere market hucksters selling their wares to the highest bidder—cheapjacks advertising themselves by patter and clatter—members of a ring which bolsters up those who are affiliated and boycotts those who are not, irrespective of the worth of the work done. With the creation of the interviewer, reticence on the one side is destroyed—on the other, honour goes by the board. What is not given in one form is filched in another; and he who refuses to be "drawn" is thrawed independently, and has to submit to his fate willing or unwilling. The public does not read unless it can run as it reads. A book is boiled down to a review, and the review is condensed into a newspaper article. Three lines of small print discuss and dismiss a work that is the outcome of a life's study, and those three lines are written by a man who does not know the very alphabet of the subject. Save in one or two noteworthy exceptions, where the editor, himself a scholar, knows how to choose his contributors, young lions are fatuously credited with literary, scientific, political, and artistic omniscience; and the general utility man, who knows absolutely nothing from the root-work, weaves the crowns or lays on the lash as the fancy takes him, or as he is the friend of the author's, or the reverse.

Compare one of these smart young men with the erudite scholars of the past generation—the men whose work was as close and perfect as a bit of Japanese enamel—who have chapter and verse for every assertion, and could put their fingers on references and quotations of which our modern young lion knows about as much as he does of Chinese—and then measure the distance of the downward step that literature has made. What was once solid heart-of-oak is now the flimsiest veneer. What was once mastery of the whole subject is now a quick study, a book of well-chosen extracts, and a serviceable memory when called on. That which was once a grave and honourable profession has now degenerated into a noisy, pushing, self-advertising trade; and he who would teach is not always abreast of those whom he undertakes to instruct. The classics are discarded for personal gossip; the continuity to be found in history runs into the sand out of which a new political fad is built; the human nature which has never varied in essence from the earliest times up to now is glibly supposed to be undergoing a transformation which will enable men to stand on their heads and talk with their heels; the golden apple has become the "purry pome," and the democratic wave has covered the garden of the Hesperides with mud and slime. Literature is not the honourable profession it was when practised by the learned gentlemen and scholars of the past generation, and it does not confer the same dignity—because the standard of self-respect has fallen like the standard of qualifications—because Dulcamara has displaced Bacon, and Dr. Marigold[1] is the best representative of a philosopher the rank and file of modern literature can show.

SOURCE

Fortnightly Review 47 (1 April 1890).

SELECTED SECONDARY READING

Anderson, Nancy Fix. *Woman Against Women in Victorian England: A Life of Eliza Lynn Linton.* Bloomington: Indiana University Press, 1987.

Broomfield, Andrea. "Much More than an Antifeminist: Eliza Lynn Linton's Contribution to the Rise of Victorian Popular Journalism." *Victorian Literature and Culture* 29.2 (2001): 267–83.

Van Thal, Herbert. *Eliza Lynn Linton: The Girl of the Period.* London: Allen and Unwin, 1979.

---

[1] Character in an 1865 short story by Dickens.

CHRISTINA ROSSETTI
(FEBRUARY 1895)

Alice Meynell

ALICE THOMPSON (1847–1926) was born in Barnes, Surrey. Her father was a Cambridge graduate of independent means and a friend of Charles Dickens, and her mother was a concert pianist. Alice and her sister Elizabeth, who later became an artist, were raised primarily in Europe, where their father supervised their education. By the time the family returned to England in 1864, Alice was fluent in French and Italian and had already revealed a talent for poetry. The family converted to Roman Catholicism during the 1870s.

Encouraged by the poets Aubrey de Vere and Alfred Tennyson, Alice published her first volume of poetry, *Preludes*, in 1875. One of the early admirers of her work was the journalist Wilfred Meynell, whom she married in 1877. Their marriage was a happy and highly collaborative partnership. Besides raising seven children, the Meynells jointly edited a number of periodicals, including the Catholic *Weekly Register* (1881–98) and the literary magazines *The Pen* (1880) and *Merry England* (1883–95). Alice wrote numerous essays on literature and the arts for each of these publications. In addition, she contributed essays to the *Scots* (later *National*) *Observer* and the *Dublin Review*, and from 1894 on she published weekly articles in the *Pall Mall Gazette*. Her *National Observer* and *Pall Mall Gazette* essays were later republished as *The Rhythm of Life* (1893) and *The Colour of Life* (1896). In recognition both of her own work and of her efforts to raise the professional standing of women of letters, in 1896 she was elected president of the Women's Society of Journalists.

From the 1890s on, Meynell returned to poetry, publishing a number of volumes, including *Other Poems* (1896), *Later Poems* (1902), and *A Father of Women and Other Poems* (1917). The reception of her poetry was such that she was a serious candidate for the post of Poet Laureate in 1895. In 1901 and 1902, she undertook a lecture tour of the United States, and in 1914 she was elected to the Academic Committee of the Royal Society of Literature. Her *Last Poems* (1923) was published posthumously.

Meynell's essay on "Christina Rossetti" appeared in the *New Review* a couple of months after Rossetti's death. Written in Meynell's characteristic compressed prose style, the essay examines seriously the strengths and deficiencies of Rossetti's work, especially the charge that her versification was faulty. Beginning with the warning that "Poetry is the rarest thing in the world"—and that even "fine poets" have only "rare great moments"—Meynell admits that "We are not to reverence the versification of Christina Rossetti as we have learnt to reverence that of a great and classic master." But although Rossetti's poetry evinces a "characteristic carelessness" and the occasional flat line, what matters is that it remains "purely poetic" because "It proves art present, and present essentially." Taking as an example the poem "Convent Threshold," Meynell argues that while it may fail to meet technical ideals of imagery, grace, and music, it remains an "immortal song of love and ... cry of more than earthly fear." In the end, Meynell insists, Rossetti will be remembered for doing "a very serious service to English versification by using afresh this voice of poetry—the voice that sings in musical time."

THERE IS ASSUREDLY BUT ONE opinion as to the poet who has lately passed from earth, though that opinion varies in degree. All who have human hearts confess her to be a sad and a sweet poet, all who have a sense of poetry know how rare was the quality of poetry in her—how spiritual and how sensuous—somewhat thin, somewhat dispread in her laxer writing, but perfectly strong, perfectly impassioned in her best. To the name of poet her right is so sure that proof of it is to be found everywhere in her "unconsidered ways," and always irrefutably. How does this poet or that approach the best beauties of his poem? From the side of poetry, or from the side of commonplace? Christina Rossetti always drew near from the side of poetry: from what to us, who are not altogether poets, is the further side. She came from beyond those hills. She is not often on the heights, but all her access is by poetry. Of few indeed is this so true.

Poetry is the rarest thing in the world. Moreover, being rare, it has its own rarities, which are to the poem what the poem is to "customary life's exceeding injocundity." We do no wrong to a fine poet in speaking of his rare great moments. His manner of approaching these—his direction—gives us the pleasure of giving him a long welcome. It is the daily life of his muse. Even poets who are not great have had fine moments: approaching them, doubtless, through commonplace, but certainly reaching them. And approach is so important, so significant of origin, so marked with character, so charged with memories, so full of preparation, so indicative of sequestered life, that one might well consider it the history of all that lives and grows. It is, in short, life with direction. And, even if so to consider it be to yield to some temptation to digress, let a few words, to set it forth, be excused here. Approach is fit to dwell upon, and has leisure, and no beaten or definite pathways. It is the day by day, the waking and sleeping, the temper and the nature. In love it is all the justification, for without a whole approach, love is profanity. In poetry approach is as perceptible as the quarter of the wind. Whence comes this flight of song? Over soft seas or dry lands? Either flight crowns the same heights. See, too, how much is approach in the art of architecture. A great building may be held to be as it were organic beyond its apparent boundaries, and to have the land, the city, the street, for its approaches; for its accessories the climate and the cloud. And it is worth while to note that a people which has lost almost all besides in

the building of its towns, has still the sense of access. Its architects of
the Renaissance turned that sense too consciously to artifice. They
were too much aware of their own instinct. They took too large and
too deliberate, too courtly, a gesture. They swept too far, and trusted
so little to the felicity whereby a great church makes itself a centre—
somewhat as the sunset disposes the clouds radiant from a centre in
its brows—that they seem now and then to work against the natural
good luck and to convince you of over-much purpose. Bernini[1] knew
too well that he had the sense of distance, and by taking thought he
added many a rood to the outposts of St. Peter's; and you wonder that
the sky does not close with his design.

In poetry approach is, needless to say, far more subtle. It is the unap-
parent history of a poem. Some poets let us see but little of it. Others
permit us to trace their way to their successes, and we sometimes see that
they have trudged a common or a difficult path, and one that has known
our own feet and our friends'. Christina Rossetti allows us to see how
purely poetic was all her least success and her unsuccess. We willingly
linger in an easy world which is, with her, not only easy but perpetually
beautiful. No less easy was her supreme success: for it is impossible to
think that she did herself any violence by close work upon her art. All
she touches is fine poetic material, albeit material that is often somewhat scattered. She has no unhandsome secrets of composition, or difficulties of attainment. She keeps the intimate court of a queen. The
country of poetry is her home, and she is a "manifest housekeeper," and
does nothing out of it. As for the stanzas and passages—but they are
oftener whole brief lyrics—in which she reaches the point of poetic
passion, they have the stress of purpose which, when it knows how to
declare itself, is art indeed. The moment of poetic passion solves all
doubts as to art. Not that it can possibly take the place of art or make
amends for art absent, as some strange criticism would have us think. It
proves art present, and present essentially. Not a verse that *manifests* the
life with which it was written can be a verse of less than triumphant art.

When we are judging the work of any poet under the rank of absolute
greatness, we can hardly do otherwise than judge the technique with a

---

[1]   Gian Lorenzo Bernini (1598–1680), Italian architect and artist.

more or less separate judgment. It may be a paradox to some readers, nevertheless it seems to be a great truth: that the more splendid the poetry the more august in importance is what, with lesser work, would be called the "mere form." It rises to such dignity that in the highest poetry the verse, the versification, is the very Muse. But fine poetry of a lower rank is to be judged in parts; and what I claim for it here is that some little failure, or fault, of mere technique by no means prevents or bars the art of a true expression. We are not to reverence the versification of Christina Rossetti as we have learnt to reverence that of a great and classic master. She proves herself an artist, a possessor of the weighty matters of the law of art, despite the characteristic carelessness with which she played by ear. That thought so moving, feeling so urgent, as the thought and feeling of her "Convent Threshold" are communicated, are uttered alive, proves her an artist. This is to be insisted upon, because during her life it was said with hesitation, by a critic of evident authority, "At its best her work is almost art":[1] so conspicuous had the obvious and as it were external faults seemed to him. To hazard another paradox: technique is not all external. In this poem—it is impossible not to dwell on such a masterpiece—without imagery; without beauty except that which is inevitable (and what beauty is more costly?); without grace, except the invincible grace of impassioned poetry; without music, except the ultimate music of the communicating word, she utters that immortal song of love and that cry of more than earthly fear: a song of penitence for love that yet praises love more fervently than would a chorus hymeneal:

> To-day, while it is called to-day,
> Kneel, wrestle, knock, do violence, pray.
> ...
> I turn from you my cheeks and eyes,
> My hair which you shall see no more.
> Alas for joy that went before!

---

[1] This comment is attributed to Tennyson in an 1862 letter from the critic Francis Turner Palgrave (1824–97) to Christina's brother, the editor William Michael Rossetti (1829–1919).

> My words were slow, my tears were few,
> But through the dark my silence broke.

In "Amor Mundi," also, there is terror, though it be terror that is not instant, but that flies and sings, as ominous as a bird of warning— terror suggested, not suffered, as it is profoundly suffered in "The Convent Threshold." In "The Three Enemies," again, fear is uttered, not sharply but, with a constant sense of

> The sadness of all sin
> When look at in the light of love.

And, by-the-bye, while the lax ways of Christina Rossetti's versification are matters of frequent criticism, the artistic perfection of these twelve stanzas of "The Three Enemies" should be insisted on. Equally perfect are "Uphill," "Advent," and some ten more: all pieces written with the full number of syllables. She has here a strong and gentle brevity without haste, a beauty of phrasing, a finality, a sense of structure and stability, with the freedom of life, scarce possible to surpass. Wherever she writes by rule, she uses that rule admirably well. It is only in the lax metres which keep—more or less—musical time rather than account of numbers, that one might wish she had more theory. Her versification then is apt to be ambiguous and even incorrect. Take the beautiful lyric at the end of *The Prince's Progress*, though many other passages might be cited. It seems, in one stanza, that the poet has chosen to let the beats of her time fall—punctually and with full measure of time—now upon a syllable and now upon a rest *within the line*, so that the metre goes finely to time, like a nursery song for the rocking of a cradle. But then the succeeding stanza is, as often as not, written with no rule except that of numbers and accents. One stanza throws doubt upon the others. Read the poem which way you will, there is no assurance as to the number of beats which she intended. It may be answered that ambiguity is difficult to avoid in a language which interchanges accent and quantity, and has few syllables which may not be used as long or short according to a writer's will; and that there is not much to hinder any man from reading Michael

Drayton's[1] "Agincourt" or his "Trent" as laxly dactyllic poems (one must, for convenience, take Coleridge's permission to use such words, made for quantitative verse, to describe the mixed verse of English poetry):

Fair stood the wind for France.

This is a line of four beats, and makes fine "march-music." But it may be read with two. If Drayton cannot help ambiguity, it is the fault of the language. This is true. But at least his ambiguity is just so much as is inevitable. He gives you the alternative throughout this "Ballad of Agincourt."

Now, even if Christina Rossetti has more than the inevitable ambiguity, and really mingles her measures, she has done a very serious service to English versification by using afresh this voice of poetry— the voice that sings in musical time. It had been much neglected since Coleridge,[2] and *he* used it so seldom! That is, he used redundant syllables freely, but a rest within the line most rarely:

Is the night chilly and dark?

This is one of the most beautiful of all lines written with a mid-line rest. Christina Rossetti sweetly wrote with rests in her unpremeditated art; and others have caught the sound of this metre and have used it beautifully—Irish poets especially, as it happens. The great iambic line, the national heroic line, need have nothing to fear from this young and elastic metre. For the two ways are separately right, as in another art are the ways of Gluck and Wagner.[3] But it will be an excellent thing if poetry in the future, when in the mood for greater movement, shall spring upon such a fantastic foot as that of

[1] Michael Drayton (1563–1631), English poet who wrote a number of long narrative poems on heroes, both legendary and historic.
[2] Samuel Taylor Coleridge (1772–1834), English Romantic poet. The line that follows is from his poem "Christabel."
[3] Christoph Willibald Gluck (1714–87) and Richard Wagner (1813–83), German Romantic composers.

Coleridge's line, just cited, or of Christina Rossetti's three-beat line in *The Prince's Progress*:

> Hark! the bride weepeth!

It will be well for our writers that they should take this strong, controlled, and leaping movement, that goes on living feet or living wings, instead of the precipitate, and therefore rather helpless, haste of metres for a long time too exclusively in use for the swifter lyrics:

> Before the beginning of years,[1]

for instance, or:

> Cannon to left of them.[2]

These two verses are those of great poets. But does not the metre of these even rather trip and fall? And in lesser hands we know that these anapaests and dactyls produce the most popular effect a really vulgar music. They are so slight, too, that they flatter our national way of speaking slippingly, without taking hold. If Coleridge's hint comes to be better obeyed, it will be much for the sake of Christina Rossetti's lovely example.

Those last words seems to rebuke for their slightness all the things written in this brief article, as they suggested themselves to a lover of her poetry. Her lovelier example is in the motive of all her song. Its sadness was the one all-human sadness, its fear the one true fear. She, acquainted with grief, found in grief no cause of offence. She left revolt to the emotion of mere spectators and strangers. When one of the many widows of the monarchs of France heard of the murder of her son and whispered, "I will not say, my God, that it is too much, but it is much," she told one of the secrets of sorrow. The poet and saint who has now passed from a world she never loved, lived a life of sacrifice, suffered

---

[1] Line from Algernon Charles Swinburne's (1837–1909) "Atalanta in Calydon."
[2] Line from Tennyson's "Charge of the Light Brigade."

many partings, unreluctantly endured the pains of her spirituality; but she kept, in their quickness, her simple and natural love of love and hope of joy, for another time. Such sufferings as hers do indeed refuse, but they have not denied, delight. Delight is all their faith.

SOURCE

New Review 12 (February 1895).

SELECTED SECONDARY READING

Badeni, June. *The Slender Tree: A Life of Alice Meynell.* Padstow, Cornwall: Tabb House, 1981.

Leighton, Angela. *Victorian Women Poets: Writing Against the Heart.* London: Harvester Wheatsheaf, 1992.